Decolonizing Wesleyan Theology

Wesleyan and Methodist Explorations

EDITORS

Daniel Castelo
Robert W. Wall

DESCRIPTION

The *Wesleyan and Methodist Explorations* series will offer some of the best Methodist Wesleyan scholarship for the church and academy by drawing from active participants in the international guilds of Methodist scholarship (Oxford Institute of Methodist Studies, Wesleyan Theological Society, American Academy of Religion—Methodist Studies Section, and others).

There is an urgent need within Wesleyan Methodist scholarship for constructive theological work that will advance the field into interdisciplinary and creative directions. The potential for the series is vast as it will seek to establish possible future directions for the field.

Another key concern of this series will be to tap the emerging field of theological interpretation of Scripture located in and for particular ecclesial traditions. Theological interpretation offers insight to historical study, especially the reception of Scripture and its effects within the Methodist church, as well as exploring the epistemic gains to particular biblical texts and themes. Theological interpretation offers insight into the holy ends of these gains for the life of the church in worship, instruction, mission, and personal devotions for a people called Methodist.

The series will seek out great monographs, while also considering superior and adapted doctoral dissertations and well-conceived and tightly focused edited volumes.

EDITORIAL BOARD

Carla Works
Karen Winslow
Sangwoo Kim
Matt Sigler
Ashley Dreff

Hal Knight III
Priscilla Pope-Levison
Sharon Grant
Frederick L. Ware
Dennis Dickerson

Decolonizing Wesleyan Theology

*Theological Engagements from the
Underside of Methodism*

EDITED BY
Filipe Maia

CASCADE *Books* • Eugene, Oregon

DECOLONIZING WESLEYAN THEOLOGY
Theological Engagements from the Underside of Methodism

Wesleyan and Methodist Explorations Series

Copyright © 2024 Wipf and Stock Publishers. All rights reserved. Except for brief quotations in critical publications or reviews, no part of this book may be reproduced in any manner without prior written permission from the publisher. Write: Permissions, Wipf and Stock Publishers, 199 W. 8th Ave., Suite 3, Eugene, OR 97401.

Cascade Books
An Imprint of Wipf and Stock Publishers
199 W. 8th Ave., Suite 3
Eugene, OR 97401

www.wipfandstock.com

PAPERBACK ISBN: 978-1-6667-9348-2
HARDCOVER ISBN: 978-1-6667-9347-5
EBOOK ISBN: 978-1-6667-9346-8

Cataloguing-in-Publication data:

Names: Maia, Filipe, editor.

Title: Decolonizing Wesleyan theology : theological engagements from the underside of Methodism / edited by Filipe Maia.

Description: Eugene, OR : Cascade Books, 2024 | Series: Wesleyan and Methodist Explorations | Includes bibliographical references and index.

Identifiers: ISBN 978-1-6667-9348-2 (paperback) | ISBN 978-1-6667-9347-5 (hardcover) | ISBN 978-1-6667-9346-8 (ebook)

Subjects: LCSH: Methodist Church—Doctrines. | Theology, Doctrinal.

Classification: BX8331.3 .D43 2024 (print) | BX8331.3 .D43 (ebook)

02/12/24

CONTENTS

List of Contributors | vii

Introduction: Decolonizing Wesleyan Theology | xi
FILIPE MAIA

Chapter I   The Wesleyan Quartet: Wesleyan Theology in the Decolonial Turn | 1

                   FILIPE MAIA

Chapter II   Grace that Liberates and Unites in the Mission of God: Liberation Theology and Wesleyan Theology in Latin America | 26

                   PABLO GUILLERMO OVIEDO

Chapter III   A Decolonial Physic: Medical Science, Healing, and the Ecology of Knowledge in Methodism | 49

                   PABLO MANUEL FERRER

Chapter IV   Wesleyan Methodism and the Interruption of Ancestral Bodies in Angolan Liturgical Practices | 66

                   ELVIRA MOISÉS CAZOMBO

Chapter V   Ministering While Single: An Angolan Perspective on Methodism and Marriage | 84

                   VIRGÍNIA INÁCIO DOS SANTOS

CONTENTS

Chapter VI Trapped between the Pew and the Altar: Wesleyan Traditions and Decoloniality; An African Feminist Perspective | 99

LILIAN CHEELO SIWILA

Chapter VII Decolonizing the Church of Empire: The Church on the Move for Justice, Peace, and Life | 115

J. C. PARK

Chapter VIII Water and Sand: Illuminating Native Theologies with a Wesleyan Lens of Spiritual Experience | 137

AMELIA KOH-BUTLER

Index | 161

LIST OF CONTRIBUTORS

Elvira Moisés Cazombo is an elder and district superintendent at The United Methodist Church (UMC) in Angola and a professor at the Faculty of Theology at the Methodist University of Angola in Luanda. She holds graduate degrees in literature and culture of the Ancient Near East and in biblical studies. Cazombo has also served at the General Board of Global Ministries of the UMC and in several other capacities within Angolan Methodism. She is the author of "Sabedoria feminina em provérbios bíblicos e na cultura Bantu," in *Abrindo Sulcos: para uma teologia afro-americana e caribenha*, edited by Maricel Mena Lopes and Peter Theodore Nash (Sinodal, 2003).

Pablo Manuel Ferrer received his doctorate in biblical studies from the Instituto Superior Evangélico de Estudios Teológicos (ISEDET), in Buenos Aires, Argentina. He teaches in several institutions and regularly offers seminars and workshops. He is a member of the Methodist Church in Argentina and the author of numerous articles and book chapters, including "Romanos 6–7: Reencontrar las dicotomías en el texto. Y en la vida," in *Revista de Interpretación Bíblica Latinoamericana (RIBLA)* 87 (2022/2); and the chapters "Pragmalingüística" and "Hermenéutica de los sujetos," in *Nuevas aproximaciones al texto bíblico. Métodos exegéticos y hermenéutica en el siglo 21*, edited by Néstor Míguez (La Aurora, 2022).

Amelia Koh-Butler's doctorate in missiology (intercultural studies) from Fuller Seminary led her to gathering many culture-language resources for missional worship. She is the convenor of the Worship and Liturgy Committee of the World Methodist Council and local minister of the Multilingual

Eastwood Uniting Church Congregation in Sydney, Australia. Publications include articles, book chapters, and liturgical resources.

Filipe Maia is assistant professor of theology at Boston University School of Theology (United States) and co-convener of the World Parish Webinar. He is the author of *Trading Futures: A Theological Critique of Financialized Capitalism* (Duke University Press, 2022) and co-editor with David W. Scott of *Methodism and American Empire: Reflections on Decolonizing the Church* (Abingdon Press, 2023).

Pablo Guillermo Oviedo is a graduate of the Instituto Superior Evangélico de Estudios Teológicos (ISEDET, Buenos Aires, Argentina) and of the Perkins School of Theology, Southern Methodist University (United States). He studied history at the National University of Córdoba (Argentina). He is a professor of theology and history at the University of the Latin American Educational Center (UCEL), and an elder and district superintendent in the Methodist Church in Argentina.

J. C. Park received his PhD from Emory University in Systematic Theology. He has served for more than three decades as professor and president of the Methodist Theological University in Seoul, South Korea. He has taught and written on the intercultural and interfaith interpretation of Asian and Wesleyan Christianity in Korea. He also published *Crawl with God, Dance in the Spirit: A Creative Formation of Korean Theology of the Spirit* (Abingdon, 1998); "Christian Perfection and Confucian Sage Learning: An Interreligious Dialogue in the Crisis of Life," in *Wesleyan Perspectives on the New Creation* (Kingswood, 2002); and "Inter-living Theology as a Wesleyan Minjung Theology," in *Methodist and Radical* (Kingswood, 2003). He was the keynote speaker at the World Methodist Conference in 2006. He taught at Iliff School of Theology (1995) and Candler School of Theology (1999). Having served as the chair of Theological Education Committee of the World Methodist Council (2006–16), he has been the president of the World Methodist Council since 2016.

Virgínia Inácio dos Santos is a theologian and philosopher. She serves as dean of the School of Theology at the Methodist University of Angola and is a pastor at the United Methodist Church in Angola.

LIST OF CONTRIBUTORS

Lilian Cheelo Siwila is an associate professor in the School of Religion, Philosophy and Classics at the University of Kwa Zulu Natal, South Africa. She is a lecturer in Theology and Gender Studies and head of Systematic Theology and Gender Studies. She is involved in a number of theological and research-related organizations in the field of Gender, Theology, and Culture. She is a member of the Circle of Concerned African Women Theologians, and active member of a number of ecumenical bodies. She has published widely in internationally recognized journals and books, including edited book volumes.

INTRODUCTION
Decolonizing Wesleyan Theology

Filipe Maia

In August 2018, a group of scholars, pastors, and ecclesial leaders met at Wesley House in Cambridge, UK, to imagine and plot the decolonization of Methodist and Wesleyan traditions. Standing on British territory and under the shadow of the prestigious Cambridge University, the gathering embodied the ambivalent legacy of the Wesleyan tradition, birthed in the midst of British imperialism while cherished by Methodist communities in the postcolonial world. We were Methodist scholars and leaders from the Global South, immigrants in the diasporas of the Global North, all coming to Wesleyan theology via the complex entanglement between missionary movements and western colonialism.

While steeped in Wesleyan traditions, the group gathered in Cambridge embodied a Methodism that could not have been envisioned by John Wesley nor the missionaries who set out to spread "scriptural holiness" to all corners of the planet. In those corners of the world, Methodism gained new edges. Those of us meeting in British territory had returned to the birthplace of our theological and spiritual tradition with a difference. We noticed that claiming our Methodist roots demanded a reinterpretation of the tradition. The gathering showed that the Wesleyan theological tradition has been pluralized in the context of colonial and neocolonial expansion. One of the ideas suggested by the group in Cambridge was the organization of an edited volume under the working title, *Decolonizing Wesleyan Theology*. This was more than a title: it was a task.

This volume is one response to that task. It gives testimony to the Methodist roots that grow in territories and bodies that uproot longstanding colonial forces. It has been envisioned, nurtured, and curated as a work of decolonial love. Authors in this volume write from multiple locations in the Global South where our Wesleyan heritage is giving new contours to the tradition. Readers will most likely notice that the language of decline, so common in Methodist circles in North America, is rarely, if ever, mentioned. This is no indication that Methodism flourishes without difficulties in the Global South, but rather a statement about how contributors are less interested in thinking about the numerical decline of Christendom and more committed to a renewed Wesleyan theology that meets the harsh realities of a world still embedded in the structures of colonialism. The decolonial approaches to Wesleyan theology offered in this volume give witness to a tradition that gains strength and vitality in decolonial struggles and in the engagement with traditions and ways of knowing that have been suppressed by western modernity.

The essays in this volume offer perspectives into a Methodism that lives and flourishes on the underside of colonial powers. From all corners of the planet, communities of faith in the Wesleyan tradition experiment with theological imaginaries and ecclesial practices that are transforming the face of global Methodism. *Decolonizing Wesleyan Theology* gives voice to these experiments while seeking to deepen the reflection in decolonial theologies and spiritualities. As authors revisit the history of the Methodist movement, they witness to the different shapes Methodism gained in the colonies—old and new. As they revisit Wesley's own writings and other important themes in Wesleyan theology and practice, they inhabit the cracks of our founder's theology and turn it in unforeseeable directions.

It is worth mentioning that the volume that you are now engaging is but one element of the ongoing task of decolonizing Wesleyan theology and traditions. In fact, it is appropriate to approach this volume as a snapshot of an ongoing conversation. This book is the fruit of a larger project that involves monthly conversations among a global network of Methodist theologians and leaders. The "World Parish Webinar" has been a platform where we have been shaping conversations in the direction of a decolonial Methodism. Since January 2020, we have been gathering monthly and our group has grown into a global parish, a "people on the move," to borrow the expression from J. C. Park, developed in his essay later in this volume. This group has been called out as an assembly—an *ekklesia*—to retrain our theological ways of knowing and to conjure up a decolonial Wesleyan theology. We have been put on the move through these webinars: we have become a migrant church, pilgriming through many locations as we pursue the task of decolonizing the Wesleyan tradition. The World Parish Webinar became a Pentecost of sorts, a place where we share good news with the accents of a multitude of locations, where we do not pursue the homogeneity of Empire, but relish on the difference that resists the colonial dream of sameness, of a single voice, of one Wesley, of one homogenous church body. The webinar is ongoing and is convened through Wesley House in Cambridge. If you would like to join the conversation you are welcome to do so. Information can be found at Wesley House's website.

Decolonizing Wesleyan theology entails the appreciation of difference and alternative forms of knowledge production, different modes of theological imagination, the recognition and negotiation of alternative inheritances. The essays included in the volume embody these principles as they construct a decolonial Wesleyan theology. Combining Wesleyan theology and decolonial theories, this volume offers a unique contribution to Methodist studies, global Methodism, and decolonial theologies.

Decolonizing Wesleyan Theology presents eight reflections that lead readers into deeper engagements with Methodism. The first chapter, which I wrote, revisits methodological discussions about the Wesleyan quadrilateral from a decolonial perspective. It introduces key concepts and insights from decolonial theory and brings them to bear on a reflection on theological method. I suggest in the chapter that the engagement with decolonial theory loosens the angles of the Wesleyan quadrilateral, shifting its shape into a decolonial *quartet*. This Wesleyan decolonial quartet is attentive to the scripts, traditions, ways of knowing, and experiences that have been put under erasure by colonial forces.

Chapter 2, written by Pablo Guillermo Oviedo, proposes a historical and theological retrieval of key ideas from the itinerary of Wesleyan theology in Latin America and the Caribbean. It stresses the interaction between Methodist movements in the continent and Latin American liberation theologies. Oviedo argues that this process has produced a new theological and missionary synthesis. The chapter concludes with a reflection on the challenges faced by Latin American Methodism in the twenty-first century; namely, the advance of racism, xenophobia, and hatred of the poor in Latin America.

In chapter 3, Pablo Manuel Ferrer revisits Wesley's medical pamphlet, *Primitive Physic*, as a way to identify how Wesley attempted to find traditional or popular forms of medical knowledge. The chapter investigates the gospel of Mark and its account of a healing narrative, which Ferrer identifies as providing clues to thinking with multiple forms of medical knowledge. Borrowing from decolonial thinker Boaventura de Sousa Santos, Ferrer proposes an "ecology of knowledge" where different kinds of medical sciences/knowledge can coexist.

Elvira Moisés Cazombo addresses in chapter 4 the historical roots of Methodist missionary activity in Angola and the liturgical practices instituted by missionaries. She suggests that the Methodist mission in Angola failed to account for how native communities communed with sacred, ancestral forces and thus introduced a form of worship that neither respected nor accounted for the precolonial worship practices. Cazombo argues that this neglect still causes tensions in Angolan Methodism, which must be addressed through intercultural communication and the retrieval of African traditional religion and practices.

Chapter 5 is written by Virgínia Inácio dos Santos and also addresses the Methodist context in Angola. Santos reflects on the encounter of traditional marriage practices and family systems in the Angolan context and the Methodist tradition. The chapter ponders the social pressure imposed on people to get married and how this impacts the ministry of single pastors in the United Methodist Church in Angola. For Santos, these challenges reflect unsolved tensions in Angolan society and have a harmful impact on women and single people in ministry.

The next chapter, by Lilian Cheelo Siwila, engages liturgy from a South African feminist and decolonial perspective. The chapter reflects on experiences of the "church within a church," that is, groups of Methodist women that, within a congregation, create their unique space. Siwila considers these groups in their ambivalence—at times, they offer South African women liberative experiences, other times, they reinscribe oppressive dynamics. Liturgical practices in here are the key to identifying the decolonizing potential of these women groups in South Africa.

In chapter 7, J. C. Park proposes a critical discourse about peace and reconciliation from the perspective of Korean Methodism. Park bases his reflection on the "Joint Declaration on the Doctrine of Justification" (JDDJ) and connects it with new realities of global Christianity. In particular, Park considers global migration as a driving concern for the church in the twenty-first century. "The Church on the Move" is the image that orients Park's reflections as he envisions a Spirit-filled movement that transposes the walls that continue to divide our world today.

The closing chapter, by Amelia Koh-Butler, proposes a meditation on Aboriginal communities in Australia as sources for a decolonial Wesleyan theology and practice. Koh-Butler invites her readers into a conversation that retrieves ancient stories and honors land, sand, water, and wind. In dialogue with voices from Pasifika-Oceania, the chapter provides nonlinear reflections and stories that put into question traditional Western theological categories. Koh-Butler concludes by suggesting pathways for the retrieval of ancient wisdom and its integration into Wesleyan theology.

I should like to acknowledge the many contributions that made this volume possible. As mentioned, the support from Wesley House has been paramount for the World Parish Webinar where many of the essays included in this volume were presented and discussed. Andrew Stobart, Paul Chilcote, Jacqui Rivas, David Field, Amelia Koh-Butler, J. C. Park, Adam Ployd, and Lilian C. Siwila have all shared their gifts in the leadership of the World Parish webinar. To them and to all the leadership and administrative staff at Wesley House, as well as to all participants in the webinar series, I express my gratitude.

The gathering of Methodist and Wesleyan scholars at Wesley House in 2018 that ignited this project was convened with support from the General Board of Higher Education and Ministry of The United Methodist Church. Thanks are due to Amós Nascimento and Matthew Charlton for their support. J. C. Park, Andrew Stobart, and Hendrik Pieterse were also involved in the initial conversations when this project was gaining shape. I express my gratitude to Dean Bryan Stone and his assistant, Jaziya Osman, from Boston University School of Theology, for offering student workers who contributed to this volume. I'm very grateful for support received with the English adaptation of chapters 2 and 3 provided by Daniel Montañez. Thomas Roane and Diego Salazar Galvis offered editorial and proofreading support to several chapters. Translations for chapter 4 and 5 from Portuguese have been done by me. Finally, I thank Matt Wimer, George Callihan, and Charlie Collier at Wipf and Stock for their care for this volume.

Chapter I

THE WESLEYAN QUARTET
Wesleyan Theology in the Decolonial Turn[1]

Filipe Maia

Yet again we find ourselves tackling the Wesleyan quadrilateral. In a process that I should like to describe briefly in the following pages, the quadrilateral has risen to the center of multiple discussions in Wesleyan theology and, more broadly, on theological method. The theme has become an obsession for Methodism. Soon we shall actually be more properly calling it a "fourfold *syndrome*."[2] I confess to suffering from it, and other syndromes too. In particular, I'm affected by a decolonial concern that most debates around the Wesleyan quadrilateral may not attend to ways in which colonial imaginaries inflect our theological method. Therefore, my driving concern in this chapter is to integrate a decolonial gesture into the fourfold syndrome that dwells in Wesleyan theology. For this shall be my argument: it is precisely this proneness to a fourfold pattern that will open up possible decolonial pathways into Methodist theology. The fourfold syndrome that

---

1. Portions of this chapter have been presented at the World Parish Webinar, convened by Wesley House, Cambridge (United Kingdom) in December 2020 and at the 70th Wesleyan Week organized by the Faculty of Theology of the Methodist University of São Paulo (Brazil) in May 2021. I would like to express my gratitude to Hendrik Pieterse, Andrew Stobart, Martin Barcala, and José Carlos de Souza for offering feedback to my presentations.

2. Outler, *Wesleyan Theological Heritage*, 28.

nourishes the Wesleyan quadrilateral will gain a subterranean habit in the decolonial theological method I seek to elaborate in the pages to follow. I will be suggesting that a decolonial reading of the quadrilateral will shift its shape and transpose us into a more fluid, indeed more musical, *quartet*.[3]

This chapter will first situate the emergence of the Wesleyan quadrilateral in the ecclesial context of United Methodism. I then present a summary of decolonial theory while attending to the theological implications and insights that theorists in the tradition may offer. The third section of the chapter is where I offer a decolonial reading of the four elements that constitute the quadrilateral—Scripture, tradition, reason, and experience. In closing, I offer some remarks to rehearse the tunes of the Wesleyan quartet.

The Wesleyan Quadrilateral in Context

Wesleyan theology in the past century strived to identify its uniqueness by means of an appeal to the quadrilateral. In the amalgamation of the Anglican *via media*, Wesley's brand of Pietism, and twentieth-century concerns about theological method, the quadrilateral became a belated signature of Wesleyan theology. Belated because the term itself is neither present in John Wesley's writings nor fully developed as a theological method until it was first introduced by Methodist theologian Albert C. Outler.[4] Still, as Randy Maddox has suggested, "a conjoined consideration" of the four elements of the quadrilateral as "criteria in [Wesley's] theological judgments is not

---

3. I first heard the expression during a lecture offered by Charles Wood at Perkins School of Theology in the spring of 2010. I was not able to identify written sources pointing in the direction of the quartet, but I express my gratitude to Dr. Wood for introducing me to the analogy that directs my reflection in this chapter.

4. The development of Outler's thinking on the quadrilateral can be traced back to an essay published in 1968 where he speaks of the "accent" of Wesleyan theology. Outler, "Thologische Akzente," cited in Maddox, "'Honoring Conference,'" 57. As I will suggest later in the chapter, the term quadrilateral first appears in the context of a preparatory commission in The United Methodist Church. For later developments in Outler's account of the quadrilateral, see Outler, "Wesleyan Quadrilateral—in John Wesley," in *Wesleyan Theological Heritage*, 24–30; and Outler, "Through a Glass Darkly." For more extensive treatments of the quadrilateral and its development in twentieth-century Methodist theology, see Thorsen, *Wesleyan Quadrilateral*; and Gunter et al., *Wesley and the Quadrilateral*. The absence of the quadrilateral from Wesley's writings has led Ted Campbell to suggest that it has gained a somewhat "mythical" status in Methodist theology. See Campbell, "Wesleyan Quadrilateral," in Langford, *Doctrine and Theology*, 154–62.

entirely inappropriate."[5] By the early 1960s, such attunement to a combined set of sources for theological reasoning was already occupying the minds of Wesleyan scholars.[6] Outler appears to have been impacted by this debate in a 1968 essay where he introduces Wesley's "fourfold complex" as a preferable theological method in contrast to what he perceived as "biblicism, traditionalism, rationalism, and narcissism."[7] At fault in these approaches was a theological single-mindedness that Outler judged to be insufficient to address the theological and ecclesial challenges of the twentieth century.

The ecclesial context that lifted the quadrilateral to the center of Wesleyan theology is noteworthy. While Outler's essay that spoke of the "fourfold syndrome" in Wesleyan theology did not include the term "quadrilateral," the expression would soon appear in documents of the Theological Study Commission of The United Methodist Church. The initial vision for the commission was that the two denominations merging to form the UMC, the Evangelical United Brethren and The Methodist Church, would come together to formulate a doctrinal statement for the new denomination. But the members of the commission opted instead to maintain previous statements from both denominations as "landmark documents" and then craft a new document on the "theological task" of the church. This document, presented as an interim report in 1970, contains the first reference to the quadrilateral.[8] A version of the document was eventually approved and included in the 1972 *Book of Discipline of the United Methodist Church*—minus the reference to the quadrilateral. It appears, as Maddox suggests, that General Conference delegates read the quadrilateral as downgrading

---

5. Maddox, *Responsible Grace*, 36.

6. See, for example, Williams, *John Wesley's Theology Today*, where Williams introduces the four elements—Scripture, tradition, reason, and experience—of what later would be baptized as the quadrilateral. As Campbell indicates, Williams's book became the standard textbook for introduction to Wesley's theology in the English-speaking world, making his references to these four sources a preparatory path of sorts for the later reception of the quadrilateral. Campbell, "Wesleyan Quadrilateral," in Langford, *Doctrine and Theology*, 155–56.

7. Outler, "Thologische Akzente," cited in Maddox, "Honoring Conference," 57.

8. For an account of the work of the Theological Study Commission on Doctrine and Doctrinal Standards, see Campbell, "Wesleyan Quadrilateral," in Langford, *Doctrine and Theology*. See also Outler, "Introduction to the Report," in Langford, *Doctrine and Theology*, 20–25. Outler later confessed that the expression "quadrilateral" was an allusion to the "Lambeth Quadrilateral" from 1888, a list of four sources used by the Anglican Communion as criterion for churches wishing to unite with Anglicanism. Outler, "Through a Glass Darkly," 86.

the role of Scripture.⁹ The approved language speaks of the theological task of the church as being guided by four *interdependent* sources: Scripture, tradition, reason, and experience.¹⁰

Despite the rejection of the language about the quadrilateral in the *Discipline*, the term disseminated quickly. Outler himself was often disappointed about the reception of the term and the insinuation that it entailed doctrinal indifferentism. To his mind, what the quadrilateral represented at its inception was rather a new moment for theological reasoning. Outler recalls the excitement of that fateful year, 1968. He speaks of the joy wrought by the spirit of ecumenism, which helped United Methodists overcome the traditional Protestant dichotomy between Scripture and tradition and count themselves as indissolubly part of a Christian tradition. Outler writes: "United Methodists were becoming less WASPish, less chauvinist, less bourgeois, less nationalistic. Not much less, but enough less so that everybody could be optimistic."¹¹ For Outler, the quadrilateral symbolized the newness of the period and the possibility of a Wesleyan theology that was ecumenical, open-minded, and pluralistic. Pluralism, Outler insisted, did not mean doctrinal indifferentism. For him, "the Wesleyan principle of pluralism holds in dynamic balance both the biblical focus of all Christian doctrine and also the responsible freedom that all Christians must have in their theological reflections and public teaching."¹²

Despite Outler's insistence on theological pluralism and his power over the theological debate in United Methodism, the quadrilateral remained a point of confusion and conflict in the denomination. A study commission was assembled at General Conference in 1984 for the purposes of refining the statement and clarifying the special role of Scripture in the quadrilateral. In 1988, the statement was amended to indicate that the quadrilateral does not question the centrality of Scripture and to illustrate how scriptural wisdom is received and interpreted through the other three components of the quadrilateral. Ultimately, a reference to the four sources of theological knowledge remained in subsequent editions of the *Discipline* of the United Methodist Church. Its most common formulation reads: "the living core of

9. Maddox, "Honoring Conference," 58–59.
10. Gunter et al., *Wesley and the Quadrilateral*, 9–10.
11. Outler, "Through a Glass Darkly," 82.
12. Outler, "Introduction to the Report," in Langford, *Doctrine and Theology*, 21. In fact, Outler was always very fond of the notion of theological "pluralism" and equally dumbfounded by the "episcopal mandate" not to use the term as well as the evangelical pushback against pluralism. See Outler, "Through a Glass Darkly," 80–81.

the Christian faith was revealed in Scripture, illumined by tradition, vivified in personal experience, and confirmed by reason."[13]

The generating impetus behind the quadrilateral was Outler's suggestion that the pull of Wesleyan theology was never to formulate strict doctrinal affirmations. The quadrilateral revealed a concern for a *way* of doing theology that may not be exclusively Wesleyan, but was nevertheless central to Wesley's theological and pastoral project. The distinguishing mark of Methodism, in this view, is not a fixed doctrinal position or a set of authoritative confessions. Rather, Wesleyan theology is distinct about the way it goes about doing theology. "[We] can see in Wesley a distinctive theological *method*, with Scripture as its preeminent norm but interfaced with tradition, reason, and Christian experience as dynamic and interactive aids in the interpretation of the Word of God in Scripture."[14] Outler was resolute in his understanding of the usefulness of the quadrilateral for contemporary Methodism and, more broadly, to Christian theology. He stressed that the quadrilateral "is a good deal more sophisticated than it appears" and that its full potential for "contemporary theologizing" is not yet realized.[15] As a theological method, the quadrilateral "preserves the primacy of Scripture, it profits from the wisdom of the tradition, it accepts the disciplines of critical reason, and its stress on the Christian experience of grace gives it existential force."[16] As is normally the case, Outler's ideas are theologically elegant and contextually valid.

Among other things, the debate around the quadrilateral signals to the rifts and tensions in Methodism, particularly in its North American context. On the one hand, liberally inclined theologians like John Cobb favored the quadrilateral as a way to reclaim a mode of theological reasoning that is fluid and open to the demands of the contemporary world.[17] Liberals tended to deploy the quadrilateral to avow modernizing energies in Methodist denominations claiming that the import of experience ought to challenge literalist interpretations of the Bible.[18]

---

13. United Methodist Church, *Book of Discipline*, para. 104, section 4.
14. Outler, *Wesleyan Theological Heritage*, 25.
15. Outler, *Wesleyan Theological Heritage*, 25–26.
16. Outler, *Wesleyan Theological Heritage*, 26.
17. See Cobb, *Grace and Responsibility*, 173–76; Cobb, "Is Theological Pluralism Dead in the U.M.C.?," in Langford, *Doctrine and Theology*, 162–67.
18. For greater context for these theological disputes in the 1990s, see the introduction of Gunter et al., *Wesley and the Quadrilateral*.

On the other side of the spectrum, conservative Wesleyan theologians argued that the quadrilateral was an easy way out of doctrinal discussions and became an alibi for a denomination that did not want to think deeply about the content of its faith. For William Abraham, the "attempt to make the quadrilateral the benchmark of United Methodist identity is unconstitutional . . . [and] intellectually wrongheaded."[19] Theological indifferentism is the catchphrase here. Conservative Methodists found themselves wary of the quadrilateral for its apparent downplaying of the authority of Scripture and the perceived trivialization of Christian doctrine by means of the affirmation of the category of experience.

The attack on the quadrilateral, especially in the current climate in North American Methodism, is fueled by the perceived threat of "theological pluralism" and fear of a loss of the denominational identity and connection to the broader Christian faith.[20] Today, this position informs much of the controversy in The United Methodist Church and the formation of the Global Methodist Church. In this polemic, the quadrilateral has emerged once again to the forefront of the ecclesial debate.[21] Abraham treats the quadrilateral as faulty theological reasoning and as the main culprit for a church that has forgotten its normative teachings:

> [The quadrilateral] was incoherent because it excluded the classical faith of the church as normative; because it was a mere stopgap held together by the personality and reputation of Outler; because the quadrilateral is not built for purpose as a theological method or as a theory of knowledge in theology; and because it was only a matter of time before a passionately committed network would seek to impose their particular vision of the faith on the church as a whole. Add to these problems the fact that the quadrilateral made it impossible to achieve genuine consensus on mission and practice, and we arrive at the crisis that is now upon us.[22]

In Abraham's reading, the pluralization of theological sources can only lead to confusion and the neglect of the sole source of theological

---

19. Abraham, *Waking from Doctrinal Amnesia*, 56–57. On a subsequent essay, Abraham raises the ante in his attacks of the quadrilateral in "What Should United Methodists Do." For similar arguments, see Morris-Chapman, *Whither Methodist Theology Now?*; and Morris-Chapman, "Beyond the Quadrilateral."

20. See Walls, *Problem of Pluralism*.

21. Abraham, "Doctrine or Death," 35; Dunnam, "Theological Accountability," 71.

22. Abraham, "Doctrine or Death," 35.

knowledge—revelation. For Abraham, the quadrilateral does not even bother to take into account this category.[23]

"Doctrine of Death," the title of one of Abraham's essays, invites responses that can only abide by the terms of the polemic. But my journey through the quadrilateral in this chapter obeys different modes of theological reasoning that shall make me unequipped and disinterested in engaging in the polemic. My gesture in the direction of the quartet will evade the assumption that the only alternative to doctrinal purity is death—an assumption that is nothing but ironic for colonized communities whose existence have always been challenged by the spread of Christian orthodoxy in the modern period. More importantly, I will be stressing that the decolonial task that I embrace in here does not dismiss the relevance of the theological category of revelation nor the sources for the discernment of theological truth.

Rather, the decolonial turn in theology shifts the underlying assumptions about authority of the sources named in the Wesleyan quadrilateral.[24] On the one hand, my contribution in this chapter certainly seeks to echo Outler's commitment to pluralizing the debate on theological method. On the other hand, my hope is also to evoke the decolonial possibilities of the "fourfold syndrome" in Wesleyan theology. Decolonial theory will support this methodological debate by providing tools to question how the authority of any given source is construed and how it might eclipse other sources. In my discussion of the quadrilateral, I want to carve a space for the recognition of the *erasure* of texts, traditions, reasons, and experiences. I want to suggest that in the construction of Christian authority and in the establishment of authoritative sources of theological knowing this erasure is paramount. But, more specifically, I will argue that in excavating sources that have been deemed improper for the discernment of theological truth, something very much like *revelation* takes place.

The Decolonial Turn

A concern for the production of knowledge is the signature mark of decolonial theory. Decolonization entails resisting and transforming dominant theological imaginaries while offering ways of knowing that incorporate traditions and the wisdom of colonized and otherwise subjugated peoples.

---

23. Abraham, *Waking from Doctrinal Amnesia*, 63.

24. From a feminist postcolonial lens, Kwok Pui-lan has engaged the categories of the quadrilateral in *Postcolonial Imagination and Feminist Theology*, 53–76.

For Christian thought, decolonization entails resistance to dominant theological imaginaries and the opening up to ways of knowing that incorporate and deepen traditions and wisdom that come from colonized communities.²⁵ Given the fact that the question of method and of sources of theological knowledge is at the center of the debate about the quadrilateral, Wesleyan theology can benefit from a direct engagement with decolonial theories. This section offers a broad summary of the insights coming from decolonial thinkers as I prepare the ground for a decolonial account of the Wesleyan quadrilateral.

There is an affinity between decolonial thought and postcolonial theories that responded to the anticolonial struggles, especially in the 1950s and 1960s. Figures like Frantz Fanon, Edward Said, Gayatri C. Spivak, and Homi Bhabha are central in this tradition. The decolonial turn shares much of the insights offered by these critics while arguing that colonial power might be more ingrained than what postcolonial theory has sustained. With attention to the Latin American and Caribbean contexts, decolonial thought approaches colonialism not only as a historical and political force, but also as an *epistemic* force. That is, colonialism shaped structures of thought and knowledge production that were inaugurated and enforced at the expense of the burying of the thinking and worldview of colonized peoples. For this reason, decolonial theorists argue that it is insufficient to articulate critiques of colonialism that deploy distinctively western categories and patterns of thought.²⁶

For Walter Mignolo, the modern/colonial nexus is one that spans from the late fifteenth century to "the current state of globalization" and is one that was built on a particular epistemological framework that "subalternized" all forms of knowing outside the metropolitan centers of knowledge and power.²⁷ Therefore, the critique of coloniality ought to stem from a different ecology of knowledges, in the apt phrase from decolonial thinker Boaventura de Sousa Santos.²⁸ Decolonial theory stresses that colonialism

---

25. The literature on theology and decolonization is growing at a fast pace. A brief and non-exhaustive list of works in the field is: Isasi-Díaz and Mendieta, *Decolonizing Epistemologies*; González-Justiniano, *Centering Hope*; An and Craig, *Beyond Man*; Mendoza-Álvarez and Courau, *Decolonial Theology*.

26. For an account of the history of decolonial theory and its departure from the disciplines associated with "Area Studies" (where many postcolonial critics were located), see Grosfoguel, "Epistemic Decolonial Turn."

27. Mignolo, *Local Histories*, 13.

28. Santos, *End of Cognitive Empire*, 8, 13–16.

was more than the expansion of power of European nation-states. Rather, colonialism involved the creation of the world in the image and likeness of colonial power. In the words of Eleanor Craig and An Yountae, "Coloniality is the universalization and normalization of matrices of power that historically enacted colonization itself and the presumption of superiority that these forces collectively grant to discourses articulated from colonizing and western perspectives."[29] Resistance to colonialism, in this sense, requires the excavation of suppressed forms of knowledge and a renewed system of knowledge production.

Decolonial theory emphasizes that the modern emphasis on knowledge and rationality is embedded in what the Peruvian sociologist Aníbal Quijano has termed "coloniality of power."[30] Quijano points out that coloniality was the byproduct of a "systematic repression" of the "ways of knowing, of producing knowledge, of producing perspectives, images and systems of images, symbols, and modes of signification," including of beliefs and imaginaries of a supranatural realm.[31] This in turn had the effect of foreclosing the "cultural production" of subjugated peoples as well as an efficacious way to socially and culturally control colonized populations. The power of colonialism was more than the power of swords, armies, and economic imperialism. It was a power of conquest through knowledge, or rather: the invention of a mode of knowing that is in itself a mode conquering. At the same time, European culture and cultural production turned into a "universal cultural model."[32] This model was normative on a global scale for it was consolidated by colonial power but it was also *seductive* precisely because it was a channel to access power. In this manner, subjugated peoples were seduced to master the protocols of European knowledge and culture for the sake of gaining space at the colonial table.

To counter epistemic conquest, Quijano invites his readers into an "epistemic decolonization" that shall give room for new "intercultural communication, to an exchange of experiences and significations, as the basis of

---

29. An and Craig, *Beyond Man*, 3–4.

30. Quijano, "Colonialidad y Modernidad"; Quijano, "Colonialidad del poder." Walter Mignolo stresses how the concept of "coloniality" is a "double-faced concept" because it offers, on the one hand, the critical analytic to question colonialism and its epistemic apparatus and, second, because it already points to "utopian" possibilities for alternative futures. Mignolo, "Decolonizing Western Epistemologies," in Isasi-Díaz and Mendieta, *Decolonizing Epistemologies*, 20.

31. Quijano, "Colonialidad y Modernidad," 12.

32. Quijano, "Colonialidad y Modernidad," 12–13.

another rationality that may aspire, with certain degree of legitimacy, to be universal."[33] With Quijano, decolonial theorists will therefore stress that in order to resist colonialism, we must excavate modes of knowing that have been suppressed by coloniality and seek ways to change the paradigm of knowledge production. Catherine Walsh points out that the decolonization "implies the recognition and undoing of hierarchical structures of race, gender, heteropatriarchy, and class" that were introduced in the colonial era and "continue to control life, knowledge, spirituality, and thought, structures that are clearly intertwined with and constitutive of global capitalism and Western modernity."[34] Of note in the passage is the recognition that colonialism also entails the control of spirituality. In the hierarchies of coloniality, there is also the hierarchy of religious traditions, ranked according to their proximity to the heights of colonial Christianity and its claims to doctrinal and epistemic purity and superiority.

According to decolonial theorists, the good news is that we have been witnessing to awakening and dissemination of new ways of knowing. For Mignolo, our time has witnessed the rise and the dissemination of a "border gnosis," a new form of knowledge that emerges from the underground and the fractures of the modern/colonial geopolitical world. The use of the word gnosis is meaningful for Mignolo because it rejects the dichotomy between faith and knowledge, between knowing as an "episteme" and knowing as "doxa," or opinion. Border gnosis includes both and thinks in the complexity of knowledge/faith/opinion.[35] With the Caribbean philosopher and poet Eduard Glissant, Mignolo refers to border thinking as one that does not seek to find a synthesis out of the encounter of two different categories—be they languages, cultures, or religions. Border thinking exists, lives, and breathes something new, something that is not a simple synthesis of antagonistic forces.[36]

For Santos, what we have before us is the rise of the "epistemologies of the South." He refers to the "ecology of knowledge" that is nurtured by this emergence as the "recognition of the copresence of different ways of knowing and the need to study the affinities, divergences, complementarities, and contradictions among them in order to maximize the effectiveness

---

33. Quijano, "Colonialidad y Modernidad," 19–20.
34. Mignolo and Walsh, *On Decoloniality*, 17.
35. Mignolo, *Local Histories*, 9–10.
36. Mignolo, *Local Histories*, 78.

of the struggles of resistance against oppression."³⁷ The emerging epistemologies of the South take shape out of the encounter of four movements. The first is what Santos calls the "sociology of absences," a concept used to address how in hegemonic forms of knowing communities of knowledge are made absent. Second comes the "sociology of emergence," a reference to the communities whose knowledge comes to the surface and the communities that claim them as such. Thirdly, once this emergence has been recognized, Santos calls forth an "ecology of knowledge"; this speaks to the need to think of knowledge production in ecological terms, and stress the connections needed for knowing. Finally, Santos speaks of the need of "intercultural translation" as a way to translate and communicate knowledge across cultural, linguistic, and epistemic difference.³⁸

Decolonial epistemology is therefore relational; it is a thinking-with. In the concept coined by the Andean indigenous thinkers Nina Pacari, Fernando Huanacumi Mamani, and Félix Patzi Paco, this is *vincularidad*—perhaps translatable as "linkage" or "relationality." This speaks to a mode of thinking relationality that stresses interdependence among all living organisms.³⁹ Similarly, Chicana thinker Gloria Anzaldúa invites decolonial thinkers to inhabit the space of *nepantla*. This is a Nahuatl term that Anzaldúa embraced to name and inhabit an in-between zone, a liminal space of grave transformative potential. Anzaldúa theorizes *nepantla* as a "space between two bodies of water, the space between two worlds."⁴⁰ It is a space where one is neither this nor that, for one is indeed changing. The indetermination of *nepantla* causes anxiety and confusion for it is a time/space marked by the loss of control and the impossibility of clinging to one definitive identity. In *nepantla*, one wrestles with the more-than-one as the one is turning into something else. In the words of AnaLouise Keating, *nepantla* "includes both radical dis-identification and transformation. We dis-identify with existing beliefs, social structures, and models of identity; by so doing, we are able to transform these existing conditions."⁴¹ The knowing of a decolonial theology takes place in this dis-placement, in this dislocation to a place where the unknown

37. Santos, *End of the Cognitive Empire*, 8.
38. For fuller accounts of these four categories in Santos' work, see Santos, *Epistemologies of the South*, chapter 4; Santos, *End of Cognitive Empire*, 25–34.
39. See Mignolo and Walsh, *On Decoloniality*, 1–2.
40. Anzaldúa, *Borderlands*, 237.
41. Keating, "From Borderlands," 9.

is welcomed as such, where one resists rigid boundaries—of thought, of nation-states, of identities, and of theologies.

From the Quadrilateral to the Decolonial Quartet

For Methodist theology, the quadrilateral has served as an identity marker, but might we approach it as more than that? Might the quadrilateral be the creative, difficult, transformative point where Methodist theology becomes ready to become something *else*? In what follows, I suggest that decolonial theory offers a refreshing twist to the quadrilateral. Admittedly, this twist will morph the axes of this quadrilateral into something more than right angles. As these angles lose their rigidity, I wonder if we may approach the fourfold pattern of Wesleyan theology with a more colorful, indeed musical, gesture. Instead of a quadrilateral, one may picture the confluence of Scripture, tradition, experience, and reason as a quartet. The musical analogy here speaks to the impossibility of separating multiple voices. It is rather their interrelation in their difference that renders the quartet its harmony. As we have seen, decolonial theory cherishes the thinking that happens through a polyphony of voices, which has been a quality of the quadrilateral. In the decolonial Wesleyan quartet, this polyphonic way of thinking does not strive for doctrinal univocity, but rather relishes in the theological newness that emerges when we encounter multiple voices, particularly those who have been silenced in the past.

A decolonial Wesleyan theology will recognize that the Bible has been an important script for the coloniality of power. Mignolo, in fact, refers to Christianity as the first "global" religion in the sense that it was the first "local history" that presented and imposed itself as a global design.[42] In the words of postcolonial feminist theologian Kwok Pui-lan, the "introduction of the Bible and Christian faith to foreign lands was used to justify the political and military aggression of the West."[43] Through the Christian/colonial expansion, the provenance of the Scripture as interpreted by Christian expansionists was erased and the Bible came to be presented as a global book, one with the force of erasing so many local stories, so much scriptural wisdom across the colonized world. In the hands of Protestant missionaries in the colonial era, *sola scriptura* meant that the Christian canon *alone* had

---

42. Mignolo, *Local Histories*, 21.
43. Kwok, *Postcolonial Imagination*, 61.

revealing power at the expense of other scripts that sustained, inspired, and liberated communities for centuries.[44] The colonial interpretation of *sola scriptura* assumes not only the exclusivity of the Christian canon, but also its independence from everything else. The Bible is portrayed to colonized peoples as the sole means of admittance into divine grace and its political correlate, civilization, all the while the colonial mediation is conveniently downplayed. As postcolonial theorists have insisted, being introduced to Christian Scripture was a rite of passage whereby colonized peoples had to be baptized into the cultural protocols of the colonizers.[45]

The focal point of a decolonial reading of the Wesleyan quartet is to problematize the erasure of scripts in the name of the one Scripture. The colonial bent in Christian thought eclipses this polyphonic nature of Scripture itself for the sake of a monotone approach to Scripture. In the age of colonial expansion, monotonous theology became the tool for the Christian-colonial nexus.

It would be a mistake to understand this argument as somehow questioning the centrality of Scripture to the Christian faith. The point here is problematizing the erasure of so many other scripts and ways of knowing in the name of a homogenizing Scripture.[46] And more: the point of the decolonial quartet is to affirm that scriptural authority as the rule of faith for Christian communities cannot entail the separation of the Bible from the many other voices that are always already echoing when we come before Scripture. Much of the commentary about the role of Scripture in the Wesleyan quadrilateral focuses on Wesley's assertion that he was a *homo unius libri*, a man of one book. But we have yet to consider how Wesley deals with the concept of *authority*. In not confronting this question, we

---

44. Homi Bhabha's influential exposition of the arrival of the "English Book" in India is central to this claim. He points out that in the colony the "discovery of the book installs the sign of appropriate representation: the word of God, truth, art creates the conditions of a beginning, a practice of history and narrative." Bhabha, *Location of Culture*, 149.

45. Tamez, "Bible and the Five Hundred Years," in Sugirtharajah, *Voices from the Margin*, 12–19; Dube, "Consuming a Colonial Cultural Bomb," in *Postcoloniality, Translation*, 17–28; Sugirtharajah, "Postcolonial Exploration," in *Postcolonial Bible*, 91–117.

46. Kwok highlights five characteristics of postcolonial criticism with regards to biblical interpretation, to which I subscribe entirely: (1) exposing the co-optation of the Bible by western imperialism; (2) a commitment to counterhegemonic narratives and voices within Scripture; (3) insistence on situating the Bible in dialogue with the multi-faith context of the third world; (4) receptivity to indigenous perspectives and critique; (5) an appeal to alternative forms of hermeneutical frameworks, like postmodernism. Kwok, *Postcolonial Imagination*, 64.

run the risk of conforming to the model of authority that assumes that power resides in a scriptural text that comes from above, disconnected and disinterested in the material reality where life meets Scripture. This top-down approach to authority and to power cannot be perceived apart from its colonial inheritance. And it is this model of scriptural authority that is questioned by the decolonial turn.

In the decolonial quartet, the edges of Scripture are not closed off at the closing end of the biblical canon. The canon of revelation multiplies itself constantly when it is enfleshed in the life of the faith community. Translating the Bible, both its text as well as its message, is always already a pluralizing process.[47] For decolonial theology, this process can be life-giving and liberative for it is through it that subjugated peoples inscribe their voices in a holy book. This inscription of the life of suppressed peoples in Scripture is what sustains the vitality of Christian Scripture. Decolonizing our understanding of Christian Scripture is to open ourselves to the communing that takes place between the life-world as illumined by a divine liberating word. Colonial theologies enclose this line of communication and of communing and thus interrupt the possibility of an encounter with a "traveler unknown" whose paths are never restricted to any one canon.[48] Decolonizing the quadrilateral and opening ourselves to the Wesleyan quartet offers us the chance of encountering in the biblical canon a symphonic combination of multiple voices and sounds. It also affords the possibility that echoes of so many other voices and harmonies might too resound in our biblical encounters.

The second voice of the quartet sings the ancestral tunes of tradition. The historical roots of the Wesleyan account of tradition—and its reception in the debate about the quadrilateral—lead us back to Anglican theological debates in the seventeenth century. This is the historical period when Anglicanism is defining its theological position as a *via media* between Roman Catholicism and Protestantism and hence developing a unique blend of the reformed idea of *sola scriptura* aligned with a certain sense of tradition that, while not authoritative in determining biblical interpretation, does offer

---

47. I base this argument on Walter Benjamin's insightful suggestion that the task of the translator is not merely to transport words from one linguistic system to another. Rather, Benjamin envisions translation as a process that transforms the "host" language as it made to welcome the words and worldviews coming from a foreign language. See Benjamin, "Task of the Translator," in *Illuminations*, 69–82.

48. The reference comes from Charles Wesley's hymn, "Come, O Thou Traveler Unknown," in *United Methodist Hymnal*, 387.

the context with which one approaches Scripture. For Ted Campbell, it is possible to track two historical moments that Anglican sources determined as authoritative to inform their understanding of Christian tradition.[49] The first refers to the first four centuries in Christian history. In his writings, Wesley treats the pre-Constantinian period as unique. According to Wesley, ecclesial practices and theological emphases systematically observed in Christian communities of the period ought to be treated as normative for the church.[50] The second period is precisely the founding documents of the Church of England. For Wesley, these documents revitalized the Christian faith in the British Isles precisely because of their faithfulness to the creeds of the primitive church. For this reason, whenever Wesley spoke of a Christian tradition, he referred to these Anglican sources: the Articles of Religion, the Homilies, and the Book of Common Prayer.[51] We do well to recognize that what Wesley identified as tradition was not a very "traditional" way of thinking about tradition. By and large, Wesley thought of tradition as the ante-Nicene tradition or the pre-Constantine era, particularly the Greek fathers.[52] As many Wesleyan scholars have pointed out, the venture into the Greek tradition, a bit uncommon for a western theologian, was quite generative for Wesley.

While Wesley's claims about the purity of the primitive church are historically inaccurate and theologically questionable, it remains significant that he remained so concerned about the Constantinian turn in Christian history.[53] Wesley undeniably noticed that succumbing to the power of the Roman Empire had a detrimental impact in the vitality of the Christian witness. One wonders why Wesley would not have noticed the same danger operative in his own Anglican Church, whose global prominence was fueled by the expansion of the British Empire. Wesley's own commitments to the British monarchy will not make him the ideal voice

---

49. Campbell, "Interpretative Role of Tradition," in Gunter et al., *Wesley and the Quadrilateral*, 65.

50. Campbell, "Interpretative Role of Tradition," in Gunter et al., *Wesley and the Quadrilateral*, 69.

51. Gunter et al., *Wesley and the Quadrilateral*, 71.

52. Maddox, *Responsible Grace*, 42–43.

53. According to Maddox, Wesley was influenced by the restorationist vision about the primitive church embraced by Puritans and Anabaptists, though he eventually came to realize that one ought not to treat this period as free from mistakes and sin. In Maddox's perspective, Wesley's was not a "totally naive primitivism." Maddox, *Responsible Grace*, 43.

to speak on behalf of decolonizing of the tradition that sustains his name. But Wesleyans need not succumb to our founder's monarchical passions so long as we notice that even the tradition that comes to claim Wesley's inheritance is from the outset inflected by voices that do not fit comfortably within the canons of empire.

Humming along the harmonies of the quartet, a decolonial Wesleyan theology will need to investigate and appreciate traditions that are not one. More precisely: we shall need to recognize that the Methodist tradition inhabits a global parish comprised of wisdom and beliefs that transcend parochial knowledge. The decolonization of our Wesleyan theological imaginaries ought to acknowledge traditions that were historically deemed improper for Christian reasoning. Therefore, before anything else, the Christian tradition that is open to its decolonization will need to recognize that the historical formation of the notion of one authoritative Christian tradition took place at the expense of the burying of so many other traditions.

Theologian Willie Jennings takes to task Alaisdair MacIntyre's moral philosophy according to which a tradition is a self-contained system that, once appropriated by a subject, offers resources for self-critique and internal development. For MacIntyre, the task of theology is always embedded within a tradition that informs the parameters of the endeavor but that also trains people into a deepening relation with this tradition. Jennings, however, questions the self-coherence of the Christian tradition in the modern period. At stake for Jennings is how Christian "tradition" has been coded within the protocols of colonial modernity and the racial discourse that it engendered. In Jennings's perspective, MacIntyre treats Christian tradition "[carrying] within itself the apparatus of judgment," thus allowing the tradition to "cultivate the ability to make judgments in regard to the excellence of its practices, its practitioners, and even its conceptual tools for making judgments." Yet, Jennings concludes, "the colonialist moment encases this Christian apparatus of judgment in new worldly power."[54] This suggests that an uncritical endorsement of a Christian tradition in modern times quickly succumbs to what colonial Christianity has deemed as part of the tradition—and also that which this tradition has excluded. Indeed, how many traditions have been suppressed, rejected, extinguished so that we could have a Christian tradition? How many voices and ways of knowing have been obscured by the right angles of the Wesleyan quadrilateral?

54. Jennings, *Christian Imagination*, 107.

A decolonial quartet confronts these questions at the core of the theological debate. The decolonization of theological imaginaries will recognize traditions that have not been deemed appropriate for Christian theological reflection and the traditions that have elevated themselves as the arbiters of all other traditions. Decolonization entails the acknowledgment that the formation of a Christian tradition entailed the erasure of a multitude of traditions. In the decolonial quartet, the voice of tradition is attentive to power relations constituted in the colonial era as well as the traditions that emerge in decolonial struggles. In the Wesleyan tradition, this means situating our tradition and our inheritance in open dialogue with pre- and para-Wesleyan traditions so that we can recognize and appreciate their impact in our way of doing theology.

Moving on to the third voice of the quartet, reason, means entering the hegemonic category in the modern-colonial matrix. For decolonial theory, reason is a premier site where coloniality takes its seat. The determination of the "rational" element in colonized and subjugated populations was a notable element of western expansion in the colonial era. Under the name of "reason," colonial forces portrayed their ways of knowing as singular and as exclusive. In Enrique Dussel's work, one cannot approach the Cartesian, "I think, therefore I am," without a prior account of the colonial attitude, "I conquer, therefore I am."[55] Modern rationalism, in Dussel's view, was modulated by a particular mode of reasoning that is in itself a form of conquest.

One repercussion of the modern account of reason is the formation of a concept of religion that must constantly negotiate the basis for its existence in tension with rationality. The modern study of religion is marked by the dichotomy of knowledge versus faith and the constant need to identify the proper boundaries between the two. In the most thorough articulation of this dispute, Kant famously situated religion within the bounds of "practical reason." That had the effect of placing religion within the confines of individual preference whereas political matters were meant to be located at the "secular" sphere. Recent analyses by Nelson Maldonado-Torres, An Yountae, and Rafael Vizcaíno are leading decolonial theory in the direction of the questioning of the category of "secularism," as the counterpart to the colonial understanding of religion.[56] The decolo-

---

55. See Dussel, *Invention of the Americas*.

56. See Maldonado-Torres, "Secularism and Religion," in Moraña, *Coloniality at Large*; An, "Myth of the Secular Revolutionary"; Vizcaíno, *Decolonial Responses*;

nial turn in religious studies, philosophy, and theology is undergoing a complete questioning of the epistemic categories that informed modern religious studies and the rationality that sustained it.

Decolonial theology will therefore challenge the received modern mode of reason. If colonial reason seeks to know in order to conquer, the decolonial reason will seek to be in relation as a form of knowledge. As I have been suggesting, decolonial theorists insist on the formation of pluralizing epistemologies that account for the multiple forms of reasoning. In Santos' vocabulary, this entails an ecology of knowledges. In this account, one partially accepts the *critical* inheritance of the Enlightenment, but expands the role of reason to integrate ways of knowing that have been suppressed. Critical reasoning, in its Kantian iteration, meant setting the limits and boundaries of human reason. Decolonial reasoning, rather, inhabits a commitment to border thinking, to the thinking that appreciates complexities, and negotiates differences, rather than suppressing it. This thinking-with may inaugurate a new type of reason that bears witness to ancient wisdom and resists extractivist methodologies and epistemologies, in Santos's phrasing.[57]

We are now in the position to move to the fourth voice in the Wesleyan quartet—experience. As several scholars have argued, the category of experience is perhaps Wesley's greatest contribution to Anglican discussions on theological method. By the time Wesley was receiving his theological training at Oxford University, the Anglican tradition had well established itself on a triad theological method of Scripture, tradition, and reason. For Outler, Wesley's "genius" was to add the experience of "vital faith" to the Anglican triad. The crux of the matter for Wesley was the concern that affirming doctrinal orthodoxy was radically different from experiencing vital faith. With this fourth voice, "Wesley was trying to incorporate the notion of *conversion* into the Anglican tradition."[58] Outler further suggests that the appreciation of experience gave Wesley a distinct, if not divergent, notion of authority. "The effect of such changes [to Anglican practice and theological method], was to put the question of authority into a new context: to relate it more nearly to individual's conscience, to small group consensus, and also to link it practically with the idea of 'accountable discipleship.'"[59] We might

---

Vizcaíno, "Secular Decolonial Woes."

57. Santos, *End of Cogntive Empire*, 130.
58. Outler, *Wesleyan Theological Heritage*, 27.
59. Outler, *Wesleyan Theological Heritage*, 27–28.

supplement Outler's account in here to stress that placing "authority into a new context" engenders an altogether different understanding of authority. Such authority lies no longer in the hands of church hierarchy not even in the exclusive realm of doctrinal confessions and canonical formulations. By playing with the Anglican triad of theological sources, Wesley may have opened up a new pathway into discerning theological truths under a different pattern of authority.

The emphasis on experience had a dual role in Wesley's theology. First, it confirmed Wesley's theological anthropology and the centrality of the senses as God-given dimensions of human life meant to open ourselves up to divine revelation and to God's graceful actions in saving us. Secondly, Wesley also believed that experience is capable of perceiving and discerning God's self-revelation in creation.[60] Maddox further suggests that Wesley's use of the category of experience suggested, on the one hand, the inner experience of assurance of faith, which he appropriated from Pietism. But experience in Wesley also entails a communal dimension connected to the type of "social religion" that he considered to be the real essence of Christianity.[61]

Locating experience at the level of communal discernment affords decolonial horizons to the Wesleyan quartet. In a decolonial view, experience cannot be located in the hands of a sovereign subject who commands and controls it. Rather, Wesley's "social religion" suggests that religious experience puts the life of faith at the center of the social tensions of the life of the community and of society. The assurance of faith that Wesley sought to experience and nurture in his followers ought to be codified not simply as the assurance that one is justified by God's grace. While acknowledging its importance, we also need to think of a collective experience of the assurance of justice, confirming that the work of the people is just, that the God's grace is present in the work of justice. As Methodist liberation theologian Elsa Tamez has suggested, justification by faith, the core theological tenet of the Protestant Reformation, must not be treated as a pious pursuit of the believer alone.[62] The faith that justifies is also the faith that seeks justice for a world marred by injustice.

The quadrilateral has been accused of being a convenient theological trick that allows people to make theological claims based on self-serving

60. Gunter et al., *Wesley and the Quadrilateral*, 122.
61. Maddox, *Responsible Grace*, 45–46.
62. Tamez, *Amnesty of Grace*.

sources. The more common site for the attack is experience, which is perceived by some as an unreliable source for theological truth. This is a lengthy debate with a long history, especially in twentieth century theology. The decolonial turn, however, sheds some light into this legacy. It suggests that the tense nature of the debate is rather a symptom of the fact that centering the category of experience might actually expose the experiences that were once deemed normative for theological reasoning. That is to say, the experience of the interpreter of a tradition or of Scripture is always already at stake. But seldom has this experience been named and acknowledged until movements in the twentieth century have made it a central category for Christian theology. The accusations against experience are therefore statements that subtly attack the emergence of experiences, particularly that of women, that heretofore had been suppressed in theology. Centering the category of experience along decolonial lines allows that presumed normative experiences, which often fall under the radar, are exposed.

In the decolonial Wesleyan quartet, Scripture, tradition, reason, and experience form an ecology of knowledges. The interaction of these categories is not one where each category seeks primacy over the other. The analogy of the quartet is helpful in this case: one does not come to any voice of the quartet in isolation. While it is possible to account for each voice distinctively, one must always be attuned to how the other voices influence and support each other. The interaction between the voices forms an ecology of knowledge with the potency to generate a decolonial Wesleyan theology. Scripture is inscribed with different scripts, tradition is expanded, reason is decolonized, and experience is socialized.

Fourfold Syndrome

Still, this endeavor will gently lead us back to Outler's reflection. Late in his life, when reflecting back on the controversies generated by the quadrilateral, Outler admitted that in more than one occasion he regretted having coined the term. He in fact warned his readers not to take the quadrilateral too seriously, definitely not literally. For him, the term was designed as a "metaphor for a four-element syndrome." It was not formulated to downplay the authority of Scripture, he insisted. Rather, the quadrilateral confirms that the biblical canon is "illuminated by the collective Christian wisdom of other ages and cultures," it safeguards the Christian faith against "obscurantism" by deploying the "disciplines of critical reason," and, finally, by situating the site of reception of biblical revelation in the actual experience of individuals and communities.[63] Outler goes on to speak of how Wesley's corpus constantly portrays the authority of Scripture in tandem with the core dimension of the Christian message, namely, *salvation*. He really insists on that and claims that few Methodist theologians have abided by the principle of *analogia fidei*. Wesley himself seems to invoke a musical meditation when speaking of the role of Scripture as having to mediate by the analogy of faith. Wesley will speak constantly about the whole *tenor* of Scripture, an expression that Outler stresses as a "catch phrase" in the Wesleyan corpus.[64] Well, is that not a convenient expression for the Wesleyan quartet?

Outler will persist on his passion for the fourfold pattern. "The 'quadrilateral,'" he says in conclusion, "requires of a theologian no more than what he or she might reasonably be held accountable for, which is to say, a familiarity with Scripture that is both crucial and faithful; a taste for logical analysis as something more than a debater's weapon; plus, a vital, inward faith that is upheld by the assurance of grace and its prospective triumphs, *in this life*."[65] With Outler, I must linger for a little while in the image of a "fourfold syndrome." For a syndrome, one must recall, is a set of symptoms that take place simultaneously or in an associated fashion. The symptoms that form a syndrome may be distinct, but their intricate and complex entanglement is what constitutes their relations as a syndrome. A fourfold syndrome is thus the combination of the symptoms one witnesses in Scripture, in tradition, in reason, and in experience. The force of Outler's metaphorical depiction of the quadrilateral is indeed escaping the corners of ninety-degree angles. They might be well breaking into the symphonic contours of a quartet.

The quadrilateral's capaciousness was confirmed by a group of lay Methodists in Brazil in the 1980s. From discussions about Wesleyan theology during Sunday school, this group suggested that the category of "creation" ought to be present as yet another source for theology in Wesley's writings. Brazilian Methodist theologians like Rui de Souza Josgrilberg and José Carlos de Souza picked up the insight and systematized it to suggest a Wesleyan "pentalateral" where creation also serves the role of a

---

63. Outler, *Wesleyan Theological Heritage*, 28.
64. Outler, *Wesleyan Theological Heritage*, 30.
65. Outler, *Wesleyan Theological Heritage*, 36.

source of theological knowledge.⁶⁶ I understand in this move as an indication of the decolonial aptitude of the quadrilateral because it speaks to a theological method that is open to maneuvering and improvisations that enlarge its axes. The creative touch afforded by the adding of creation to the quadrilateral suggests that our theological knowing is open and ready for a decolonial turn and improvisation.

The Wesleyan proneness to thinking about theological sources through a fourfold pattern may open up our methodological discussions to some decolonial pathways. The quartet, I have been suggesting, speaks to a methodological nimbleness that allows the theologian to investigate and integrate multiple sources of knowing into our theological reflection. The quartet also responds to a decolonial radicalism that demands a constant movement in the direction of the colonial roots of western modernity. This movement toward the roots of coloniality is not just a form of critique. Decolonial theory supports a theological program that seeks moments of *revelation* in the excavation of suppressed scripts, traditions, modes of reasoning, and experience. Coloniality buried ways of knowing but a decolonial commitment will not treat as dead that which has been buried. Underneath the wreckage wrought by coloniality there remains a subtle, quiet, and yet decisive process of epistemic composting. That which has been buried continues to shift form and eventually makes the soil fertile for life to creep back in again. The theological knowledge that colonial Christianity buried is nourishing a subterranean uprising of decolonial wisdom. The Wesleyan quartet finds its decolonial edge in there.

Bibliography

Abraham, William J. "Doctrine or Death." In *The Next Methodism: Theological, Social, and Missional Foundations for Global Methodism*, edited by Kenneth J. Collins and Ryan N. Danker, 31–41. Franklin, TN: Seedbed, 2022. Kindle.

———. *Waking from Doctrinal Amnesia: The Healing of Doctrine in the United Methodist Church*. Nashville: Abingdon, 1995.

———. "What Should United Methodists Do with the Quadrilateral?" *Quarterly Review* 22.1 (2002) 85–88.

An, Yountae. "The Myth of the Secular Revolutionary: On Fanon's Religion." *Contending Modernities*, April 7, 2022. https://contendingmodernities.nd.edu/decoloniality/the-myth-of-the-secular-revolutionary-on-fanons-religion/.

---

66. Josgrilberg, "A Motivação Originária"; Souza, "Um modo de fazer"; Souza, "Creation." For summaries of this debate in Brazilian Methodism, see Ribeiro, "Teoria e Prática"; Souza, "Wisdom of God in Creation."

An, Yountae, and Eleanor Craig. *Beyond Man: Race, Coloniality, and Philosophy of Religion*. Durham: Duke University Press, 2021.
Anzaldúa, Gloria. *Borderlands: The New Mestiza = La Frontera*. 2nd ed. San Francisco: Aunt Lute, 1999.
Benjamin, Walter. *Illuminations: Essays and Reflections*. New York: Schocken, 2007.
Bhabha, Homi K. *The Location of Culture*. London: Routledge, 2004.
Cobb, John B. *Grace and Responsibility: A Wesleyan Theology for Today*. Nashville: Abingdon, 1995.
Dube, Musa W., and R. S. Wafula. *Postcoloniality, Translation, and the Bible in Africa*. Eugene, OR: Pickwick, 2017.
Dunnam, Maxie. "Theological Accountability." In *The Next Methodism: Theological, Social, and Missional Foundations for Global Methodism*, edited by Kenneth J. Collins and Ryan N. Danker, 66–78. Franklin, TN: Seedbed, 2022. Kindle.
Dussel, Enrique. *The Invention of the Americas: Eclipse of "the Other" and the Myth of Modernity*. New York: Continuum, 1995.
González-Justiniano, Yara. *Centering Hope as a Sustainable Decolonial Practice: Esperanza En Práctica*. Lanham: Lexington, 2022.
Grosfoguel, Ramon. "The Epistemic Decolonial Turn: Beyond Political-Economy Paradigms." *Cultural Studies* (London, England) 21.2/3 (2007) 211–23.
Gunter, W. Stephen, et al., eds. *Wesley and the Quadrilateral: Renewing the Conversation*. Nashville: Abingdon, 1997.
Isasi-Díaz, Ada María, and Eduardo Mendieta, eds. *Decolonizing Epistemologies: Latina/o Theology and Philosophy*. Transdisciplinary Theological Colloquia. New York: Fordham University Press, 2012.
Jennings, Willie James. *The Christian Imagination: Theology and the Origins of Race*. New Haven: Yale University Press, 2010.
Josgrilberg, Rui de Souza. "A Motivação Originária da Teologia Wesleyana: o Caminho da Salvação." *Caminhando* 8.12 (2003) 103–24.
Keating, AnaLouise. "From Borderlands and New Mestizas to Nepantlas and Nepantleras: Anzalduan Theories for Social Change." *Human Architecture* 4, special issue (2006) 5–16.
Kwok, Pui-lan. *Postcolonial Imagination and Feminist Theology*. Louisville: Westminster John Knox, 2005.
Langford, Thomas A., ed. *Doctrine and Theology in The United Methodist Church*. Nashville: Kingswood, 1991.
Maddox, Randy L. "'Honoring Conference': Wesleyan Reflections on the Dynamics of Theological Reflection." In *The Renewal of United Methodism: Mission, Ministry, and Connectionalism*, edited by Rex D. Matthews, 55–97. Nashville: General Board of Higher Education and Ministry, The United Methodist Church, 2012.
———. *Responsible Grace: John Wesley's Practical Theology*. Nashville: Kingswood, 1994.
Mendoza-Álvarez, Carlos, and Thierry-Marie Courau. *Decolonial Theology: Violence, Resistance and Spiritualities*. Concilium 2020/1. London: SCM, 2019.
Mignolo, Walter. *Local Histories/Global Designs: Coloniality, Subaltern Knowledges, and Border Thinking*. Princeton Studies in Culture/Power/History. Princeton, NJ: Princeton University Press, 2000.
Mignolo, Walter D., and Catherine E Walsh. *On Decoloniality: Concepts, Analytics, Praxis*. Durham: Duke University Press, 2018.

Moraña, Mabel, et al., eds. *Coloniality at Large: Latin America and the Postcolonial Debate*. Latin America Otherwise. Durham: Duke University Press, 2008.

Morris-Chapman, David Pratt. "Beyond the Quadrilateral: The Place of Nature in John Wesley's Epistemology of Theology." *Hervormde Teologiese Studies* 78.2 (2022) 1–8.

———. *Whither Methodist Theology Now? The Collapse of the "Wesleyan Quadrilateral."* Tiverton: Methodist Sacramental Fellowship, 2010.

Outler, Albert Cook. "Through a Glass Darkly: Our History Speaks to Our Future." *Methodist History* 28.2 (1990) 77–91.

———. *The Wesleyan Theological Heritage: Essays of Albert C. Outler*. Edited by Thomas C. Oden and Leicester R. Longden. Grand Rapids: Zondervan, 1991.

Quijano, Aníbal. "Colonialidad del poder, Eurocentrismo y América Latina." In *La Colonialidad del saber: Eurocentrismo y ciencias sociales: Perspectivas Latinoamericanas*, edited by Edgardo Lander. Buenos Aires: Consejo Latinoamericano de Ciencias Sociales, 2000.

———. "Colonialidad y Modernidad / Racionalidad." *Perú Indígena* 13.29 (1992) 11–20.

Ribeiro, Cláudio de Oliveira. "Teoria e prática: como os estudos wesleyanos podem contribuir para que as igrejas caminhem na missão?" *Revista Caminhando* 8.2 (2003) 236–59.

Rieger, Joerg. *Grace Under Pressure: Negotiating the Heart of the Methodist Traditions*. Nashville: General Board of Higher Education and Ministry, The United Methodist Church, 2011.

Rieger, Joerg, and John Vincent, eds. *Methodist and Radical: Rejuvenating a Tradition*. Nashville: Kingswood, 2003.

Santos, Boaventura de Sousa. "Beyond Abyssal Thinking: From Global Lines to Ecologies of Knowledges." *Review* (Fernand Braudel Center for the Study of Economies, Historical Systems, and Civilizations) 30.1 (2007) 45–89.

———. *The End of the Cognitive Empire: The Coming of Age of Epistemologies of the South*. Durham: Duke University Press, 2018.

———. *Epistemologies of the South: Justice Against Epistemicide*. New York: Routledge, 2014.

Souza, José Carlos de. "Creation, New Creation and the Theological Method in Wesleyan Perspective." Oxford Theological Institute, 2002. https://oxford-institute.org/2002-eleventh-institute/working-groups/.

———. "Um modo de fazer teologia equilibrado, dinâmico e vital." *Revista Caminhando* 4.2 (1993) 12–20.

Souza, Luis Wesley de. "The Wisdom of God in Creation: Mission and the Wesleyan Pentalateral." In *Global Good News Mission in a New Context*, edited by Howard Snyder, 138–52. Nashville: Abingdon, 2001.

Sugirtharajah, R. S., ed. *The Postcolonial Bible: Bible and Postcolonialism*. Sheffield: Sheffield Academic, 1998.

———, ed. *Voices from the Margin: Interpreting the Bible in the Third World*. 25th anniversary ed. Maryknoll, NY: Orbis, 2016.

Tamez, Elsa. *The Amnesty of Grace: Justification by Faith from a Latin American Perspective*. Nashville: Abingdon, 1993.

Thorsen, Donald A. D. *The Wesleyan Quadrilateral: Scripture, Tradition, Reason and Experience as a Model of Evangelical Theology*. Grand Rapids: Zondervan, 1990.

United Methodist Church. *The Book of Discipline of The United Methodist Church 2016*. United Methodist Publishing, 2016.

The United Methodist Hymnal. Nashville: United Methodist Publishing, 2017.

Vizcaíno, Rafael. *Decolonial Responses to Secularism from the Underside of Modernity.* PhD diss., Rutgers University, 2020.

———. "Secular Decolonial Woes." *The Journal of Speculative Philosophy* 35.1 (2021) 71–92.

Walls, Jerry L. *The Problem of Pluralism: Recovering United Methodist Identity.* Wilmore: Good News, 1986.

Williams, Colin W. *John Wesley's Theology Today: A Study of the Wesleyan Tradition in the Light of Current Theological Dialogue.* Nashville: Abingdon, 1960.

Chapter II

GRACE THAT LIBERATES AND UNITES IN THE MISSION OF GOD

Liberation Theology and Wesleyan Theology in Latin America[1]

PABLO GUILLERMO OVIEDO

THE GLOBAL CRISIS OF our current epoch is marked by neoliberal globalization and its effects have unfortunate human and ecological dimensions. In this chapter, I propose a theological reflection that contributes to the debate on how we can renew and decolonize ourselves as ecclesial communities of grace in our Latin American contexts. In the words of Zygmunt Bauman, one of the features of our time is the "liquidity of life," which he describes in terms of a loss of historical memory and lack of empathy.[2] For this reason, a historical-theological perspective is fundamental. As Rubem Alves affirmed, "[the] historian is someone who recovers forgotten memories and disseminates them as a sacrament to those who have lost their memory.... The historian is not an archeologist of memories ... [but] a sower of visions and of hopes."[3] The vision and hopes that

---

1. Sections of this chapter have been previously published as: "Teología de la liberación," and in "Unity that Liberates." The author would like to express his gratitude for permission to reprint portions of these essays.

2. Bauman, *Liquid Life*, 2–4.

3. Alves, "Las ideas teológicas," 363.

I want to sow in this chapter relate to the missionary relevance of various key themes in Wesleyan theology. I want to do so from a hermeneutic that positions itself on the margins and from the bottom-up, which I believe has been one of the great contributions of Latin American liberation theology, a tradition that has deepened Wesleyan theology in Latin America and the Caribbean for almost forty years.

To address this, is it necessary to keep in mind some assumptions. First of all, Latin American liberation theologies are considered by most of its authors an ecumenical interpretation of the Christian faith that has its point of departure the suffering, struggles, and hopes of the poor.[4] It is also considered a critique of society, systemic injustices, and the ideologies that sustain them. Moreover, it is a critical exercise born from the praxis of faith and of the activity of the church and of Christians, always from the point of view of the poor. Second, Wesleyan theology in the Latin American context has been treated as a "practical theology" of divine grace, in the sense that it is not a "theology that applies the data of the dogma to lived reality, but is rather a theology that discovers in that reality the action of God and the call of God to whom the dogma refers."[5] And finally, let us not forget that Wesleyan and Methodist traditions of Latin America made significant contributions to the formation of liberation theology. The influence has been a two-way street.[6]

Taking these assumptions into consideration, my working hypothesis can be formulated in the following manner: there is a reciprocal influence between liberation theology and Wesleyan theology in Latin America and theologians in the Wesleyan tradition were not only influenced by liberation

---

4. I understand that there is not a single form of liberation theology, which is why it is more appropriate to speak of Latin American liberation theologies. In this chapter, when I say Latin America, I refer to South America, Central America, and the Caribbean, as well as those who live in North America and produce Spanish-Portuguese-speaking theology. Some correctly use the indigenous name, Abya Yala, to refer to the region. I opted for the more traditional nomenclature for the sake of understanding.

5. González, *Juan Wesley*, 45.

6. The influence of Latin American Liberation Theology (LALT) and the emerging ecumenical movement toward the middle of the twentieth century in Latin American Wesleyan theology was very clear, as we will see. Similarly, the contribution of Methodist theologians to LALT and to the ecumenical movement has been highly valued in Latin America. Theologians and ecumenical leaders such as José Míguez Bonino, Julio de Santa Ana, Elsa Tamez, José Duque, Emilio Castro, Mortimer Arias, among others, contributed a particular theological vision that enriched the Latin American theological construction."

theology but also contributed to its development. This encounter was due to significant theological affinities both in method (theology as reflection-praxis of God's action in history) and in theological themes. Latin American Wesleyan theology contributed considerably in the development of themes like sanctification and liberation, divine grace, and Christian and human unity. I will argue that there is a mutual influence, especially through the contributions of many Methodist theologians of the Wesleyan tradition throughout the Americas. I will be suggesting that this fruitful dialogue between Wesleyan and liberation theologies offered a decolonizing impetus for Christian communities in Latin America. A decolonizing outlook and the critique to western modernity were important commitments in Latin American liberation theology from the beginning.[7] Furthermore, these are also key themes for Wesleyan theology in the global south and for the missionary ministry of Methodist churches in South America.[8]

In a time filled with disputes over the meaning of the Wesleyan tradition at a global level, I believe that a central part of Wesleyan identity, inspired by the theology and practice of John Wesley, is the focus on God's grace as manifested and embodied in situations where life is put under pressure, where profound changes and social displacement are present, and oppression is experienced.[9] This commitment to pursuing divine grace in times and sites of oppression connects Methodism to liberation theology in Latin America.

My chapter is divided in three parts. First, I establish the historical connection and interaction between Wesleyan theology in Latin America

---

7. For the pioneer work in the philosophy of liberation, see: Enrique Dussel, *Globalización*, 91–92, 96–98. In this regard, Dussel declares that modernity is "the 500-year system" that entered the twentieth century in deep crisis and that this crisis is not exclusive of Europe but a worldwide phenomenon. See Dussel, *Invention of the Americas*. Walter Mignolo is another author who most recently articulated the links between modernity and coloniality: Mignolo, *Local Histories*, 3.

8. Even though most of the founders of Latin American liberation theology studied in the European or North American contexts, their approaches to theology were evidently against the primacy of western thought and they could therefore be understood as offering a decolonizing effort in theology. For more perspectives from Protestant theologians, see Míguez Bonino, *Faces of Latin American Protestantism*, and Westhelle, *Voces de protesta en América Latina*. Westhelle argues that Bartolomé de las Casas was a pioneer in this task of recognizing otherness in Latin American theology in the sixteenth century in the midst of the harshness of Spanish colonialism. A more recent engagement, which includes two Methodist authors (Míguez and Rieger), can also be found in Míguez, Rieger, and Sung, *Beyond the Spirit of Empire*.

9. Rieger, *Grace Under Pressure*.

and the rise of liberation theologies. I go on to reflect on the continuities and ruptures in the history of Methodism in the continent and how the climate produced by liberation theology actually allowed Methodist theologians in Latin America to rediscover Wesley's theology. This historical itinerary takes me to the second and third sections of the chapter where I articulate some dimensions of a Wesleyan theology of grace and liberation and a decolonial ecclesiology of intersubjectivity, from the margins. In these times of oppression by what I should call the system of Mammon, I stress the need to recover visions from indigenous peoples about good living and creation, a spirituality of tenderness against growing violence and hospitality in the style of Jesus. For me, these are key decolonizing missionary and theological challenges for this crucial hour of our peoples.

An Itinerary of Latin American Wesleyan Theology

I hope to demonstrate in this section that the interaction between Wesleyan and liberation theologies produced continuities and ruptures in the interpretation of the Wesleyan tradition in Latin America. This itinerary that can be perceived in two different moments, first in the 1960s and 1970s and later in the 1980s. This second moment generated a rediscovery and resignification of Wesleyan theology in Latin America that led to new theological and missionary synthesis at the beginning of the twenty-first century. I argue that this synthesis offers theological and ecclesial challenges that must be attended by Christian communities, especially those in the Wesleyan tradition. This is a precondition for our faithfulness to God's work in this new time, the *kairos* of Latin America.

Let us begin by mentioning that Methodism in its arrival to Latin America experienced what Mortimer Arias has called "distorting meditations."[10] Methodism arrived in Latin America in the nineteenth century carrying commitments that were at once politically liberal and religiously pietistic. This mixed inheritance will have a lasting impact on Latin American Methodism.[11] On the one hand, the coming of Methodist

---

10. Arias, "As mediações distorcionantes," 73.

11. Míguez Bonino, *Protestantismo y liberalismo*, 21. Míguez Bonino reconsiders this discussion later in his career in *Faces of Latin American Protestantism*, chapter 1. Regarding the thesis of Jean-Pierre Bastian on the introduction of Protestantism in Latin America, Míguez Bonino affirms that its value consists in having recognized the concurrence

missionaries converged with the arrival of political and economic liberalism in Latin America and the institutions that represented it. North American Methodism arrived in Latin America with the promise of a new world: democracy, education, the regression of superstitious religiosity, and the urge to bring about economic and cultural development similar to those of the United States. This gospel of development found traction among immigrants who were receptive to liberal anticlerical preaching. In several countries in the region, Methodist leaders contributed to republican causes that were being introduced in the continent. In the River Plate basin, for example, we see a disposition toward the construction of a new reformist, democratic, and progressive project for society.[12] In the case of Argentina, this Methodism made great contributions to education, to the formation of unions, and in the fight for civil rights.[13]

On the other hand, North American Methodist missionaries brought with them a certain form of pietism that was individualistic and escapist. This theology was deeply anti-Catholic and caused Latin American Methodists to clash with Roman Catholics. These tensions had the effect of inhibiting the development of Methodism because it granted the tradition a strictly oppositional identity. In this sense, as Arias suggests, the Wesleyan legacy was distorted.[14] The distorting tendency was a part of the missionary agenda but it found a local context highly conducive to its exacerbation and perpetuation. Some central themes in Wesleyan theology like enthusiasm, Christian perfection, and holiness nearly disappear in this context. Methodist historian Daniel Bruno describes this as "a slide towards what we could call, on the one hand, a process of homogenization with orthodox Protestantism, and post-war evangelicalism from the United States, on the other."[15] As this homogenization gained roots in the

---

of factors both exogenous (the North American capitalist advance) and endogenous (fundamentally, the struggle of the liberal Latin Americans for modernization).

12. Amestoy, "Los orígenes del metodismo," 100.
13. Andiñach, "Methodism in Latin America," 141.
14. Arias, "As mediações distorsionantes."
15. Bruno, "Modelo para rearmar." Bruno describes three processes that impacted Methodism in Latin America. First, a process of theological homogenization that tended to erase the Wesleyan theological identity. Second, starting from the end of the nineteenth century, Methodism suffered a polarization between a formal and respectable religion and a subjectivist evangelicalism. Finally, this polarization made daring and relevant theological themes of original Methodism invisible, thus making it difficult to construct a Latin American Methodist theology.

twentieth century, Methodists in Latin America were virtually disconnected from Wesleyan theology.

Things began to change in the second half of the twentieth century, a period that coincides with the consolidation of the ecumenical movement in Latin America and the emergence of liberation theology. In fact, Protestant movements and theologians are among the precursors of this new moment in Latin American theological reflection.[16] But what made Protestant theologians who shared a liberal and pietist heritage join the early days of Latin American liberation theology? My modest answer is twofold. First, Methodists in the continent were confronted by the failure of the project of capitalist development which was always part of the missionary agenda and had been adopted uncritically by Latin American Methodists.[17] The second feature in the story is the birth of the ecumenical student movements such as the Latin American Union of Evangelical Youth and the Christian Student Movement. These organizations exposed Protestant youth to European theology and opened them up to the dialogue between Catholicism and Marxism. The Protestant leadership that would later give rise to Church and Society in Latin America (ISAL is the acronym in Spanish) was generated in these student associations. In the spirit of the ecumenical ethos of these movement, Latin American Protestants, including several Methodists, started to realize the limitations of North American liberal Protestantism. Under the influence of Marxism and European theology, they decided to get out of the narrowness of the pietistic worldview and its conservative morality. In Bruno's words, Methodists decided to "participate in the ideological struggle" and abandoned the "dualistic conception" that separated the church from the world.[18]

In the early stages in the development of Latin American liberation theology, the Methodist contribution was significant. Methodists like José Míguez Bonino, Julio de Santa Ana, Elsa Tamez, José Duque, Emilio Castro, and others were active in the period. Yet, between 1960 and 1970, their contribution to liberation theologies rarely mentions their Methodist roots. This is the period that I refer to as the "silencing" of the Wesleyan

---

16. Arias, "El itinerario protestante hacia una teología de la liberación." In this essay, Arias reconstructs the different milestones and the process of an evangelical theology in LA, which, although quite timid in its beginnings, evolved to earn a place in the international environment with its own profile. On this matter, see also Gotay, *El pensamiento cristiano revolucionario en América Latina y el Caribe*, 50.

17. Bruno, "Modelo para rearmar," 124.

18. Bruno, "Abordaje y periodización," 41.

legacy in Latin American. There is a silence with regards to the Wesleyan heritage and its potential contribution to liberation theologies. In these decades John Wesley or the Wesleyan tradition almost do not appear explicitly in theological writings by Wesleyans. The underlying assumption behind this silence appears to be the notion that Wesley was too attached to the liberal Protestantism of the missionaries and to North American individualism and imperialism.[19]

A new period begins as a result of the meeting of Latin Americans at the Oxford Institute in 1977 in England. The central theme of the gathering was "Sanctification and Liberation: Theologies of Liberation in Light of the Wesleyan Tradition," with Míguez Bonino, K. Dickson, and James Cone participating as speakers.[20] After the event, Latin American Methodists decided to meet in San José, Costa Rica, in February 1983, an event that marked the first effort to gather Methodist theologians from across Latin America.[21] A similar meeting took place one year later in Piracicaba, Brazil. These events generated the first serious attempt at collaborations that sought to produce Wesleyan theology from a Latin American perspective. These meetings indeed marked the beginning of a new time for Wesleyan studies in the continent.[22]

Twenty years later, a new meeting of Wesleyan theology was convened, this time in São Paulo, Brazil, in 2003. The next meeting took place in 2009 in Buenos Aires, Argentina. This itinerary from 1983 to 2009 shows how Wesleyan thought was slowly permeating the theological reflection of Methodist theologians in Latin America. These four meetings are captured in the four volumes that reflect the itinerary of a unified Wesleyan theological tradition in Latin America.[23] By tracking this itinerary, one notices the growth and development of Wesleyan theological

19. González, *Juan Wesley*, 17; Míguez Bonino, "Wesley in Latin America," 173.

20. Runyon, *Sanctification and Liberation*.

21. The book that documents this meeting is Duque, *La tradición protestante*.

22. Bruno, "Reseña histórica," 13. Bruno writes: "The truth is that from the beginnings of the 1980s, the interest for rediscovering the Wesleyan tradition in light of the social and theological challenges of LA, became more and more palpable, although the frequency of the meetings does not show it."

23. The four volumes that document the work generated by these gatherings are the following: Duque, *La tradición protestante*; Míguez Bonino et al., *Luta pela vida*; Ribeiro et al., *Teologia e prática*; Centro Metodista Estudios Wesleyanos, "IV Encuentro latinoamericano de estudios Wesleyanos." A new meeting is being scheduled to commemorate the fortieth anniversary of the first gathering, which provides the hope that this tradition will continue to flourish.

themes in Latin America. Bruno, editor of the final volume, affirms that the goal of these publications is to "encourage the will to continue delving into the questions that emerge when we get ready to read our traditions, not as finished formulations, but as answers from the past that can help us to generate new questions in our present."[24]

Since that first meeting in Costa Rica, we witness the recuperation of Wesleyan theological themes that had been eclipsed by North American Methodism missionaries as well as the integration of Wesleyan theology on the Latin American context approached from the vantage point of liberation theologies. I maintain that this integration enriched both of these traditions in Christian thought and practice.

I would like to express a general theological assessment of this itinerary of Latin American Wesleyan theology. If we observe the themes and content of the four Latin American meetings of Wesleyan studies, we perceive a shift from an emphasis on sanctification in the earlier gatherings to the theme of grace, which is more central to the two more recent meetings. This does not mean that sanctification has been abandoned, but that it has been resignified from the perspective of grace. In the first two meetings (Costa Rica in 1983 and Piracicaba in 1984), conversations were centered on the distorting mediations of the Wesleyan legacy in Latin America, themes that then trigger the reflection about holiness and the association between sanctification and the liberation of the poor. The dialogue presupposes an ecumenical commitment as a criterion for Latin American Wesleyan theology and is clearly staged in fruitful dialogue with liberation theologies.[25]

Decades later, and already entering the twenty-first century, the other two gatherings (São Paulo in 2003 and Buenos Aires in 2009) emphasized pastoral and missionary themes. On a theological level, the dialogue moves toward grace, justification, and salvation.[26] The central theme of the fourth meeting was "Grace and Salvation: Wesleyan Themes in a Latin American Perspective," and the category of grace is present

---

24. Bruno, "Reseña histórica," 15.

25. Roman Catholic theologian Hugo Assmann observes that the ecumenical ethos characterizes Methodism in Latin America and praises the tradition for its theological flexibility in addition to the emphasis on sanctification, its ecumenical openness and absence of sectarianism, its human warmth, its social holiness. See Míguez Bonino et al., *Luta pela vida*, 191.

26. See book index in Oliveira et al., *Teologia e prática*.

in the theological, ecclesiological, missionary, and pastoral reflections shared at the gathering.[27]

I hope to have shown how this theological and pastoral interaction between liberation and Wesleyan theologies in Latin America emerges in large part thanks to the ecumenical movement. As I suggested, the rediscovery and resignification of Latin American Wesleyan theology led to a new theological and missionary synthesis in the beginning of the twenty-first century. The affinities between liberation theology and Wesleyan theology are well captured in Míguez Bonino when he stressed the dynamic character of the Methodist identity, thirty years ago: "If there is a Methodist heritage . . . such heritage demands the pursuit of local and universal forms of visibility that best express *the missional and communal call of the people of God* in our post-confessional, divided and conflictive world."[28] This was derived from the certainty that the heart of Wesley's ecclesiology is the linking of the emphasis on the koinonia of believers and the emphasis on the missionary character of their vocation. There appears the importance of the unity of the church, liberation and mission in Latin American Wesleyan theology.[29]

This itinerary that Latin American liberation theology and Wesleyan theology is relevant because large sectors of Latin American Methodism, starting in the second half of the twentieth century, were able to *enculturate* and *incarnate* themselves in the struggles of the Latin American people. I believe that this process is a witness to the decolonization of Methodism in the continent. As I indicate in the next section, through its enculturation and incarnation in the reality of the Latin American peoples, Methodism

---

27. See index in *Revista Evangélica de Historia* 6 (2010), 7–8. Here, the theme of piety and spirituality also appears, which does not happen in the first two books. At the time, this is noticeable in Argentine Methodism, as argued by Sosa, "La Oración." In retrieving the issue of spirituality, one reevaluates a central theme in the Wesleyan heritage.

28. Míguez Bonino, "¿Conservar el metodismo?," in Duque, *La tradición protestante*, 338.

29. Míguez Bonino, "Fue el metodismo un movimiento liberador?," in Duque, *La tradición protestante*, 73. Also, see Míguez Bonino, "Methodism and Latin American Liberation Movements" in Rieger and Vincent, *Methodist and Radical*. In the essay, Míguez Bonino clarifies how Methodism in Latin America was opening to the consciousness of liberation in the second half of the twentieth century. An earlier essay by Míguez Bonino makes a similar point, "Wesley in Latin America." Also, see the excellent book from De La Torre and Floyd-Thomas, *Beyond the Pale*, especially the article from Harold Recinos, "John Wesley." Finally, see Recinos "Barrio Christianity and American Methodism," in Rieger and Vincent, *Methodist and Radical*.

was able to incorporate new ways of knowing and establish the initial contours of a deep dialogue between Wesleyan theology and the spiritual and ethical traditions that are indigenous to our region. This is an unfinished process but its emerging possibilities are exciting.

A Latin American Wesleyan Theology: New Creation in Liberating Grace

Taking into account this historical and theological itinerary, a central theme emerges, namely, to rethink the vitality of historical Christianity and its missionary challenges. And that is its intercultural diffusion. The theological method generated in the Latin American liberation theology crystallized a new and more complex perspective of the hermeneutical circle. Ideological suspicion, critical rereading of the history of interpretation, and political action are incorporated as decisive elements in biblical interpretation and doctrinal elaboration. Philosophy is no longer the exclusive interlocutor of the theological discourse as human sciences and popular participation have now joined the theological endeavor.[30]

Thus, Christian theology and mission are understood and lived as an interaction with God's mission in our history, in our context, and in God's activity in all of creation. We start from the premise that missiologist Carlos Cardoza-Orlandi proposes about the *missio dei*, about the relationship between the gospel, Christian mission, the church and the world, namely, that the different theologies and practices of mission that emerged in the twentieth century were "the response of the co-participation of the communities of faith in the mission of God in the world."[31] In Cardoza-Orlandi's words: "the theologies of mission . . . have their foundation in the praxis of Christian communities in their determined context."[32] And for this reason the visions of the mission change according to the new demands and challenges that these contexts pose. Cardoza-Orlandi continues: "The mission continues to change. One of the factors that has changed our reflection and action in mission is the contribution and missionary activity of the so-called 'third world,' of the countries of the periphery."[33]

---

30. Segundo, *Liberation of Theology*.
31. Cardoza-Orlandi, *Una introducción a la misión*, 73.
32. Cardoza-Orlandi, *Una introducción a la misión*, 74.
33. Cardoza-Orlandi, *Una introducción a la misión*, 114. My study focuses on my context of the Protestant and Wesleyan tradition in the third world along with its

For all this, we must connect this theme of grace with the theological theme of the new creation, very present in Wesley, and taking the latter as the hermeneutical key to understand Wesleyan theology in Latin America.[34] Moreover, following Joerg Rieger, I suggest that a component of Wesleyan identity is to claim that God's grace is manifested and embodied more clearly in situations where life is put under pressure. In this sense, it is interesting to note that in the current social context of Latin America, poverty and exclusion have worsened due to the current advance of neoliberal politics. I believe that this context must be kept in mind when we consider how Latin American Wesleyan theology went from emphasizing the theme of sanctification to the theme of grace in the earlier part of the twenty-first century. The pressures imposed by neoliberal globalization force Wesleyan thought to connect the theology of grace to the theme of the new creation.

Seen in this way, Wesleyan theology is a path of grace as an active commitment of faith in different life situations, where the grace of God manifests itself there where the power of God operates from the "bottom-up," where God's grace acts in ways that are distinct from the top-down approach of neoliberalism.[35] This is where we experience the new creation in Christ, in hope, and in action. And more in this time of the COVID-19 pandemic where it has highlighted the other pandemics, including the structural-global injustice of the capitalist system and the gap between rich and poor and all its implications, which has added violence in the dimensions of race, gender, and ecology, along with the growing hatred of the marginalized of history. This has theological implications and ecclesiological and missionary

---

dynamics and missionary and theological experiences. My intent is to consider how this tradition interacted with Latin American liberation theology and was embodied in the struggles of our peoples for justice and full life.

34. Ultimately, a Wesleyan ethical and theological proposal in Latin America must seek a "new creation" because, as Runyon asks: "Christ's purpose was not to limit or restrict the love of God . . . but to demonstrate the very life of God in a mission toward all humanity. Can our mission be any less?" (Runyon, *New Creation*, 220). That is to say, according to Wesley, final salvation would not be outside of human history, but would be the transformation of this history. Final salvation is the theme with which Wesley concludes his sermon, "The New Creation." Wesley writes: "a state of total holiness and happiness far superior to that enjoyed by Adam in paradise . . . a deep, intimate and permanent union with God . . . and of all creatures" (Wesley, "New Creation," in *John Wesley's Sermons*, 500).

35. Rieger, *Grace Under Pressure*, 53–54. For further reflections from Rieger, see "What Do Margins and Center Have to Do with Each Other?," in Rieger and Vincent, *Methodist and Radical*; Rieger, "Between God and the Poor." I have addressed some of these themes in Oviedo, "El Espíritu de Dios."

challenges for Christian churches today, especially for Protestant-Evangelical communities and those of Wesleyan heritage.

New Creation and Liberating Grace: Renewing Christology and Subjectivities from the Margins

Many have claimed that one of the hallmarks of Wesleyan theology is the experience of divine grace. "Wesleyan theology is a thorough-going theology of grace," writes Richard Heitzenrater.[36] Wesley was a theologian of grace with an all-encompassing emphasis on sanctification that returns the believer to their responsibility before the God of grace. Albert Outler, in his edition of Wesley's Sermons, states:

> The heart of Wesley's gospel was always a very vivid sense of grace at work at every level in creation and in history, in individuals and in communities.... The "Catholic substance" of Wesley's theology (which it includes the Protestant and the Catholic, the Western and the Eastern) is the theme of participation—the idea that all life is grace and all grace is the mediation of Christ by the Holy Spirit.[37]

In search for alternative modes of subjectivity centered on the grace of God from the encounter with other sufferers, I find support in the theological proposal of the book *Beyond the Spirit of Empire*. The three authors, Nestor Míguez, Joerg Rieger, and Jung Mo Sung—the first two, Methodist scholars—argue that in the face of the challenge between growing individualism and community, we must see how this process is manifested in the margins. They argue that we have to pay attention to what is really happening on the ground, as this gives us a clearer understanding of the fact that the oppressed retain a kind of subjectivity and agency, even in the conditions of postmodern or postcolonial empire.[38]

How does this affect our theological understanding and our Christian mission? If we start from the renewing experience of grace in the Holy Spirit

---

36. Heitzenrater, *Wesley and the People*, 290.
37. Wesley, *Works*, 1:98–99.
38. Míguez, Rieger, and Sung, *Beyond the Spirit*. For the concept of a "postcolonial empire," see Rieger, *Christ and Empire*, chapter 7. The term appears to be contradictory, but Rieger clarifies it in his account of new Christology from below. The author seeks to reclaim Paul's notion of the lordship of Christ in relationship to empire as manifested in different periods of history. For another excellent contribution to the postcolonial debate and its import to theology, see Nausner, "Homeland as Borderland."

and not from the spirit of empire, life and mission should be carried out from the margins. An anthropology and subjectivity of grace is present from a Christology from below and from the margins. God's design for the world is not to create another world but to recreate what God has already created in love and wisdom. Jesus began his ministry by affirming that being filled with the Spirit is to liberate the oppressed, restore sight to the blind, and announce the coming of the reign of God (Luke 4:16–18). He undertook the fulfillment of his mission by opting for those who were on the margins of society because their situations gave testimony to the sin of the world, and his longing for life was combined with the designs of God.

A renewed grace-centered Wesleyan Christology from the margins would be an interesting task ahead, I think, for Latin American Wesleyan theologians. The figure of Jesus in Latin America is perhaps the theological issue that needs to be the most reviewed and liberated. There is an important contribution from Latin American liberation theology that serves as a basis for the urgent transformation of Christology.[39] Much of the criticism around Latin American Christology has to do with the intention not to justify the suffering of the majority from pain and despair, or into the trap of triumphalism and abuse by the powerful.

The need for a Spirit-centered Christology in an updated and pertinent Trinitarian hermeneutical key has already been mentioned by several theologians in Latin America.[40] For our Wesleyan theology, this is important. Míguez Bonino warns us that renewal and mission are inseparable, which is why it is necessary to rethink the totality of the church in light of the incarnation of the Son since we will clash with Wesley's spiritualism and individualism that were common in his time. Míguez Bonino comments that "the Wesleyan Christ sometimes seems only concerned with souls and little connected with his concrete reality, due to his weak doctrine of the humiliation of the Christ and his earthly life."[41]

In an article entitled "Jesús was born in Guatemala," Methodist theologian Edgardo Colón-Emeric proposes a hermeneutical approach to the

---

39. To mention the primary ones: Boff, *Jesus Christ Liberator*; Míguez Bonino, *La fe en busca de eficacia*; Míguez Bonino et al., *Jesús*; Sobrino, *Christology at the Crossroads*.

40. Míguez Bonino writes that Evangelical Christological reductionism is present in broad sectors of Latin American Protestantism as he describes it as an "individualistic, Christological-soteriological in a basically subjective key, with emphasis on sanctification" (*Faces of Latin American Protestantism*, 40). See also Meeks, *Trinity, Community and Power*; Recinos and Magallanes, *Jesus in Hispanic Community*.

41. Míguez Bonino, *Hacia una eclesiología evangelizadora*, 72. He takes this idea from Deschner, *Wesley's Christology*, 2.

Christological issue from a Wesleyan perspective. He argues that in order to avoid the recurring temptation of theology of projecting our ideologies or moral visions onto the figure of Jesus, he states, citing Míguez Bonino, that the solution to this enigma is "a hermeneutics that respects not only the original historicity of the text but also the singularity of the readers locus."[42] He affirms:

> A Latinx Wesleyan Christology starts from the mystery of the conception and birth of Jesus but does not stop there. A Christology centered on the mystery of the incarnation to the exclusion of the transfiguration underappreciates the possibility of the status quo being swept up by the Holy Spirit into the history of salvation. All cultures, historical ages, and peoples bear the marks of sin. We can profess faith with Gonzalez in the "God made flesh in one culture for all cultures," only if we read the "for" missiologically. Latinx Wesleyan theologians would benefit from engaging the theological vision of Saint Oscar Romero whose Christological thought centers on the transfigured Christ who transfigures the people of God and the land of El Salvador.[43]

We need to renew our vision of Jesus the Christ, especially of the Christ who is present in everyday life today, transforming the lives of so many and revealing himself in those who are on the periphery, on the margins of our peoples.

The voice and wisdom of indigenous or native peoples represent the historical and current margins of Latin American societies. What I believe is that in this time we must transform Christology from two fundamental hermeneutical keys (which challenge us from the margins of Latin America): one from the struggle for equality in all its forms (especially gender embodied by feminist theology)[44] and another from the cultural contributions of indigenous peoples. Methodist theologian Nestor Míguez affirms that theology must undergo a paradigm shift in response to the concept of "good living" (*sumak kausai* in Quechua) and in relation to the question of ecological care of the earth (of "mother earth," or Pachamama).[45]

---

42. Colón-Emeric, "Jesús Was Born in Guatemala," 116.

43. Colón-Emeric, "Jesús Was Born in Guatemala," 115.

44. On the topic of the struggle for gender equality and a feminist theology, see Oviedo, "Between the Encounter with Others and the Other," in Rieger and Vaai, *Methodist Revolutions*.

45. Míguez, "Teología en América Latina."

I believe with Míguez that some of the theologies of indigenous peoples are making an important eruption in Christian theology. The concept of "good living" and the question of caring for "mother earth," both of which are central and dynamic elements in various ancestral religions, especially in the Andean region, have become a true epistemological axis taken up by various Latin American theologies.[46] As Míguez maintains, the concept of "good living" is assimilated to that of a full life in the Gospel of John, and is distinguished from the consumerist idea of a good life as an accumulation of goods of the market utopia. Jesus with his promise to "come so that they may have life and life in abundance" (John 10:10) can be redefined from this cultural axis.

The decolonization process, which does not wish to return to an impossible past prior to the conquest, seeks the integration of the plurality and diversity of Latin America peoples and cultures with the goal of constructing liberated and mutually committed peoples. Míguez writes about the concept of *suma qamaña*, often translated as the "good life" as "living well together": "*Suma qamaña* naturally touches upon the 'totality of living conditions,' but it is fundamentally about freedom and collective dignity, family life and spiritual well-being . . . equality and integrity." Míguez then concludes: "this concept of *suma qamaña* allows recovering most of the affirmations of the Latin American Liberation Theology as they were formulated in its beginnings."[47] The concept emphasizes community, balance, and harmony with the ecosystem, which is sought with our common home on earth and not separated from it. Because we are relational beings, the main value that should guide relationships is mutual care and not competition.[48]

These worldviews have provided a true epistemological turn taken up by various Latin American theologies. They share an affinity with the Hebrew and biblical worldview of Shalom and the year of jubilee in the prophetic tradition, which Jesus makes his own (see, for example, Luke 4:16–21). The current capitalist development model, focused on productivity and individual consumption leaves no room for solidarity, to share

---

46. See Míguez, "Theology," 15. A pioneer of this discussion has been Leonardo Boff, *Cry of the Earth*; Boff, *La dignidad de la tierra*. In these books we can observe the definitive turn toward ecology in Boff's theology. We also observe commitments that echo his past work, namely, the notion that the poor represent an epiphany of the divine, combined with a renewed pneumatological vision that informs Boff's eco-spirituality.

47. Míguez, "Juntos por la vida," 254–55.

48. See the ecclesial document from Iglesia Evangélica Metodista Argentina, "El 'Buen Vivir.'"

goods in fairness and respect for life. In this sense, "Living well expresses a different relationship between human beings and their social and natural environment. Living well incorporates a human, ethical, and holistic dimension to the relationship of human beings both with their own history and with their nature."[49]

This is the challenge of working toward an intercultural theology that affirms that dignifying and salvific presence of God in all cultures and that allows the confrontation of each religious and cultural tradition with its own limitations. This is also a way to take a critical look at the set of values that each culture sustains, rethinking the memory of Jesus and his ethical legacy as a path of justice and love that is shared by other ethical traditions in the history of humanity. Therefore, strengthening a decolonizing vision of faith and promoting interreligious and intercultural dialogue is a path toward fraternity and sorority, which in turn allow for the possibility of abundant, just, and dignified life for peoples.[50]

This brings us to yet another fundamental challenge. Facing the fact that Latin America has become a society of high aggression and violence, we now face the challenge of formulating a paradigm of care and tenderness. A "theology of tenderness proposes non-violent resistance and a revolution that also includes the overcoming and dismantling of the structural components of the exploitation and imperial colonization, and the construction of a new relational mode."[51] This new way of relating must be motivated by a spirituality of tenderness and empathy. As some Latin American theologians state in a recent book, it is from the transforming practice of "spirituality as an urgent resource for restoration, insurgency, and emancipation, and no longer only for the celebration of faith. Spirituality should be seen as a mechanism of transformation for all strata of society."[52]

The figure of Jesus, historically used to oppress, condemn, and maintain the status quo through an escapist apocalyptic paradigm, must be presented in Latin America from a critical Christology as a model of humanity that stands in opposition to violent systems to show us maternal, humane, compassionate, and empathetic care for vulnerable people and for all of creation.[53] Likewise, mission from the margins invites the

49. Regazzoni, "El anuncio del Reino," 17.
50. Oviedo, "Teología latinoamericana, "13–16.
51. Míguez, "Teología en América Latina."
52. Segura and Grellert, *Ternura*, 350–51.
53. Oviedo, "Jesús liberador y amigo."

churches in Latin America to rethink mission as a vocation that the Spirit of God inspires, and to join the work of God (*missio dei*) in this time of misfortune. This works for a world in which the fullness of life is possible for everyone, especially for those who suffer the most, and to do so in a cooperative way with other Christian churches, other faiths, movements, and social organizations. Míguez affirms in the edited volume that was inspired by last call of the World Council of Churches:

> The mission of the Christian faith today in Latin America is fourfold: it includes caring for and enjoying the goods of creation, working to build a worthy city, with agreements and conflicts, and engaging in the search of social and economic justice in the continent that supports the most unequal distribution of wealth and thus proclaim and live in open dialogue—with the others—original peoples, women and their voices and many other excluded—a testimony of our hope in the life that we receive through the grace of God the Creator, Jesus Christ the Messiah and the vivifying breath of the Spirit, the community of the divine trinity that inspires the human community.[54]

These actions, as I stated above, are key challenges of our Latin American Wesleyan identity: Christian and human unity for the mission of God. Two indisputable marks of Wesleyan theology: the *grace of God* from Jesus the Christ and *the unity from and for the mission of God*, understood as the integral sanctification, *the new creation*, that God wants to do in all his creation.

By Way of Conclusion

The fruitful synthesis between Wesleyan theology in Latin America and Latin American liberation theologies marks the challenge of elaborating and promoting an embodied theology of divine grace and of unity from and for the mission from the margins and from below with a corresponding anthropology: an alternative subjectivity to empire and a sense of community that questions the power that oppresses and kills, which in turn experiences the new creation. This theological and missionary synthesis (which has at its center a pneumatological Christology of grace and tenderness) is emerging: between God's renewing grace, the personal-social sanctification, and

---

54. Míguez, "Juntos por la vida," 266.

the macro-ecumenical vocation should mark the journey of the Christian communities in Latin America at this time.

Part of the visions and hopes that we want to sow at this time is to propose the importance and missionary relevance of key themes for Christian and Wesleyan theology, from a hermeneutic of the new creation, which is positioned on the margins and from below. In a time of misery, we offer the grace of God manifested in Jesus Christ. In a time of fragmentation and division of our peoples, we offer Christian and human unity. In a world marked by post-truth, fascism, xenophobia, agorophobia, racism, and patriarchal machismo, we offer the new creation as a key theological theme that sustains a vision for a new world and alternative subjectivity.

This experience of grace and of the Spirit for an alternative community should continue to promote ecclesial and ecumenical unity and in interreligious dialogue, in addition to the work for life and human rights with other actors of civil society. At the same time and always, respecting diversity.[55] As Joerg Rieger says, "Theology is a matter of life and death."[56] Theology has historically functioned in death-dealing ways. A revision is necessary so that it can be life-giving.

From this perspective, I would like to close this chapter mentioning theological challenges that remain open and important for Latin American Wesleyan theology. I present these challenges under two categories that I conceive of as related: *theological* challenges and *ecclesial* challenges. First, we will need to resignify our idea of God and our relationship with God as "other." Equally important as the continual transformation of the church by grace acting in times of oppression, bringing liberation and equality, is the transformation of our image of God. I believe that for this change to occur, we will need to play close attention to the trinitarian theology offered by Latin American liberation theologians and in the worldwide Wesleyan tradition. Moreover, we will need to center our Christology on grace and tenderness that functions in the direction of justice. Renewing our image of God and rejecting idolatrous images is key at this time.[57] The second theological challenge is to resignify our relationship with all creation and with

---

55. Oviedo, "Zona de promesas."

56. Rieger, *Grace Under Pressure*, 75.

57. We see a beginning of this work in Rieger, Míguez, and Sung, *Beyond the Spirit*. Also in the recent collective book by Zavala, *Abajo los muros*. There we find essays on the subject of the image of God: May, "Religiones y divinidades"; and Míguez, "La doctrina de la gracia o la ley del mercado."

others, in the direction of shaping an alternative mode of subjectivity that I believe will need to be conceptualized as *intersubjectivity*.[58]

The ecclesial challenges that we face are fourfold. First, Wesleyan and Methodist communities in Latin America will need to find ways of collaborating in the *missio dei* while remaining committed to the margins and in a ground-up manner. Secondly, our communities will need to consolidate themselves as "communities of a liberating grace." That means they shall not be caves of darkness but homes of life where the new anti-imperial subjectivity is practiced. They shall be based on solidarity, they will be prophetic, inclusive, evangelizing, service-oriented, and renewed in the Spirit of grace of Jesus of Nazareth. Thirdly, these communities will need to commit themselves to the new creation that God is forming in Latin America. These communities will need to become true ecological democracies. Fourth, our Wesleyan communities will be committed to the unity and diversity in the face of interreligious and intercultural challenges. They shall work to resist fundamentalism, patriarchy, and violence against women, xenophobia, racism, neofascism and its hatred of diversity. They shall favor the poor, the excluded, and the migrants—those to whom God has opted.

As I suggested in a recent article about the multiple pandemics that have been made invisible by the COVID-19 pandemic, these hidden calamities are the real challenge for a decolonial, relevant, and transformative Wesleyan theology:

> Our God, the God of Jesus Christ, is not a solitary God, but the God of life, of solidarity with the victims and those who suffer. . . . This is our hope. The last word is not death but Life, full and definitive. As Jesus affirms: "I have come so that they may have life and life in abundance" (John 10:10). This continues to be a challenge that must be re-signified as part of a process of decolonization that seeks the integration of the plurality and diversity that is America today, as a construction of liberated peoples in equality and at the same time mutually committed. This is a challenge that calls us to join in the work that God is doing in our midst—as John Wesley liked to say—we must advance the extension of his kingdom of grace and justice. What is at stake is human life and the life of

---

58. In reality, Wesley's works offer us solid theological and ethical clues to address the environmental crisis and place it at the center of our missionary concern. Some of the most obvious Wesleyan clues are: (1) the idea of integral salvation; (2) the concept of the human being as a steward of creation, never a conqueror; (3) the presupposition that creation has intrinsic value because it is the manifestation of divine work, and (4) the union between nature and human history.

creation. Our faith in the living God is at stake, acting in the midst of the pandemics.[59]

I believe that once again the Christian communities are challenged to preach and bear witness to the gospel of Jesus' grace to the people and peoples in Latin America in all their misfortunes, to connect interculturally with the new faces of the mission, the others that emerge in a new historical conjuncture marked by growing exclusion: women victims of patriarchy, children, young people, indigenous groups, and many others. But not from patronizing charity or using others as means to increase their membership. For this reason, I believe in the transforming and revolutionary power of the gospel that is present in our Wesleyan tradition. As theologians of the Wesleyan tradition affirm in a the recently-published edited volume, *Methodist Revolutions*: "If religion is indeed always social, as Wesley realized, its practitioners need to come to terms with the challenges of their times and places in order to become part of the transforming work of God. Just as there can be no nonrevolutionary Gospel, there can be no nonrevolutionary Methodism."[60]

The margins, which actually constitute the majority of our humanity today, are the source of our commitment. With power concentrated in less than one percent of humanity, and with the resources of creation being devastated to satisfy the luxury of the wealthiest ten percent, while almost half of humanity still suffers in poverty, it is necessary to ask where life is. The Gospel is always a questioning of the existing powers from the power of the life of the lowly ones. Let us remember that in our history of faith it was in the margins of Galilee, and in the crucified messiah among the marginalized where the transcendence of those excluded from history is manifested. For this reason, we hope that our communities, rooted in the experience of the grace of Jesus the Christ, come out of the confinement of religious selfishness toward the encounter of others, who today reveal the face of Christ on the margins (according to the parable of the final judgment in Matthew 25), and to do it together with other churches and religions, indigenous peoples, and sectors of civil and political society.

In this time marked by the system of Mammon and its devastation of creation, of growing individualism that makes it difficult to create a community and people in solidarity, of colonization of mentalities and the

---

59. Oviedo, "Introducción."

60. Rieger and Vaai, "Introduction: Revival, Reform, and Revolution," in *Methodist Revolutions*, 15.

domestication of emancipatory desire, the gospel is the power and grace of God that liberates, it is openness to new times and possibilities, to a new humanity, to a new creation.

Bibliography

Alves, Rubem. "Las ideas teológicas y sus caminos por los surcos institucionales del Protestantismo brasileño." In *Materiales para una historia de la teología en América Latina*, edited by Pablo Richard, 343–66. San José, Costa Rica: DEI, 1981.

Amestoy, Norman Rúben. "Los orígenes del metodismo en el rio de la plata. Las sociedades metodistas en el marco liberal (1867-1900)." *Revista Evangélica de Historia* 5.2 (2004) 83–100.

Andiñach, Pablo. "Methodism in Latin America." In *The Oxford Handbook of Methodism Studies*, edited by William Abraham and James Kirby, 139–54. Oxford: Oxford University Press, 2009.

Arias, Mortimer. "El itinerario protestante hacia una teología de la liberación." *Vida y Pensamiento* 8.1 (1988) 49–59.

———. "As mediações distorcionantes na transmissão do legado original do Wesley." In *Luta pela vida e evangelização*, edited by José Míguez Bonino, 73–95. São Paulo, Paulinas/UNIMEP, 1985.

Bauman, Zygmunt. *Liquid Life*. Cambridge: Polity, 2005.

Boff, Leonardo. *Cry of the Earth, Cry of the Poor*. Ecology and Justice. Maryknoll, NY: Orbis, 1997.

———. *La dignidad de la tierra. Ecología, Mundialización, Espiritualidad, La emergencia de un nuevo paradigma*. Madrid: Trotta, 2000.

———. *Jesus Christ Liberator: A Critical Christology for Our Time*. Maryknoll, NY: Orbis, 1978.

Bruno, Daniel. "Abordaje y periodización para una historia del metodismo en Argentina." *Revista Evangélica de Historia* 7 (2012) 11–44.

———. "Modelo para rearmar: el metodismo latinoamericano y sus opciones teológicas." *Revista Evangélica de Historia* 6 (2010) 123–38.

———. "Reseña histórica de la reflexión Wesleyana en América Latina." *Revista Evangélica de Historia* 6 (2010) 11–15.

Cardoza-Orlandi, Carlos F. *Una introducción a la misión*. Nashville: Abingdon, 2003.

Centro Metodista Estudios Wesleyanos, ed. "IV Encuentro latinoamericano de estudios Wesleyanos." *Revista Evangélica de Historia* 6 (2010).

Colón-Emeric, Edgardo. "Jesús Was Born in Guatemala: Towards a Latinx Wesleyan Christology." *Wesleyan Theological Journal* 54.2 (2019) 102–17.

De La Torre, Miguel A., and Stacey M. Floyd-Thomas, eds. *Beyond the Pale: Reading Theology from the Margins*. Louisville: Westminster John Knox, 2011.

Deschner, John. *Wesley's Christology: An Interpretation*. Dallas: Southern Methodist University Press, 1960.

Duque, José, ed. *La tradición protestante en la teología latinoamericana, primer intento: Lectura de la tradición metodista*. San José, Costa Rica: DEI, 1983.

Dussel, Enrique D. *Globalización, exclusión y democracia en América Latina*. Mexico City: Contrapuntos, 1997.

———. *The Invention of the Americas: Eclipse of "the Other" and the Myth of Modernity*. New York: Continuum, 1995.
González, Justo. *Juan Wesley: Desafíos para nuestro siglo*. Buenos Aires: ISEDET, 2004.
Gotay, Samuel S. *El pensamiento cristiano revolucionario en América Latina y el Caribe*. Salamanca: Sígueme, 1980.
Heitzenrater, Richard P. *Wesley and the People Called Methodists*. 2nd ed. Nashville: Abingdon, 2013.
Iglesia Evangélica Metodista Argentina. "El 'Buen Vivir' como transversal a los temas de la Gran Parroquia." March 2021. https://iglesiametodista.org.ar/el-buen-vivir-como-transversal-a-los-temas-de-la-gran-parroquia.
"Index." *Revista Evangélica de Historia* 6 (2010) 7–8.
Meeks, M. Douglas, ed. *Trinity, Community and Power*. Nashville: Kingswood, 1995.
Mignolo, Walter. *Local Histories/Global Designs: Coloniality, Subaltern Knowledges, and Border Thinking*. Princeton Studies in Culture/Power/History. Princeton: Princeton University Press, 2000.
Míguez, Néstor. "Juntos por la vida y la teología contemporánea latinoamericana." In *Nuevas concepciones de misión y los cambios de contexto*, edited by Kenneth R. Ross et al., 254–55. Buenos Aires: La Aurora, 2017.
———. "Teología en América Latina." Nestor Míguez, n.d. https://nestormiguez.com/wp-content/uploads/articulos/Teologia-en-America-Latina.pdf.
———. "Theology." In *Christianity in Latin America and the Caribbean*, edited by Kenneth R. Ross, Ana Maria Bidegain, and Todd M. Johnson, 360–71. Edinburgh: Edinburgh University Press, 2022.
Míguez, Néstor, Joerg Rieger, and Jung Mo Sung. *Beyond the Spirit of Empire: Theology and Politics in a New Key*. London: SCM, 2009.
Míguez Bonino, José. *Faces of Latin American Protestantism*. Grand Rapids: Eerdmans, 1997.
———. *La fe en busca de eficacia*. Sigueme: Salamanca, 1977.
———. *Hacia una eclesiología evangelizadora*. São Paulo: Editeo, 2003.
———. *Protestantismo y liberalismo en América Latina*. San José: DEI, 1983.
———. "Wesley in Latin America: A Theological and Historical Reflection." In *Rethinking Wesley's Theology for Contemporary Methodism*, edited by Randy L. Maddox and Theodore Runyon, 169–82. Nashville: Kingswood, 1998.
Míguez Bonino, José, et al., eds. *Jesús: ni vencido ni monarca celestial*. Buenos Aires: Tierra Nueva, 1983.
———. *Luta pela vida e evangelização*. São Paulo: Paulinas/UNIMEP, 1985.
Nausner, Michael. "Homeland as Borderland: Territories of Christian Subjectivity." In *Postcolonial Theologies: Divinity and Empire*, edited by Catherine Keller, Michael Nausner, and Mayra Rivera, 118–32. St. Louis: Chalice, 2004.
Oliveira, Claudio et al., ed. *Teologia e prática na tradição wesleyana. Uma leitura a partir da América Latina e Caribe*. São Paulo: Editeo-Umesp, 2005.
Oviedo, Pablo G. "El Espíritu de Dios: el desafío de la comunión y la misión en un mundo fragmentado. Pneumatología trinitaria hoy." *Cuadernos de Teología* 27 (2008) 79–103.
———. "Introducción." *Apuntes* 41.1 (2021) 1–5.
———. "Jesús liberador y amigo. Espiritualidad y liberación desde el margen: un diálogo entre los místicos (Teresa de Jesús) y la teología latinoamericana de la liberación." *Apuntes* 38.1 (2019) 25–40.

———. "Teología de la liberación y teologia wesleyana en América Latina." *Teología y Cultura* 17 (October 2020) 59–77. https://teologiaycultura.ucel.edu.ar/.

———. "Teología latinoamericana: actualidad y desafíos." *El estandarte evangélico* (2012–13) 13–16.

———. "Unity that Liberates for an Embodied Mission." *International Review of Mission* 111 (November 2022) 187–382.

———. "Zona de promesas. Una Latinoamérica globalizada y fragmentada es mi parroquia. La teología wesleyana ante los desafíos políticos y ecuménicos." In *Abajo los muros; perspectivas wesleyanas en perspectivas contemporáneas*, edited by Pedro Zavala, 55–82. México: Cupsa, 2018.

Recinos, Harold. "John Wesley." In *Beyond the Pale: Reading Theology from the Margins*, edited by Miguel A. De La Torre and Stacey M. Floyd-Thomas, 95–103. Louisville: Westminster John Knox, 2011.

Recinos, Harold, and Hugo Magallanes, eds. *Jesus in Hispanic Community: Images of Christ in Popular Religion*. Louisville: Westminster John Knox, 2009.

Regazzoni, Quinto. "El anuncio del Reino y la 'Vida Buena' (Sumak Kawsay)." *Umbrales: Revista de actualidad religiosa latinoamericana* 202 (2009) 15–22.

Ribeiro, Claudio de Oliveira, et al., eds. *Teologia e prática na tradição wesleyana: uma leitura a partir da América Latina e Caribe*. São Bernardo do Campo: Editeo, 2005.

Rieger, Joerg. "Between God and the Poor: Rethinking the Means of Grace in the Wesleyan Tradition." In *The Poor and the People Called Methodist*, edited by Richard Heitzenrater, 83–99. Nashville: Kingwood, 2003.

———. *Christ and Empire: From Paul to Postcolonial Times*. Minneapolis: Fortress, 2007.

———. *Grace Under Pressure: Negotiating the Heart of the Methodist Traditions*. Nashville: General Board of Higher Education and Ministry, The United Methodist Church, 2011.

Rieger, Joerg, and John Vincent, eds. *Methodist and Radical: Rejuvenating a Tradition*. Nashville: Kingswood, 2003.

Rieger, Joerg, and Upolu Lumā Vaai, eds. *Methodist Revolutions: Evangelical Engagements of Church and World*. Nashville: Wesley's Foundery, 2021.

Runyon, Theodore. *The New Creation: John Wesley's Theology Today*. Nashville: Abingdon, 1998.

———, ed. *Sanctification and Liberation: Liberation Theologies in the Light of the Wesleyan Tradition*. Nashville: Abingdon, 1981.

Segundo, Juan Luis. *Liberation of Theology*. Maryknoll, NY: Orbis, 1976.

Segura, Harold, and Anna Grellert. *Ternura: la revolución pendiente*. Barcelona: CLIE, 2018.

Sobrino, Jon. *Christology at the Crossroads: A Latin American Approach*. Maryknoll, NY: Orbis, 1978.

Sosa, Raul. "La Oración." *Cuadernos de Teología* 17 (1999) 79–106.

Wesley, John. *John Wesley's Sermons: An Anthology*. Edited by Albert C. Outler and Richard P. Heitzenrater. Nashville: Abingdon, 1991.

———. *The Works of John Wesley*. Bicentennial ed. Vol. 1. Nashville: Abingdon, 1984.

Westhelle, Vítor. *Voces de protesta en América Latina*. Mexico City: LSTCH, 2000.

Zavala, Pedro, ed. *Abajo los muros; perspectivas wesleyanas en perspectivas contemporáneas*. México: Cupsa, 2018.

Chapter III

A DECOLONIAL PHYSIC

Medical Science, Healing, and the Ecology of Knowledge in Methodism

Pablo Manuel Ferrer

THE IDEA OF UNIVERSALITY is central to a colonial mindset. It suggests that unity is completeness, that Being is a totality. In this chapter, I reflect about this cultural idea as it is expressed in the idea of health as construed in western civilization. I take as my point of departure John Wesley's booklet, *Primitive Physic*. Specifically, my goal is to read its preface where I identify Wesley as having to wrestle with the emergence of a modern scientific perspective on medical care as a specialized, professional discipline. I argue that Wesley's book is illuminating when approached from a decolonial lens. I then turn to Mark's gospel and read a miracle story with the framework previously worked out in the paper. In both the gospel narrative and in Wesley's work, I suggest that there is a parallel conflict around different viewpoints on health and healing, which have implications for Methodist theology and ecclesial practices today.

This chapter considers the situation of Methodist churches in Latin America and this is the context that inspired me to write it. My own existential situation, living in a third world country like Argentina, is my point of departure for reading both Wesley and the biblical text. My goal is to recognize the relationship between Wesley's *Primitive Physic*, the gospel of Mark, and our times. I work with two concepts that come from decolonial thinker Boaventura de Sousa Santos: *abyssal thinking* and the *ecology of knowledges*. I argue that the relationship between the church and western medicine ought to be understood as exemplary of abyssal thinking. Abyssal thought, according to Santos, divides cultural phenomena in two sides: the real one and the nonexistent.[1] For him, all that can be captured by hegemonic epistemologies is considered to be "real" and "visible," whereas things that are unknowable under the categories provided by colonial thought are deemed inexistent and are thus invisibilized and thrown to the other side of the abyss. I will consider how Wesley's *Primitive Physic* and the pericope in Mark 5:25–34 are suggestive examples where we can detect abyssal thought. The second concept that will be considered is the ecology of knowledges.[2] Santos says that western culture has produced an "epistemicide," that is, after splitting reality into two (abyssal thought), it goes on to kill all forms of knowledge coming from the other side of the divide.

As Methodists, we need to open our way of thinking and our ecclesiology to other forms of medical knowledge. As I will show, this is complex because western medicine and Christianity often function under the same epistemic paradigm, on the same side of abyssal thought. The matter is further complexified because of our own social position, which has been deeply impacted by colonialism. As suggested by decolonial theory, colonialism is not simply a force that shaped social and cultural issues in colonial times, but rather it continues to shape our own situation. I believe that our social position as Methodists today is impacted by abyssal thought. Our reliance on western medicine shows that we stand on the "visible" side of the abyssal divide. This side is primarily what must be decolonized.

I suggest that what we need to consider is the idea of religion as a wide space where many medical knowledges are possible. It is therefore interesting to observe how *Primitive Physic* has been received by some commentaries. One commentator remarked in derogatory fashion that Wesley relied too heavily on "folklore" medicine and a "credulity in belief in what the folk tradition contained."[3] Another writer represents Wesley as embracing "a strange mix of old wives' tales and recent insights."[4]

1. Santos, *Epistemologies of the South*, 118–33.
2. Santos, *Epistemologies of the South*, 175–81.
3. Stone, *John Wesley's Life and Ethics*, 157.
4. Turner, *John Wesley*, 41–42. The position I take in this chapter is informed by the contrary perspective on Wesley's *Primitive Physic* that is advanced by Maddox, "John Wesley."

In this chapter, I want to contrast Wesley's *Primitive Physic* with biblical narratives of miracles as examples of different forms of medical knowledge. In the context of colonial modernity, it goes without saying that this knowledge is assumed to be inferior. But I want to stress the urgent need for traditional and popular medicine and to the need to unite ecology and health. I want to stress the need to think about multiple forms of medical knowledge and encourage a true ecology of knowledge that is built on the entanglement between our environment and our health. This connection, I believe, has been exposed by the COVID-19 pandemic, which has also signaled the limitations of western culture and medical science.

Medicine and Epistemology

In Latin America, we are accustomed to understanding that our history begins with the arrival of European expeditions to the continent. This is a small illustration of how culture and our conceptions of history have been shaped by colonialism: history happened in Europe and was then expanded to the Americas. In philosophy, Li-Hsiang Lisa Rosenlee has argued that western philosophy in the modern period has built its concept of universality on ideas about race that presumed white superiority.[5] Similar patterns can be observed in disciplines like geography, politics, and the arts.

In this section, I turn my attention to medicine, health, and disease as cultural categories constructed in the context of empire. I suggest that we need to situate western modern medicine as a science in this imperial framework. The category of universality is present in medical affirmations, in concepts about health, about the human being, about diseases, and so on. These concepts have shaped what is construed as normal and abnormal. Philosopher and physician Georges Canguilhem's vision can be a helpful tool for starting to reflect on the idea of health in relation to normality. His contributions to the history and philosophy of science demonstrate the unity between epistemology and medicine. He was an heir of Gaston Bachelard who thought that every particular science produces, at every moment of its history, its own standard of truth.

There are a couple of ideas in Canguilhem which will be important for my reflection. First, he indicates that western medicine did not have a consensus in the understanding about the relationship between health and disease. Canguilhem writes that Greek medicine is based on a notion

---

5. Rosenlee, "Revisionist History," 8.

of disease that is not "localizationist but totalizing." He goes on to say that for the Greeks, the natural state of both humans and the world is one of "harmony and equilibrium." The disturbance of this balance, he concludes, "is called disease. In this case, the disease is not somewhere in man; it is the whole man."[6] What is interesting here is how this perspective differs from what became the established paradigm of western medicine. Contrary to Greek medicine, we recognize the triumph of the idea that the illness is a localized problem inside the human body. We can't understand illness as being connected to a rupture in environmental harmony. The hegemonic theory in medicine puts aside the relationship between environment (which is a topic for ecology) and health (which is a topic for medicine).

The second thing that Canguilhem shows is the incipient concept about normality and abnormality in relationship to medical science. Using the writings of Auguste Comte, Canguilhem notices an insistence in "determining the normal and its true limits of variation . . . before methodically investigating pathological cases." Canguilhem, however, observes that Comte offers no criteria to determine what constitutes normality. For Canguilhem, one must simply assume the received notion of what is the "normal state" of human health. In the end, what is presumed to be natural and normal is set apart from the medical science whose limits and specificities Comte sought to establish. In Canguilhem's words, Comte ends up having to embrace a notion of normality that is "more aesthetic and moral than scientific."[7] In this paradigm, the normal is built not in relationship to phenomena but in relationship with previous criteria of normality. Medicine will determine the normal and the abnormal and, by doing so, an entire set of categories that define who the human being is. When we consider that this paradigm is thought of as universal, we begin to recognize how it will function in colonialism by imposing what is to be deemed "normal."[8]

Decolonial theorists today have been investigating how to center medical knowledge on different epistemological grounds with non-western categories. These movements are rescuing other forms of being human. Jonathan Andrews explores some of these themes in his investigation of new developments in the history of medicine. Andrews stresses a newly-developed awareness of a "less Western-centric, geographically broader

---

6. Canguilhem, *Normal and the Pathological*, 40.

7. Canguilhem, *Normal and the Pathological*, 53.

8. Foucault similarly draws attention to the relationship between health and normality, disease and abnormality. See Foucault, *History of Madness*, 89–128.

history of medicine, more appreciative of interchanges, of pluralities and of differing racial and cultural composition in differing health contexts."[9] In a demonstration that things are indeed changing, the World Health Organization recognizes the existence of a diversity of medical theories and practices. It useful to read about it on the WHO website. In it, it is possible to read about traditional, complementary, and integrative medicine. The example I highlight is what the website says about traditional medicine:

> Traditional medicine has a long history. It is the sum total of the knowledge, skill, and practices based on the theories, beliefs, and experiences indigenous to different cultures, whether explicable or not, used in the maintenance of health as well as in the prevention, diagnosis, improvement or treatment of physical and mental illness.[10]

Moreover, the WHO is seeking to expand its attention to non-western medicine, for example, through the "Implementation of the WHO Traditional Medicine Strategy 2014–2023."[11] This is a project that looks to promote safe and effective use of traditional medicine.

Although there is currently an extended awareness about the need to rediscover other forms of medical knowledge, we still encounter complications to implement diverse medical practices. I would like to mention just two of them. The first problem has to do with the coronavirus pandemic. The pandemic reinforced the hegemony of western medical knowledge as the only solution to the disease. The second point is connected with the first and is about common sense. Even when many specialists and institutions offer alternative medical visions, they are still far from entering common sense. It means that when something wrong happens to our health, still the great majority of people believe—I stress the term believe—in the scientific medical system. Indeed, there remains so many concepts and ideas to decolonize.

---

9. Andrews, "History of Medicine," 505.

10. World Health Organization, "Traditional, Complementary and Integrative Medicine."

11. For a study on how the agenda of the World Health Organization has been shifting in the direction of incorporating both western and traditional and alternative medicines, see Doolan and Carne, "Evolution and Complementarity?," 32.

The Wesleyan Vision of Health

Before working on some of the ideas expressed *Primitive Physic*, we need to consider briefly some of the medical beliefs present in John Wesley's times, a period with many competing medical theories. I want to highlight just the ones that I understand to be present in *Primitive Physic*. First, there is a clear idea that one's health is connected with the environment. As Canguilhem shows, the debate about an intervention or not on the human body is closely linked to this point of view:

> This heterogeneity of normal and pathological states persists today in the naturalist conception, which expects little from human efforts to restore the norm, and in which nature will find the ways toward cure. But it proved difficult to maintain the qualitative modification separating the normal from the pathological in a conception which allows, indeed expects, man to be able to compel nature and bend it to his normative desires. . . . Thomas Sydenham (1624–89) thought that in order to help a sick man, his sickness had to be delimited and determined. There are disease species just as there are animal or plant species.[12]

I want to note that Thomas Sydenham is quoted in *Primitive Physic* where he is positively considered like one who gives "simple medicines."[13] Moreover, we know, also from Canguilhem, that Sydenham was considered by Daremberg (1817–72, physician, linguist, librarian, historian of medicine) as a naturalist, not a clinician. Indeed, the social idea of a clinician, or a medical doctor, was being constructed in this period. The idea of nature as providing medicine and healing still had general acceptance at the time. Of course, this was not the perspective that prevailed. The idea of human intervention on the human body without connection with its environment was being constructed. Second, it is possible to see here how the idea of a single medical science is starting to grow. We can witness to a transition away from the traditional methods of healing that are named in Wesley's *Primitive Physic*. This is why Sydenham will be considered a naturalist, not a clinician.

There has been good research done about Wesley's interest and contributions to medical science during his lifetime.[14] I just want to refer to some

---

12. Canguilhem, *Normal and the Pathological*, 41–42.
13. Wesley, *Primitive Physic*, preface 3.12.
14. See, for example, Bruno, "Juan Wesley"; Turner, "John Wesley"; Andrews, "History of Medicine"; Maddox, "John Wesley"; Leong and Pennell, "Recipe Collections."

of them. Debora Madden shows how Wesley's conception of original sin "is fused with the experimental philosophy of Robert Boyle, which sought to explain the relationship between hostile environment and disease in purely physical terms."[15] We notice in here, again, that the environment is present as a category to be considered in the diagnosis of an illness. No doubt, Wesley considered that illness is related to sin. However, there is a social aspect of sin at play in Wesley's writing that connects it to the environment. Wesley draws a connection between industry and disease to address sin, as we can read in the preface of *Primitive Physic*:

> The seeds of wickedness and pain, of sickness and death, are now lodged in our inmost substance; whence a thousand disorders continually spring, even without the aid of external violence. And how is the number of these increased by every thing round about us? The heavens, the earth, and all things contained therein, conspire to punish the rebels against their Creator. The sun and moon shed unwholesome influences from above; the earth exhales poisonous damps from beneath; the beasts of the field, the birds of the air, the fishes of the sea, are in a state of hostility; the air itself that surrounds us on every side, is replete with the shafts of death; yea, the food we eat daily saps the foundation of that life which cannot be sustained without it.[16]

We can appreciate the way Wesley understands nature like a polluted environment. This nature is toxic for human life. But it is harmful because of human sin, not because its own essence.

Against Wesley's idea about the necessary connection between the human body and the environment, the emerging medical paradigm of his time will eventually separate nature and the environment from medical reflection. Modern medicine emerges through the separation between nature and human life. Contrary to that, Madden stresses that Wesley considered that nature and the environment are necessary aspects of the healing process of any illness. Wesley's reliance on Sydenham's work shows that he believed strongly on the "providential and healing power of nature" and that "although nature determined disease, it was also the case that nature could provide the appropriate cure."[17] Sydenham offers his theological interpretation of this:

---

15. Madden, "*Cheap, Safe and Natural Medicine*," 33.
16. Wesley, *Primitive Physic*, preface, I.2.
17. Madden, "*Cheap, Safe and Natural Medicine*," 39–40.

> The Supreme Deity, by whose power all things are produced, and upon whose nod they depend, hath in his infinite wisdom, so disposed all things, that they betake themselves to their appointed works after a certain order and method; they do nothing in vain; they execute only that which is the most excellent and which is best fitted for the universal fabric and for their own proper natures. They are engines that are moved not by any skill of their own, but by that of a higher artificer.[18]

I would like to highlight a couple of strategies that I see Wesley deploying in *Primitive Physic*. These strategies allow us to separate the ideas of "simple medicine" from the "professional" one. The first strategy was the assimilation of popular medicine with pastoral care. Pastoral care was understood as healing of both soul and body. For a long time, Wesley's approach to medicine was read exclusively as a matter of pastoral care work. This entails a clear separation between medicine and spiritual care. It established "simple medicine" in the sphere of religious spaces, meanwhile "chemical-based" medicine was relegated to the scientific realm as defined by the Enlightenment. As Madden shows, "clerical medicine" was used when a physician could not be found.[19]

The second strategy was the regionalization of traditional medicine basically to exclusively rural areas. This kind of movement kept the "simple" medicine for "simple" people living in "non-civilized" places, meanwhile the "sophisticated" medicine was associated with civilization (i.e., an urban way of life). In some cases, simple medicine was considered a useful way for the poor living in the cities.[20] In the next section, I discuss some of the ideas about the reason why Wesley preferred to stay with simple medicine.

Wesley and Abyssal Thought

I would like to approach *Primitive Physic* in a rather peculiar way. I already expressed my concerns about a universal way of thinking as a symptom of empire. I now want to come back to this idea. In many commentaries I have read about *Primitive Physic*, I have found some explanations about Wesley's use of plain language. Madden argues that "Wesley's espousal of plain style" does not "simply stem from a popularising impulse but had a

---

18. Sydenham, *Works of Thomas Sydenham*, 12.
19. Madden, "*Cheap, Safe and Natural Medicine*," 48.
20. Madden, "*Cheap, Safe and Natural Medicine*," 59.

deep moral and theological imperative." Moreover, Wesley's own expertise in medical sciences "gives . . . his work a depth and originality rarely found in typical popularisers."[21] The use of plain language is therefore interpreted by Wesley as coinciding with the mission of the church (as deep moral and theological imperative) which must reach all people. Wesley in fact criticizes the ways in which medicine had become an "abstruse science, quite out of the reach of ordinary men."[22]

The plain language in *Primitive Physic*, and the recipes in it, have to do with the goal of Wesley's ministry and his writings: to reach the simple folk. Besides that, it offered an uncomplicated way to cure diseases. This complicates the social construction of medicine as a singular truth, of the notion in western culture that truth must be one, and that this one true medicine eradicates any other forms of medical knowledge. The point raised by Wesley's *Primitive Physic* demonstrates an openness to diversity in the treatment of diseases.

It was this search for diversity that created a social conflict. It was related to the control of goods—material goods, like money, and symbolic goods, like knowledge. It is noteworthy to examine some of the harsh attacks Wesley received because of *Primitive Physic*. It is possible to find some of them in an interesting collection of articles that appeared in a newspaper during Wesley's time.[23] I bring attention to one of these attacks, included in an essay by William Hawes, "Examination of Mr. Wesley's Primitive Physic."[24] In his preface, Hawes mainly criticizes Wesley's endorsement of ideas and treatments outside of a scientific worldview. Hawes considered Wesley's *Primitive Physic* as a dangerous book for people's health. Besides that, Hawes attacks Wesley for defamation because Wesley suggested that apothecary science had been invented for the purposes of making money. When I examine the abundant correspondence between Hawes and Wesley, what I find so revealing is a review that Hawes makes of *Primitive Physic*. In it, he says:

> Had Mr. Wesley prudently restricted himself within the limits of his profession, by elucidating the principles of primitive religion, he might have edified his readers much more, without either endangering their temporal welfare, or exposing his own opinions

21. Madden, "*Cheap, Safe and Natural Medicine*," 72.
22. Wesley, *Primitive Physic*.
23. Wesley, "Primitive Physic Controversy."
24. Hawes, *Examination*.

to the imputation of medical ignorance, of which he is so clearly convicted in this examination.²⁵

This short excerpt helps us to undercover the construction of the spheres of symbolic power. The problem here is that Wesley, a clergyperson, is talking about medicine. The real problem is that religion and medicine are supposed be on the same side of social thinking. If there is conflict between them, one of them will need to be erased because of its errors.

That is what Santos calls abyssal thought. It consists of "a system of visible and invisible distinctions" that dictates the structure of social reality whose fundamental consequence is to abolish everything that stands on "the other side of the line" of this separation.²⁶ "In the field of knowledge," he suggests, "abyssal thinking consists in granting modern science a monopoly on the universal distinction between the true and the false." The visibility and validity of western science is "built on the invisibility of forms of knowledge that cannot be adapted to any of those forms of knowledge." These invisible and excluded forms of knowledge are identified as "popular, secular, commoner, peasant or indigenous knowledge on the other side of the line."²⁷

Primitive Physic reveals abyssal thought in its construction. Wesley accused medical science of working to build a system that controls knowledge by placing it in the exclusive hands of professionals. Wesley reveals the epistemic abyss when he shows the line dividing those men who can perform medical science and those who perform traditional medicine. The line of the abyssal thought is being created and it is criticized by Wesley.

We must highlight where the dividing between the visible and the invisible was during Wesley's time, specifically in the conflict around medicine. At first sight, it seems that the line is the one separating science and theology, but if we go deeper, we can discover that the invisible line is between the universal-civilized world and the uncivilized world. The latter represented by the poor, the simple people who have in their hands common recipes to cure most diseases. Wesley's critical vision in *Primitive Physic* exposes abyssal thought by refusing to accept the line that divides and ultimately erases popular and traditional medical knowledge.

---

25. Wesley, "Primitive Physic Controversy," 16.
26. Santos, *Descolonizar el saber*, 29.
27. Santos, *Descolonizar el saber*, 31.

Ecology of Knowledge

Another important movement we can find in *Primitive Physic* can be understood through the concept of an "ecology of knowledge." Santos calls forth a "post-abyssal thinking" that "confronts the monoculture of modern science with the ecology of knowledge. It is an ecology," he concludes, "because it is based on the recognition of the plurality of heterogeneous knowledge . . . and on the continuous and dynamic interconnections between them without compromising their autonomy." For Santos, we need an "ecological" epistemology because every knowledge is "inter-knowledge."[28]

We should note that *Primitive Physic* does not reject scientific medicine or chemically based medicine. Instead, in *Primitive Physic* we see diverse ways of addressing diseases. Some of them will be close to the traditional medicine based on nature (plants, roots, fruits, etc.), others will be close to empirical knowledge. However, abyssal thought does not accept the possibility of diversity. There is no place for an ecology of knowledges in abyssal thought.

Primitive Physic gives a hint as to why this multiplicity of knowledge cannot coexist—*money*. Wesley uncovered the subtle interest behind the invisible line. In an ecology of knowledges, we understand there is a sharing of goods, both symbolic and material ones. We can see this openness to a diversity and the line of goods accumulation as the invisible divider line in *Primitive Physic*. Randy Maddox suggests the following:

> His opposition to the restrictions being imposed by the Royal College did not lead Wesley to reject professional medical care, in favor of sole reliance on traditional treatments. Even in *Primitive Physick*, which was devoted to self-help advice, Wesley makes clear that the best advice in some instances is to consult a good—and honest!—physician. . . . But Wesley was also convinced that many physicians unnecessarily protracted the cure of patients' bodies in order to derive the maximum fee, which is why he stressed finding an honest physician.[29]

It is possible to recognize in the passage how Wesley discovered that a worldview was being built subtly in his society. Inside this view, abyssal thought erased several forms of traditional medical knowledge that had been built along centuries in English society. It is what Santos calls

---

28. Santos, *Descolonizar el saber*, 49.
29. Maddox, "John Wesley," 10.

"epistemicide." However, what is most revealing to me is how Wesley shows that the new chemical medicine—an abyssal form of science, I would suggest—is going to produce a critical separation inside society based on power and money. The poorest in society will be relegated to the "invisible" side of the abyssal divide.

Wesley and Mark's Gospel

We have made a basic framework where we consider the social situation in England around medicine. Certainly, it is a noticeably short one. However, it can be a useful tool for reading a biblical text that is possible to be interpreted with the same framework. My main goal was not to explore Wesley's time per se but to find some similarities between his period and the gospel of Mark. So, we are going to find some clues about universality versus ecology of knowledge, and, if it is possible, to find some marks about the conflict that emerged between traditional medicine and heterodox medicine. The text we find to work with this theme is Mark 5:25–34. The goal will be exploring a short commentary the gospel narrator writes about a woman's story.

In the fifth chapter of Mark, there is a miracle story about a woman with blood hemorrhages for twelve years who is healed after meeting Jesus. Previously, in verses 25 and 26, that woman is introduced by the narrator as follows: "And a certain woman who had an issue (*rhysis*) of blood twelve years, and had suffered many things under many physicians (*hiatros*) and had spent (*dapanao*) all that she had and was no better, but rather grew worse" (Mark 5:25–26). Here we have an interesting text that helps us to discover something about medical knowledge present in the community addressed by Mark's gospel. Why does the story mention the "many physicians" the woman had to see? Undoubtedly, the woman had trusted one kind of medicine that did not work for her. Or might we say many types of medicine?

Mark's commentary can be read at least in two ways. First, the woman went to many physicians who were from the same medical context or paradigm. Or the woman understood that Jesus offered a type of medical knowledge. These two possibilities can be assumed as popular memories present in all miracle narratives in Mark.[30]

---

30. Guijarro, "Indicios de una tradición popular."

The commentary in Mark 5 could be read as an invitation to consider the ecology of knowledges. Some of them, like miracles, were settled in popular memories. If an urban/rural controversy can be imagined in Mark's gospel, we can probably understand the miracle in chapter 5 as a form of keeping alive the significance of popular medicine preserved in rural settings against urban elitism.

For some scholars, the medical care systems operative in Palestine frequently overlapped. By and large, common people utilized popular medicine based on family knowledge. Others also utilized folk medicine through forms of knowledge like exorcism, magic, amulets, and miracles. Finally, the elite and upper class utilized professional medicine, which entailed going to bath buildings, a privilege of urban elites.[31]

What Mark is doing here is highlighting other possibilities for healing. However, I suspect that those medical possibilities seem to be addressed to some subjects and discarded by others. This idea is suggested by an article that pays attention to the professional medicine, which takes into account the problems and illness of the wealthy class:

> [We] can observe that Greek medical writers make often mention to diseases connected with the lifestyle of the elite, characterized by overeating, exaggerated ingestion of certain food, alcohol consumption, and lack of physical activity; among them, especially gout (ποδάγρα), once known as "the disease of kings," and obesity (πολυσαρκία), which was conceived as an actual illness. Conversely, less attention seems to be paid to maladies and therapies of diseases that struck the lower classes, as well as to the ordinary conditions of poverty as a cause of illness.[32]

Universality, as I have been arguing, has its own normative view of the human being. Moreover, it is worth noting that in this miracle narrative in Mark's gospel there is a gender issue combined with a class issue. This kind of intersectional analysis would be something useful to explore in future decolonial essays concerning medicine.

The other thing we need to highlight has to do with the matter of economics in both the gospel of Mark and Wesley's *Primitive Physic*. Interestingly, both in Wesley and in Mark it is mentioned that there is an important problem with the cost of medicine. In fact, the woman was in trouble because she lost her money with many physicians. This goes to

31. Guijarro, "Healing Stories," 102.
32. Bonati, "(Un)healthy Poor," 18.

show how singular forms of medicine are tied to the problem of the appropriation of capital. Both in Wesley and in Mark, the problem of money is always tied to the appropriation of knowledge and the destruction of diversity of knowledge.

What happens with the text in the parallel synoptics? It is noteworthy how the accounts of the miracle offered by Matthew and Luke differ. Matthew cuts the commentary about the physicians and changed a few things in his description of the woman. First, the elimination of the commentary raises suspicions because the conflict with the physicians is totally erased in this gospel. Second, Matthew changed the definition of the illness of the woman. This illness is named as "issue of blood" in Mark, which Matthew changes to "haemorrhages" (*haimorroysa*). In Mark there is a kind of description of what is happening while in Matthew there is a name for the illness. Probably, those different definitions came from different medical contexts. While in Mark we have a popular description of the woman's illness, in Matthew we have a more professional one.[33] This change was probably motivated by the proximity between Matthew's community to some rabbinical circles and the acceptance of "professional" or urban medicine against popular one. This displacement of popular medicine is observable in other miracle narratives that Matthew had read from Mark. In Luke's Gospel, the commentary is erased in some of the manuscripts. The urban setting of Luke-Acts probably is responsible for the omission. A posterior revision, trying to assimilate the Luke Gospel with Mark, inserted it again.

Abyssal thought should be emphasized here. The community background we see in Matthew and Luke could be revealing of their places in society. The place they chose will be in one or other side of the line of the abyssal thought. As a hypothesis, Mark's community is defending the ecology of knowledges and setting itself on the popular side of the line. Meanwhile, the Matthean and Lukan communities are trying to keep themselves in the scientific, imperial, and "approved" side of the line.[34] I identified this same division of the abyssal thinking above in my reading of Wesley's position.

---

33. The concept of haemorrhage is found in some Greco-Roman medical groups. It would be, may be, a line that after evolved to the ideas of Soranus of Ephesus.

34. This can be contrasted with the passage that Luke inserts in 4:23. Here we can notice a popular saying that upholds a negative perspective about the physician. Luke takes the passage and applies it to Jesus and thus offering a negative light on those who apply the saying to Jesus. In some way, the saying changes to a positive one.

Contemporary Ideas of Health

We have been considering medical knowledge in New Testament and in Wesley's times. At this point, I would like to return to our contemporary context. In my view of South American Methodism, we have remained caught up in western notions of universality and of medical knowledge. I should like to highlight three scenarios where this conflation can be observed in our daily lives: public prayer and liturgy, educational programs, and pastoral care.

Usually in our worship, public prayer takes into account illnesses that are experienced by members of the congregations. For the most part, these prayers are offered for the safety and wisdom of the doctor who will perform the medical procedure. It is very rare to hear a public prayer asking for wisdom for a person whose medical practices are out of the western medicine. Secondly, our educational programs related to pastoral training are focused on the cure of souls. We have separated what in other times was united, that is, health as a problem that involves body *and* soul. We left the body for the specialists. By doing that, we accept the premises of western medicine. Finally, pastoral care is also framed by the idea of specialization. Pastoral care will never include care for the body or attention to environmental issues affecting the members of the church.

It is possible that we have heard about holistic approaches to health. Some in our churches write papers and public declarations about it. However, we still need to put in practice these holistic ways in our community life. We need to create churches where the problem of health is part of the entire life of the community. We need to consider how to incorporate in our church's programs the study and practice of holistic health. An important component in this reflection has to do with our indigenous medicine. We know so little about it. We need to recreate the ecology of knowledges inside our communities. We need to remember the energy of Wesley's *Primitive Physic* where the preoccupation for the needs of the poorest was a matter of both physical and environmental health.

Finally, our discourse and action should be decolonized with respect to health. We read in the gospels and Wesley how a singular form of medicine destroys the harmony of the human being and its environment, contributes to the accumulation of symbolic and economic capital, and destroys the richness we find in diverse knowledges. I have suggested that both *Primitive Physic* and miracle stories in the Bible present alternative forms of medical knowledge. These stories reveal the urgent necessity to unite ecology and health. Encouraging the ecology of knowledge today must consider the clear relationship between our environment and our health.

By doing it, we will be working to change the commonly accepted idea of the human being. Both abyssal thought and the ecology of knowledges are useful concepts that can improve our ways of life in this time, in this world. Technology, the climate crisis, the pandemic, war, and social violence work with a particular idea of the human being. Western anthropology needs be decolonized. This is an anthropology that is supported and reproduced by the western system of health. Moreover, considering intersectional analysis we will find points where health knowledge, economy, and even geopolitics are discovered working united.

As Methodists, we are a religious movement that was originated in a time in the European history when the western anthropology was being consolidated. Wesley could see the problematic emergence of chemical medicine for the well-being of the human being. Unfortunately, we lost Wesley's prophetic vision and have reproduced western anthropology. By doing it, we sustain abyssal thought and contribute to epistemicide. Health, ecology, religion, education, and science are social spheres where we need to keep a decolonial vision as Wesley and Jesus did in their own times.

Bibliography

Andrews, Jonathan. "History of Medicine: Health, Medicine and Disease in the Eighteenth Century." *Journal for Eighteenth-Century Studies* 34.4 (2011) 503–15.
Bonati, Isabella. "The (Un)healthy Poor: Wealth, Poverty, Medicine and Health Care in the Greco-Roman World." *Akroterion* 64 (2019) 15–43.
Bruno, Daniel A. "Juan Wesley y los alimentos: dones de Dios para todos." *Invenio* 19 (2016) 169–71. https://www.redalyc.org/articulo.oa?id=87745590011.
Canguilhem, Georges. *The Normal and the Pathological*. New York: Zone, 1991.
Doolan, Angela, and Greg Carne. "Evolution and Complementarity? Traditional and Complementary Medicine as Part of the International Human Rights Law Right to Health." *Bond Law Review* 32.1 (2020) 63–89.
Foucault, Michel. *History of Madness*. New York: Routledge 2006.
Grosfoguel, Ramon. "Decolonizing Post-Colonial Studies and Paradigms of Political-Economy: Transmodernity, Decolonial Thinking, and Global Coloniality." *Transmodernity* 1.1 (2011) 1–36.
Guijarro Oporto, Santiago. "Healing Stories and Medical Anthropology: A Reading of Mark 10:46–52." *Biblical Theology Bulletin* 30.3 (2000) 102–12.
———. "Indicios de una tradición popular sobre Jesús en el evangelio de Marcos." *Salmanticensis* 54.2 (2007) 241–65.

Hawes, W. *An Examination of the Rev. Mr. John Wesley's Primitive Physic . . . Interspersed with Medical Remarks and Practical Observations.* London, 1780. https://ia801601.us.archive.org/3/items/examinationofrevoohawe/examinationofrevoohawe.pdf.

Leong, Elaine, and Sara Pennell. "Recipe Collections and the Currency of Medical Knowledge in the Early Modern 'Medical Marketplace.'" In *Medicine and the Market in England and Its Colonies, c.1450–c.1850,* edited by Mark S. R. Jenner and Patrick Wallis, 133–52. New York: Palgrave Macmillan, 2007.

Madden, Deborah. *"A Cheap, Safe and Natural Medicine": Religion, Medicine and Culture in John Wesley's Primitive Physic.* New York: Clio Medica, 2007.

Maddox, Randy L. "John Wesley on Holistic Health and Healing." *Methodist History* 46.1 (2007) 4–33.

Rosenlee, Li-Hsiang Lisa. "A Revisionist History of Philosophy." *Journal of World Philosophies* 5.1 (2020) 121–37. https://scholarworks.iu.edu/iupjournals/index.php/jwp/article/view/3605.

Santos, Boaventura de Sousa. *Descolonizar el saber, reinventar el poder.* Montevideo: Trilce, 2010.

———. *Epistemologies of the South: Justice Against Epistemicide.* New York: Routledge, 2014.

Stone, Ronald H. *John Wesley's Life and Ethics.* Nashville: Abingdon, 2001.

Sydenham, Thomas, MD. *The Works of Thomas Sydenham.* Vol 1. London: Sydenham Society, 1848. https://ia902703.us.archive.org/25/items/worksofthomassydo1sydeiala/worksofthomassydo1sydeiala.pdf.

Turner, John Munsey. *John Wesley: The Evangelical Revival and the Rise of Methodism in England.* Peterborough: Epworth, 2002.

Turner, Michael K. "John Wesley, Medical Reform, and the Methodist Revival in 18th Century England." Paper for the Oxford Institute of Methodist Theological Studies, n.d. https://oimts.files.wordpress.com/2018/11/2018-10-turner.pdf.

Wesley, John. *Primitive Physic; or, An Easy and Natural Method of Curing Most Diseases.* 23rd ed. London: Epworth, 1960.

———. "The Primitive Physic Controversy: Letters and Reviews from December 1775 through August 1776." https://divinity.duke.edu/sites/divinity.duke.edu/files/documents/cswt/Primitive_Physick_Debate_%281776%29.pdf.

World Health Organization. "Traditional, Complementary and Integrative Medicine." https://www.who.int/health-topics/traditional-complementary-and-integrative-medicine#tab=tab_1.

Chapter IV

WESLEYAN METHODISM AND THE INTERRUPTION OF ANCESTRAL BODIES IN ANGOLAN LITURGICAL PRACTICES

Elvira Moisés Cazombo

The history of Methodism in Angola is embedded in the history of the country. Angola is located on the African Atlantic coast and its geography is characterized by the flow of the rivers Zaire, Kuanza, Lwey, Kuango, and Zambezi. The predominance of vegetation, dense forests, fertile soils for agriculture, and various sorts of minerals constitute the basis of Angola's economy. Communities composed of various ethnic families and linguistic groups offer a multicultural landscape where dances, initiation rites, masks, and prayers express the rich spirituality of the people and a shared belief in a single God, the Creator. A focus on Methodism in Angola helps us in understanding how Wesleyan theology coexists with the local culture. My central concern in this chapter relates to worship and liturgy as I discuss how indigenous practices have been incorporated—not without difficulties and resistance—into the practices of Angolan Methodists.

Historically, Methodism was born in England as a revival movement, was structured in the United States as a denomination, and arrived in

Africa at the height of the imperial, mercantilist, and expansionist policies of North Atlantic nations. In this context, Africa was divided into different zones for the sake of the reception of Christian evangelizing and educational missions. The encounter with the Methodism proclaimed by the missionaries was shaped by how it interacted with the traditional religion, communication instruments, and the lifestyles of the local population. This context produced both resistance and accommodation to the message of Wesleyan missionaries. In some instances, accommodating the Christian message meant the extinction of local culture.

A decolonial perspective can help in highlighting the founding marks of Methodism that bring us closer or farther from African traditional religion, including in the current reality of Methodists in Angola. Given the fact that the holy emerges in the midst of complex aspects of culture and their adaptations in reading and interpreting life, I would like to ask: have ancestral bodies and memories been suppressed or evidenced in Methodist liturgical practices in Angola? Does the Wesleyan movement provide a space for enculturation of these ancestral bodies or does it demand the abandonment of Angolan ancestral religion and culture?

To address these questions, it is important to first outline the historical trajectory of Methodism in Angola. Secondly, I will investigate the encounters between missionaries and local communities, specifically attending to the missionaries' encounters with manifestations of popular religiosity. The third section of the paper will address aspects of worship practices in Angola and the movement of bodies in liturgical spaces. My attention is here directed at the ancestral phenomenon called *xinguilamento*, a form of spiritual trance. The final section of my chapter deals with the echoes of this phenomenon in present-day Angola where the influence of Pentecostalism is reviving practices that are on the surface similar to *xinguilamento*. This is nevertheless causing tensions and confusions in Angolan Methodism, which I hope to address so that we may consider the Methodist tradition in Angola as hybrid cultural and religious reality that, amidst internal contradictions, finds ways of building avenues for the liberation of bodies to move beyond the impositions of western Christianity.

Historical Roots of Methodism in Angola

Addressing the history of Methodism in Angola is essential so that we can account for the impact of the tradition in society. As I have already indicated, there is a strong connection between the history of the church and Angolan society. Moreover, this study helps to sharpen the knowledge of the history of Africa in all of its complexities. The western view tends to conceive African history as somehow starting in the colonial era and it remains a challenge to follow the historical paths of Africa in its own terms. For the pan-Africanist leader Amílcar Cabral, the history of the continent cannot start with the arrival of colonizers nor adopt a colonial mindset, but rather it begins from the moment Africans are conscious of their heritage and identity and when they engage in anticolonial struggles for independence.[1] It in this manner that "the preconceived notion that imperialism introduced us into history at the time of colonization must be denounced. The moment colonialism and imperialism arrived, they made us withdraw from our history to enter another history," writes Cabral.[2] History from its colonialist vein is not told from the native's perspective but through the religious, colonizing, and expansionist perspective of the white man.

The evidence shows that Africa is not only the cradle of humanity but also the cradle of Christianity.[3] With regards to Angola, the established narrative places the beginning of Christianity to the fifteenth century at the onset of the arrival and subsequent colonization of these lands by the Portuguese.[4] Franciscan missionaries arrived in 1484, followed by Dominicans, Augustinians, and Jesuits in the ensuing century. The first expansionist expeditions arrived in Angola in the sixteenth century, guided by Paulo Dias de Novais who was accompanied by a delegation of Jesuit priests who all landed on the coast of the Kingdom of Congo in 1560.[5] In 1575, they arrived at Baia das Cabras, where today is located the Armed Forces Museum, on the island of Luanda. While the expansionists were involved in the slave trade and the extraction of minerals, the priests were responsible for opening the first mission centers for the purpose of catechesis and indoctrination to the natives. However, given the proximity to the slave market and mining operation, the missionaries remained caught up in disputes for the hegemony of territories and riches.

---

1. Carvalho, *A igreja no centro da sua história*, 46.

2. Carvalho, *A igreja no centro da sua história*, 46.

3. See Stanley, "History of the African Experience with Christianity," in Lamport, *Encyclopedia*, 883.

4. For a summary of the history of the arrival of the Portuguese in what is today Angola, see July, *History of the African People*, 153–57.

5. Carvalho, *A igreja no centro da sua história*, 8.

The first Protestant mission to settle in Angola was the English Baptist society, founded by William Carey, in São Salvador do Congo, in 1878.[6] This mission was followed by two missionary delegations: on February 27, 1885, William Summers and Heli Chaterlain, from England, arrived in Luanda. They had been carefully recruited by Methodist Bishop William Taylor, one of the most influential Methodist missionaries of the nineteenth century, known as "flaming torch" lit in Africa.[7] Bishop Taylor himself arrived weeks later in Luanda with a delegation of forty-five people that included missionaries, musicians, mechanics, and a homeopathic doctor. Those willing and able to work built an improvised wooden chapel and, on March 22, they celebrated the first Methodist public worship on Angolan soil. This was no mere worship. This marked the first instance of a public display of Protestant liturgy conducted by an American Methodist.

Taylor's goal was to evangelize the native population, contribute to the general spread of the Christian gospel in the region, as well as limit the advance of Islam in southern Africa and establish barriers to slave trade, which at the time was still a major fuel for capitalist growth in Europe and for providing labor for Brazil. To mitigate the wear and tear of a small budget, a strategic plan was drawn up that required that any missionary delegation should find means for its subsistence utilizing local resources, or through teaching, industry, agriculture, or trade.[8] This enabled the opening of schools, the construction of chapels, and agricultural posts. Some places even started to produce and sell alcoholic beverages. These activities made the missions self-sufficient and independent from external aid from missionary societies in the United States.

After arriving in Angola, Luanda was not Taylor's final destiny. After some time there, he followed along the Kuanza River, toward eastern Angola, where he founded the second Methodist mission in Dondo. There they were met by high temperatures, which resulted in the death of some members of the delegation and were forced to continue for roughly eighty kilometers to the village of Nhangui-a-Pepe, where they established the third mission center. The group was well received by the natives and dedicated themselves to teaching, particularly to girls, whom they taught crafts

---

6. See Grenfell, Barros, and Barros, *História da Igreja Baptista em Angola*.

7. Carvalho, *A igreja no centro da sua história*, 32. For a complete account of Bishop Taylor's life and ministry, see Tzan, *William Taylor*.

8. For more on the self-sufficiency emphasis of Taylor's mission, including how it neglected his dependency on slave labor in his native context in Southern United States, see Tzan, *William Taylor*, 15–16, 201–13; Carvalho, *A igreja no centro da sua história*, 31.

like sewing, health care, and literacy. Taylor kept firm to his plan to reach eastern Angola, so the group traveled another sixty kilometers to reach the community of Pungo-a-Ndongo. From there, they advanced to Malanje, founding the Malanje Mission in 1892, and proceeded for a few more kilometers until reaching the banks of the river Quessua.

It is unquestionable that the missionary work transformed the local context. Missionaries like Taylor were able to transform lives and broaden perspectives through biblical teaching, education, literacy programs, opening schools for girls and boys, teaching sewing, reading, and distributing Bibles, as well as encouraging the writing and reading of the Bible in native languages. All of this empowered these communities and eventually projected Angolan leaders who were actively involved in the struggle for Angolan independence in the 1960s and 1970s. This contribution is unquestionable. Equally beyond dispute, however, is the influence that missionaries had on shaping the liturgical practices of Methodists in Angola. The liturgy taught and still embraced by Methodist communities in the country is based on the hymnody brought by the missionaries, the musical instruments played by them, and the bodily postures enforced by western patterns.

Liturgy and Ancestral Traditions

People are known and recognized by their culture. All human cultures have specific characteristics by which identities are established and similarities and differences can be traced between cultures. In these identities, one sees the religious manifestation that becomes part of human existence. Religion nevertheless presents itself in complex ways both at the individual and the communal level. Though diffuse, religious phenomena share a common objective, what may generally be referred to as "the holy" or the divine. The challenges wrought by human existence, difficulties and victories, complexities and joys, compel the human person to search for answers that refer them to a higher being. Hence the need to connect with cosmic forces through the ancestors. In this ancestral connection, traditions play an important role in the binding of the social roles of a past world with the flow of present reality.

Surely the way to religious beliefs goes through the knowledge of rites and rituals. African cosmogony rests on the founding belief in the existence of two worlds: the visible and the invisible, a known and an unknown world.

In the invisible world we have God, the supreme being, and the ancestors. The latter exercise the function of intercessors. In this hierarchy, each family has its ancestor who knows and takes care of the needs of each member of their lineage. The concept of heaven is configured as a village where others are present. In the visible world, we have the family and its ethnic ramifications that, in addition to maintaining connectivity with the ancestors, keeps the obligation to preserve sacred places, such as a tree, a rock, a river, or a forest, where the ancestor can be consulted.

Liturgical rituals are called upon when there is a need to appeal to the intervention of ancestors in people's lives. The word liturgy, it should be noted, is not African. However, the equivalent in Kimbundu, the language spoken in central and eastern Angola, is *Ngungu ia isungu*, which refers to rites or steps for invoking good or bad spirits. The expression contains the term *pangu*, a reference to the proceedings of the *ijila*, that is, the way in which priests and worshippers move before the sacred.

One such practice particular to Angolan ancestral worship practices is called *xinguilamento*, a movement-based form of trance. The act is usually accompanied by music, invocational chants, drumming, prayers, and sacrifices. The word *xinguilamento* comes from the root *kuxinguila*, which describes para-somatic or parapsychic phenomena and spiritual changes and movements. The person begins to convulse with inexpressible and uncontrollable groans, suggesting that there is a fusion of spiritual and material realities in one's body. During this fusion, the material dimension of the person is fully interconnected with vital forces at the spiritual realm. In reaching into this invisible realm, the body is agitated and convulses radically until it faints and returns to its material reality.

Xinguilamento as a ritual is a form of worship directed at the spirits of the ancestors and is often compared to candomblé as practiced in Brazil.[9] It is pertinent to emphasize that *xinguilamento* does not take place anywhere, but only in the *dilombe*, a sacred space, where the trance occurs. It also obeys the rigor of having to occur on a specific day, preferably close to the house of the *soba* (king).[10] The person responsible for the sacred space are the *kimbandas*, medical priests, who work by virtue of their combined responsibilities as both priests and healers and who traditionally have authority over the social and political affairs of a village.

9. Kadiegi, *Documentários*.
10. Ribas, *Ilundo*, 53.

According to Óscar Ribas, there are two primary forms of initiation into *xinguilamento*. The first is when the *mukulu* (the ancestors) elect a person and the second is caused by other entities. The first case is referred to as the "opening of the head" (*kujukula o mutue*) and the second, "breaking the *calundu*" (*kubula o kilundu*). The election of *mukulu* is tied to other entities of the spiritual world of higher spiritual status and signifies that the person incorporating has this spiritual marking in their lives. They can go on a trance to receive communication from the invisible realm and therefore act as servants, who can reveal messages for healing physical and social illnesses, as well as offer religious mediation to strengthen lives and create aspects of interpersonal stability in the community.

In the expression "opening the head" the process takes place through the head where entities reveal aspects that humans could not discover to give rise to the *kubula kilundu*, to breaking of the spirit. This being of high hierarchy reveals what was received from the spirits of the ancestors. The kilundu spirits "represent the souls of people who lived in remote times, at a distance of centuries, being these healers, warriors, and protectors."[11] The popular wisdom of Kimbundu speakers states that "the person shall be calundu, the calundu was person." Our ancestors were persons and any of the living can become an ancestor. The proverb addresses the continuity of life in between the here and what is to come and the interconnection of the visible and supernatural worlds.

Xinguilamento is the preparation for the act of seeking the message or divining that allows the person to be in possession of the spirits of the ancestors and Nzambi (God) for the interpretation of various spiritual entities.[12] To enter a trance, the person is exposed to spiritual conditions such as: (1) the place (dilombe), a special house with materials for invoking spirits; (2) cultural prohibitions on food and clothing; (3) the degree of kinship or familiarity that blends with the possessing man or woman and the spirit; (4) then the ritual to evoke the spirits and incorporate them. This ritual allows for making alliances with the spirits and appropriating them.[13]

The act of possession does not only occur in the dilombe, house-chapel, but also and frequently in houses where a wake is taking place, in parties, or consecrations. Acts associated with *xinguilamento* like the gathering of people for weeping, welcoming rituals for and by the elders,

11. Ribas, *Ilundo*, 172.
12. Ribas, *Ilundo*, 54.
13. Ribas, *Ilundo*, 182.

drumming—all of these can trigger *xinguilamento* so as to reveal the origin of the misfortune, discover a remedy that society needs, to interrupt evil, or to receive blessings.

In short, it is evident that it is not possible to speak of African traditional religion in the Angolan context outside of *xinguilamento*, since through it the visit or connection between the ancestors and the living is established. In African theology, ancestors are not dead persons but mediators with infinite and indeterminable functions and actions. Their responsibilities follow them into the unseen world. The person does not die, but has continuity in the other realm. That is why the movement of the bodies of both those who receive the deities and those who receive the final messages are involved in any act of worship.

Drumming: A Mediating Space for Worship in African Religions

So far, we have noticed that African religion has its own characteristics and nuances that differentiate it from religions informed by a western matrix. Every religion only makes sense when people participate in liturgical ceremonies and rites. In the *makudionda* worship, prayers, requests, and invocations within the liturgy provide ways to reencounter with the divine in a worship that is dedicated to the deities, including the ancestors. These are not mere requests or pleas, but means by which spirits are called to act in favor of life in the community.

Worship being a consultation with the deities, it is usually mediated by a priest or priests, an elder or a group of elders who enjoy the respect and reverence of people in the village or ethnic group. Obviously, not every elderly person is an elder, but one of good conduct and high spirituality. The soba (king) is an elder who enjoys priestly confidence. For a soba to reach this hierarchical position, he had to undergo a careful ritual of selection among the living and be confirmed by the ancestral spirits.[14] All of this is carefully conducted on holy ground. Although there may not be a specific place built by human hands for the sake of worship, sacred places are all around us. These can be under leafy trees, by a river, or any other place chosen by natives. This

---

14. *Soba* is a male figure, which is why I use the masculine pronoun in the sentence. Interestingly, but not surprisingly, we have lost the Kimbundu word for a female queen. Today, when we reference a female political indigenous leader in Angola, we must use the Portuguese word "rainha," or queen.

is where they gather, both for worship, as well as to hear and receive advice and instructions. To approach these spaces and participate in the petitions, behavioral ritual practices must be followed: the head and the body ought to be reclined, feet ought to be bare, both hands ought to be conjoined by their palms in a sign of extreme reverence and respect. Prayers start after the authorization of the priest, the elder.

In the house of worship, wearing many amulets, one meets the sounds of the *ngoma*—drumming. The instrument is predominantly made of wood and the covering of the animal's skin determines the quality of the sound. As a percussion instrument producing a loud and vibrant sound, it serves (depending on the place) as a means of communication between villages for the convocation of the congregation for the solemn occasion, and then the invoking of nature, the creatures of the earth, spirits, the ancestors, and ultimately God. The rhythm has a divine-human language, which mysteriously invokes the spirits and provokes a trance in the human. This trance alters reality and makes the body convulse and chill as it glimpses itself from the outside. Drumming leads to dance and bodily movements elevate one both materially and spiritually as this embodied prayer joins the beats of the drum. Dance here is not a simple matter of fun, but a deep expression of piety aimed at the socialization between beings in human and divine realms. In drumming, we encounter "dance, critique, a social cry, the political and religious realm, time, communication, war, peace, marriage, and other manifestations."[15] Drumming is the expression of African religiosity.

African traditional religion is conceived through its rites and manifestations where music is a constitutive part of worship. That is why our spiritual arteries pulsate at the sound of the drums and it is because dancing is inseparable from our daily lives. This also speaks to the strong sense of the presence and accompaniment of the ancestors. Praise and worship are therefore inseparable from dancing and body movements.

Angolan Methodism: Resistance and Assimilation

These cultural aspects were part of the religious landscape that Protestant missionaries encountered in their arrival to Angolan lands. Their most common attitude was to deny or annihilate these practices, which resulted in superficial evangelization that stifled the natives' structures of religious meaning-making. Rendering African bodies static was akin to

15. Cazombo, "Presença da Religião dos Ambundu," 256.

what Frantz Fanon described through his iconic expression, "black skins into white masks."[16] Our people have music and dance running through our spiritual arteries, but the Protestant missionary ethic masked the religious expressions of the natives.

There has been a deep conflict between the cultures of the missionaries and the ones of African natives. Control over the body and the control of ideas for the sake of "purifying" them has always been at the foundation of Eurocentric and totalitarian powers, supported as they have been by imperial religious discourses embraced by the missionaries. Without attention to native spirituality and culture, they ended up neglecting or rejecting cultural realities that foreclosed the possibility of dialogue. The civilizing tendencies in Christian missions resulted in the annihilation of the many expressions of African traditional religion. These sentiments can be found in some statements by the missionaries: "In our view, the main objective of the missions of a Christian country should be to bring Christianity to peoples who live in paganism and who, in our Africa . . . are receiving the influence of various ancestral pagan cults. What we think is necessary is to bring to the African natives the Christian religion that is the basis of our civilization."[17] Missionaries simply did not understand African traditional religion and this caused much of the conflict. Their perception was that "superstitious practices were current and many villages had deeply rooted pagan beliefs."[18] Conclusions like these created an environment of monitoring African ways of life and a targeted effort to change them without concern for native communities.

In the community of Pembenji, in the vicinity of Quingua (a missionary center) there was a traditional ceremony for the healing of a sick person through the removal of evil spirits.[19] Records from the event in 1906 show an engraving of a Christian ceremony showing dozens of people from local communities bringing their "fetishes to be burned" at the feet of the missionaries.[20] It is noteworthy that many of the natives who were evangelized, instructed, and baptized in the Christian faith, became missionaries in their own right and assumed the role of teachers and evangelists. They were normally sent to small villages. In one of these villages, we hear the report

16. Fanon, *Black Skin*.
17. Silva, "Missões e Missionários," 3.
18. Blake, *Angola colonial*, 39.
19. Blake, *Angola colonial*, 39.
20. Blake, *Angola colonial*, 39.

of a native missionary, Nzengele João Webba, who reported of some people who would "sacrifice their children to the stream—such as might be born face downward, or as might creep at one or two months old, or cut upper teeth first."[21] Records of these encounters are scarce and do not report the perspective of the local community, only that traditional crafts from this village were burned. Communities brought all their belongings to be burned. In the words of Borck, paraphrasing Achille Mbembe, "Colonialism is at all times marked by killing and dying, without due process.... In fact, it is a violent process, where the 'gaze' of the white colonizer is already condemning colonized peoples."[22]

In addition to the burning of sacred ancestral sources and traditions, mission work also supported the creation of the system of segregation and apartheid. The divide-and-rule policy was more complex than one might think. The division of the African continent did not only take place in the geopolitical and economic spheres during the Berlin conference, but also in the religious sphere. The ideological disputes between Catholics and Protestants also made possible the division of native communities, disrupting the unity of African communities. In Angola, villages were subdivided into three categories: villages under the influence of Protestant missions, those under Roman Catholic supervision, and finally villages of the so-called "seculars" (*mundanos*). This system fostered religious segregation and in many localities the movement of people and goods from one village to another was prohibited.

Christianity developed differently in each of these three different spaces with diverging levels of tolerance for religious diversity. It is noteworthy that in the Protestant villages and missions, drumming, dances, and other African rituals were in some instances censored, and in others completely banned. Women's adornments and clothing were burned. Both female and male initiation rites were censored, alcohol and tobacco repudiated. Intolerance was visible. It is only in some Catholic missions that some practices were preserved, albeit still modulated by colonial forces. While in religious spaces there were prohibitions and departures from African traditions, in the so-called "secular villages," life followed its normal rhythm. Drumming, dances, initiation rites and prayers, *xinquilamento*, and other consecration rituals were performed with the usual

21. Copplestone, *History of Methodist Missions*, 576.
22. Borck, "Achille Mbembe."

dexterity. These became spaces to safeguard that which annihilated in the zones of influence of the Christian missions.

We can classify the response from indigenous populations to the arrival of Christian missionaries in two categories: assimilation and resistance.[23] Assimilation is by and large the most common response. Protestant communities in Angola assimilated what was imposed on them by the West from 1482 to 1885. Taking advantage of openness and hospitality of indigenous groups, western Protestants, sometimes through the whip and weapons, imposed a regime of religious coercion, preaching of a merciless and jealous God, and of hell as the destiny of all those who resisted their message. The control over and subsequent death of African ancestral traditions is yet another instance of the biopolitical force over the life of populations, and the necrophilic logic of "letting die" authorizes and validates the disappearance of bodies, their movements, and the rhythm that once ran in their spiritual arteries.[24]

In Protestant worship on Sundays today, sacred music is sung over piano and guitar instruments. It is the death of drumming in the villages and in the assemblies of Protestant Christians. Silent prayers are more accepted by God than prayers to invoke the *Kalundus*. Thus began the process of self-denial that gives rise to the division of the self, the idea that the African self becomes alienated from itself.

When native evangelists joined western missionaries, the church continued its program of evangelization, education, and burning what was perceived as incomprehensible, indecipherable. Abandoning traditional theology and practices became the condition for baptism and, consequently, the change of stage from the indigenous to the assimilated. This was followed by a unique experience of subjection, characterized by the falsification of the history of Africa and a state of strangeness with regards to one's own identity as African. It would be incorrect to suggest that native Angolans refused their traditional beliefs, but it is correct to say that the possibility of accepting them was always monitored by the gaze of the western colonizer and of the Christian missionary.

Every encounter is only healthy when there is a balance of forces or when the model of rationality is based on equal rights and opportunities. The absence of this is nothing more than mere feeding on the other, annihilating their religious traditions and making them easy prey. The

23. Cazombo, "Presença da Religião dos Ambundu," 182–95.
24. See Mbembe, *Necropolitics*.

atmosphere of hostility toward African cultures allowed the missionaries to lose the dimension of their primary mission and turn to the expropriation of lands and riches in the name of evangelization, to implant religious westernization. The characteristics of African traditional religion that I presented are of fundamental importance for the resistance to the Christian religion as imposed by the missionaries. Some of them remain alive within Christianity while in other instances they are kept alive precisely because of their distance from Christianity.

The Pentecostal Influence in Methodist Worship in Angola

Pentecostalism was entrenched in the mission led by Bishop Taylor. This Pentecostal trait impacted his way of doing missions and preserving cultural aspects that were not perceived as opposed to the Bible. While some traditional practices were indeed abandoned and rejected by the missionaries, the Pentecostal roots of Angolan Methodism allowed for the preservation of some memories from our precolonial times. Things began to change in more recent decades.

In the 1980s and 1990s, the Pentecostal movement led by Brazilian evangelist and businessman, Bishop Edir Macedo, broke the transcontinental border and arrived in Angola. The country had gained its independence from Portugal in 1975. After independence, the country was involved in a bloody civil war that lasted for several decades, leading people to confinement to large urban centers, loss of land and productivity due to dependence on imports and donations. While at the economic level dependence from foreign aid only grew, one cannot neglect the immense force of the intellectual and cultural influence that would come to strike postcolonial Angola. With the importation of Brazilian soap operas, films, and news reports, the idiosyncrasies of Brazilian people started to be commercialized in Angola. This dictated the context for a new foreign influence in the country. Religion was central to this endeavor: ways of preaching adopted by Brazilian preachers, lifestyle, clothing, and even accent pushed Angolans into imitating the Brazilian model. It was the start of cultural neocolonization.

With the arrival of the Brazilian Pentecostalism of Bishop Macedo and his brand of the prosperity gospel, his denomination, the Universal Church of the Kingdom of God, exploded in Angola. The church settled in central places of the city of Luanda, building imposing and luxurious temples, equipped with attractive musical instruments. In addition to the luxury and grandeur of the temples, Bishop Macedo and his leaders created a business plan to train Angolan ministers who are asked to acquire a strong Brazilian accent and to keep temples open twenty-four hours a day so that people can come to pray, hold vigils, seek baptism, or an exorcism. Many of the programs endorsed by the Universal Church are embraced by women in vulnerable positions and youth dreaming of social mobility. Typical programs include exorcism, the evangelist call to "bring one more to Christ and make them stay," prayer vigils, and going up to the mount for prayer. The influx of Brazilian Pentecostalism contributed to the emptying of traditional Protestant churches, as many Angolans seem to have encountered in Pentecostal churches a preferable worship experience where they are free to express emotions in an embodied way.

Whereas in historic Protestant churches prayers are offered in a silent and introspective manner, body movements are controlled in the singing of hymns, where the body remains still during worship, in the temples of the Universal Church, one encounters prolonged and loud prayers. People also experience spasms, shivering, and shouting. There are expressions of divination and spiritual possession, all of which point us in the direction of *xinguilamento*. In Methodist churches, either members depart for the Universal Church or the community starts to adopt some of their practices, like shouting, dancing, and other spiritual manifestations. The mobility of these practices has caused conflict and confusion within Methodist churches who fear that the Pentecostal explosion goes against the foundations of Wesleyan Methodism preached by the missionaries.

In this paradoxical environment, some elements are being incorporated into the Methodist liturgy while others are rejected. Drumming, for example, is already welcomed in the liturgy by youth choirs, women's choirs, and in festive occasions, such as thanksgiving, offerings, weddings, and even funerals. While the drums are accepted, there are still strong levels of intolerance for the incorporation of spirits as evidenced through the control of the movement of bodies. When there are instances of *xinguilamento*, people in a state of trance are silently removed from the congregation under the pretense of being possessed by demonic spirits. At times, they are warned not to manifest in this way, other times they are disciplined, even to the point of exclusion from the church community.

One example of that happened in 1991, when members of a Methodist church were excluded under the accusation of embracing "spiritualist" practices that were perverting order in Methodist worship.[25] The expulsions were intended to control the movement of "spirits" within the Methodist body. The measure seemed to work. However, after a few years, prayer groups in local churches became resilient, clandestine, and sometimes subversive, which gradually empowered the ministry of prayer. Who participates in this ministry? The majority are women, followed by a smaller percentage of young people who feel called to prayer and who receive the gifts of speaking in tongues, who receive visions from spiritual forces, and who sometimes possess gifts for healing. These prayer groups are very strong in Methodist churches and they regularly meet, often times at night. Intercessors are normally placed at the entrance of temples while the worship is taking place so as to guard against the invasion of evil spirits. My critique of these practices has been that they tend to create instability and confusion in Methodist communities that stress the "communication with the spirits" while not always educating people to understand and process this form of expressing our ancestral traditions.

While Wesleyan Methodism preached by the missionaries repressed the practice of trance expressed through *xinguilamento*, Pentecostal churches seem to be resignifying this repressed African heritage. However, I am not comfortable suggesting that Pentecostalism has brought liberation insofar as it intensifies conflicts surrounding religious identity. There is still a deep silence about how to integrate traditional worship practices into Methodist worship in a way that is life-giving. In our present context, the dominant feeling is that of fear: those who sing and clap their hands are monitored, those who pray loudly are criticized, and those who enter into trance—*xinguilamento*—are disciplined.

Methodism must be read and recognized by its discipline, by its appeal to the "religion of the heart," and by its commitment to balance. The Wesleyan balance of piety and action is what made the Methodist movement confront slavery, attend to the poor, the suffering, and the excluded, and bring them to the center of the church's ministry. This is also what led to the formation of the Methodist Church of Southern Africa with its "Bantu Ministry" that brings centers on the integration of African culture and Christianity. Here we find a form of decolonization of Wesleyan traditions. A decolonial Angolan Methodism will follow suit and integrate

---

25. Graça, "Monte Sinai, Jornada Árdua."

African traditional religion into its worship experience, freeing the body to move freely into communion with the unseen world.

One thing must be said in closing: Chiziane and Martins teach us that genuine Christianity is not incompatible with African cultures. In her study of their theologies, Paulo Sergio de Proença recalls James Cone's pioneering work in giving shape to a Black theology of liberation. Proença argues that insights from Black liberation theology and African traditional religion can support a decolonial project. He concludes by affirming that Africans have much more to teach us about God than the received legacy of "racist Christianity."[26]

In the midst of these conflicts, Angolan Methodism is divided within itself like a river in search of an outlet to continue its natural course. At times, it remembers old paths: the music, the clapping, the drumming, the gentle beat of women's feet as they sing their true melodies—these are signs that we are entering our own space for worship, perhaps even remembering a neglected past. Oh! How I miss my land, how I miss my ancestors, how I miss my ways of worship. Carvalho quotes Father Mveng, one of the experts on African art who paraphrased John 10:10, "Christ came so that we might have abundant life. Christ did not come to destroy us, but to take us where we must go."[27] Where are you mother Africa, who keep the secrets of a vital Christianity?

Conclusion

Paulina Chiziane, the first woman to publish a novel in Mozambique, insisted throughout her life and work that genuine Christianity is not incompatible with African cultures and, at the same time, it is also part of the heritage that Africans bequeathed to humanity.[28] The absence of dialogue between this heritage and the Christianity brought by missionaries caused many problems for Methodism in Africa. Immersed in a crisis of religious identity as a result of the expropriation of cultural heritage (whether by westernized missionaries or by missionaries of Brazilian Pentecostalism), Angolan Methodism is now moving toward the construction of its identity in the midst of many uncertainties. Its resignification becomes urgent, one that will need to

---

26. Proença, "Resenha," 1667.
27. Cited in Carvalho, *Teologia e prática do metodismo*, 49.
28. See Chiziane and Martins, *Ngoma Yethu*. For a study of Chiziane's work, see Cesário, "Ventos do Apocalipse."

find in African culture the ground for its resurrection. Therefore, Pentecostalism, which for the time being presents itself as an undesirable challenge to traditional churches, can become an aid for the reconstruction of religious identity. Another important axis is precisely the contribution that the "secular," unevangelized villages can offer to this process of retrieving African traditional theology. Here also lies the hope of theological institutions that seek to bring discussions about African theology to the academy in order to rescue the essence of the African.

Bibliography

Blake, Paul A. *Angola colonial fotografada por missionários metodistas*. Luanda: Fundação Antonio Agostinho Neto, 2020.
Borck, Igor Sulaiman Said Felicio. "Achille Mbembe e o escancaramento dos mundos de morte." Instituto Humanitas Unisinos, May 30, 2022. https://www.ihu.unisinos.br/categorias/160-cepat/619034-achille-mbembe-e-o-escancaramento-dos-mundos-de-morte.
Carvalho, Emílio Júlio de. *A Igreja no Centro da sua história: subsídios para a História da Igreja nos Países de Língua Oficial Portuguesa em África*. Lisboa: Núcleo, 1995.
———. *Teologia e prática do metodismo: uma experiência da Igreja em Angola*. São Paulo: Imprensa Metodista, 1983.
Cazombo, Domingos José. "Presença da Religião dos Ambundu nas Transformações Histórico-Sociais e Culturais de Angola." Master's thesis, Universidade Metodista de São Paulo, São Bernardo do Campo [Brazil], 2001.
Cesário, Irineia L. "Ventos do Apocalipse, de Paulina Chiziane, e Ponciá Vicêncio, de Conceição Evaristo: laços africanos em vivências femininas." PhD diss., Universidade de São Paulo, São Paulo [Brazil], 2013.
Chiziane, Paulina, and Mariana Martins. *Ngoma Yethu: o curandeiro do Novo Testamento*. Belo Horizonte: Nadyala, 2018.
Copplestone, J. Tremayne. *History of Methodist Missions*. Vol. IV, *Twentieth-Century Perspective 1896–1939*. New York: Board of Global Ministries, The Unity Methodist Church, 1973.
Entralgo, Armando. *África religión*. Havana [Cuba]: Editorial de Ciencias Sociales, 1979.
Fanon, Frantz. *Black Skin, White Masks*. London: Pluto, 2008.
Graça, João Manuel. "Monte Sinai, Jornada Árdua, Vida da Igreja." March 1997.
Grenfell, F. James, Virgilio Barros, and Margarida Barros. *História da Igreja Baptista em Angola: 1879–1975*. Queluz: Núcleo, 1998.
July, Robert William. *A History of the African People*. 5th ed. Prospect Heights, IL: Waveland, 1998.
Kadiegi, Marisol. *Documentários: Angola sob o olhar de uma de suas filhas*. Documentary film. Produced by Nok Nogueira, 2008. https://www.youtube.com/watch?v=7uQQb5zHqXM.
Lamport, Mark A., ed. *Encyclopedia of Christianity in the Global South*. Lanham: Rowman & Littlefield, 2018.
Mbembe, Achille. *Necropolitics*. Durham: Duke University Press, 2019.

Proença, Paulo Sergio de. "Resenha de Ngoma Yethu: o curandeiro do Novo Testamento." *Horizonte* (Belo Horizonte) 17.54 (2019) 1663–68.
Ribas, Óscar. *Ilundo: Espiritos e ritos angolanos*. Luanda: Impressão e Acabamento, 2009.
Silva, Afredo de. "Missões e missionários: a boa doutrina." *Jornal Estandarte* (1942).
Tzan, Douglas D. *William Taylor and the Mapping of the Methodist Missionary Tradition: The World His Parish*. Lanham: Lexington, 2019.

Chapter V

MINISTERING WHILE SINGLE

An Angolan Perspective on Methodism and Marriage

Virgínia Inácio dos Santos

Marriage is one of the most important institutions in Angolan society. In its traditional form, marriage has four phases: the knocking on the door, the request (the *alambamento*, which is also called "traditional marriage"),[1] the civil ceremony, and the religious ceremony. Each ceremony includes a celebration that can last from hours to one, two, or three days, and includes various cultural manifestations, including conversations, large banquets, costumes, and dances. The importance of marriage in the Angolan subconscious is not only based on legality of the act, but rather in the ideal of the conjugal life, the emotional connection with another person, and the possibility of having children. This vision means that married couples enjoy a great deal of social prestige in Angola. Conversely, unmarried people are marginalized. Religious institutions, including The United Methodist Church in Angola, which will be the focus of my analysis in this chapter, do not encourage celibate life and do not have any kind of public, institutional, or community care aimed at reducing the feeling of abandonment and disconnection that

---

1. *Alambamento* is known through different names in Angola depending on ethnic group and based on the many languages spoken in the country. The ritual consists of the delivery of a letter stating the request for the bride's hand in marriage and gifts of food, clothing, and a symbolic monetary amount.

single men and women experience. Unmarried people live on the margins of Angolan society: while welcomed by their families, they often live in a profound affective, social, and symbolic solitude.

John Wesley, founder of the Methodist movement in England, is far from being an ideal model for those who hold married life in high esteem. As is widely known, Wesley himself experienced great tensions and disagreements in his marriage. Furthermore, he upheld a type of monastic pietism in which the demands of Christian piety and service to others made the celibate life not only possible, but in some cases preferable. For historical and cultural reasons that I will not be able to consider in this chapter, this vision was never part of the Methodist identity in Angola. As I intend to demonstrate, the Bantu cultural heritage and its privileging of marriage remains very active in Methodist communities. In this context, there is immense social pressure for people to marry and stigmas directed against single people, as well as a lack of social structures to care for widows. I believe that this situation deserves attention and that intercultural dialogue and the decolonial perspective can offer something of value to Angolan Methodism.

In this chapter, I reflect on the marital relationship, the Methodist tradition in Angola, and the social pressure imposed on the unmarried. I begin with a brief description of the cultural genealogy of the Bantu people and its impact on current Angolan thinking about marriage. Secondly, I reflect on the tensions Wesley dealt with in his life and ministry to then return to the Angolan cultural context. I conclude with notes for future reflections and research on the chapter's topic.

Marriage in Traditional Bantu Culture

Angolans are part of the Bantu ethnic group.[2] The Bantu are a large ethnolinguistic family that have certain kinship relationships with the prehistoric Saharans. For example, there are Black-Sudanese linguistic forms and

---

2. I would like to note that my comments in this chapter offer a very broad account of marriage that can be thought of as transversal to the various ethnic groups in Angola but that in no way accounts for the specificities of each group. When needed, I will mention specific groups. Secondly, a note on the term Bantu: in its origins, the term did not mean anything particular to the people of a region, culture, or race. In general, the term refers to Black civilizations in various places in sub-Saharan Africa. The etymology of the word comes from the suffix "ntu," which means "person," and the prefix "ba" indicates the plural. Etymologically then, Bantu means simply a "people" as the plural of person. In some instances, it simply refers to a group of people regardless of race or ethnicity.

expressions that are very close to the Bantu linguistic variants.³ The current form of existence of the Bantu people is the result of centuries of interactions with different ethnic and linguistic groups, various displacements, social conflict, geographical mobility, and the long history of colonialism in the African continent.⁴ Despite this complex history, Bantu groups preserve common roots. In addition to the clear linguistic kinship, they preserve a background of similar beliefs, rites, and customs. These similarities grant various Bantu groups certain similarities that exist regardless of their specific racial identity. Therefore, it is possible to speak of a Bantu "people" while holding space for cultural and historical differences.

Angolans are part of the Bantu heritage and its people and culture uphold distinct epistemological resemblances with other peoples of the same ethnic origin. It should be stressed that the Angolan perspective on marriage that I describe in this chapter is within the epistemic categories of the Bantu according to which marital relations are central. That is to say: from our cosmologies and epistemologies, a wedding ceremony and the married life is a site where the entire community gathers: the ancestors, the living, and those yet to be born. Consequently, marriage has vital force in society and sustains its relations.

My goal here is not to offer a comprehensive analysis of the concepts of marriage in the context of the Bantu people, but rather to reflect in depth on the particularities of being Angolan and its relationship with this institution and its impact on the Methodist tradition.

Angolan Wedding Traditions and Family Systems

Marriage symbolizes the origin of life. It is a collective act from its conception, preparation, realization, and sustenance. The decision to marry is normally a family decision and the family also has a role in managing potential conflicts between the couple and other members of the family. In Angolan culture in general, and in particular for the BaKongo, marriage was never a personal decision.⁵ This act has always been linked to families and

---

3. Diop, *Aperçu sur les Cultures Pré-historique en Afrique*, 113.

4. For further information about the historical development of populations in the African continent, see Gatti and Gatti, *New Africa*.

5. The BaKongo people of Angola belonged to the former state of Kongo, which in historiographical writings is the State of Kongo, based in Mbanza-Kongo, today the capital of the Angolan Province of Zaire. As a whole, the BaKongo ethnolinguistic and

the parents have always found a way to get their children married. When someone cannot find a marriage partner, the family intervenes. In the past, parents were responsible for finding future spouses for their children, suggesting—with different degrees of pressure—their children to accept the proposals. In this scenario, the bride and groom had nothing to say because it was the parents who owned and organized everything. Even the economic situation in the early days of the couple's marriage depended on the funds gathered at the wedding. It was impossible not to observe all the preparatory rituals leading up to the main wedding ceremony, that is to say, the delivery of the dowry (*Nkama Longo*) from the groom's family to the bride's family. This final rite, I should stress, is no longer being practiced.

The *alambamento* ritual, which consists of the two families sitting together, confirms the transactional character of marriage. This suggests that union is not only between the couple, but a true society formed by the coming together of the two families. The children born to the couple belong to the mother's side of the family. The arrangement also means that if a woman is unable to bear children, the eldest maternal uncle is responsible to address the situation. In fact, maternal uncles and aunts have a great deal of authority over the couple's children. They are responsible for the growth and protection of their nieces and nephews. Hence, the authority that uncles and aunts have comes with a great deal of responsibilities, which include spiritual and economic responsibilities. In the social imagination, uncles and aunts have the power to bless and to curse, which is the root of the commonly held accusation of witchcraft directed against those who are seen as not exercising this authority for the good of their nephews and nieces.

The sharing of obligations and rights within families is in my view a positive habit in Angolan families. This sense of unity, when lived everywhere and strictly followed, enhances human flourishing. Shared duties and obligations, if well observed and respected, also elevate culture and society. Moreover, the family organization that I'm describing signals to the

---

cultural group is distributed in the northwest part of Central Africa, between the Republic of Angola, Republic of the Congo, Democratic Republic of the Congo, and the southern part of the Republic of Gabon. The seat of its cultural capital is in Angola, which after the country's independence returned to the old name of Mbanza-Kongo, which the Portuguese had withdrawn. See Nsaovinga, "Os Bakongo em Angola." For the discussion on the anthropological sources of study of marriage among the BaKongo, see MacGaffey, "Lineage Structure," 173–87. For further discussion of marriage in Angolan society and culture, see Oyebade, *Culture and Customs of Angola*, chapter 6.

importance of sharing responsibilities in the formation of children. For example, the uncle who is responsible for looking after the nephews and nieces from his sister's marriage does not make decisions unilaterally. He always listens to all sides when faced with a dilemma so as not to make the wrong decision. An old Angolan proverb says that "the chief does not eat the pig's head that has only one ear." That is to say: a leader never comes to a decision by listening to only one person. This speaks to the spirit of discernment, which I would say characterizes the Spirit of God.

When a woman does not have any child, it was common for the husband to be required to find another wife. What sustains this practice is the worldview that having no children means an oblivious life. For Angolans, eternity is concrete and unfolds in one's offspring. For this reason, even those people who cannot find a partner to marry and start a family are advised to at least have a child, even if one has no condition to sustain the child. In this case, it is understood that the child will be cared for by the maternal relatives of the parent. What is essential is to have a child, no matter under what social, psychological, or economic conditions. Not having them is condemning oneself to eternal death, to eternal oblivion. The eternal existence of a person is more important than the social condition of life.

The customs that I have described so far have been losing force, mainly in large urban centers. In part due to the widespread presence of Christianity in the country, very few Angolan parents would dare to choose partners for their children. The instances when this occurs are by and large in rural areas and smaller villages where one can still find couples whose marriage was fixed by their families and who performed traditional ceremonies, including *alambamento*. In general, however, the traditional way of thinking about marriage has changed a lot in connection to the population's introduction to Christianity. In families with different religious and cultural practices, it is not uncommon to witness disputes regarding the rights of parents and family members to be involved in the marriage life of other family members.

Marriage and Gender Relations

Our cultures are matrilineal in essence. This means that matters related to inheritance follow the mother's side of the family, not the father's. However, this matrilineal system does not empower women themselves. That is, women have no economic, political, or decision-making power. In this regard, my position here affirms the importance of centering women's empowerment and to create more opportunities for mutual support among women in a system that tends to put them against each other. I will be addressing the economic, political, and social dimensions of the gender issues that can be identified in the Angolan family dynamics.

With regard to economic power, the most common activities carried out by women are domestic services or as self-employed workers in retail. They contribute to the maintenance of the home, but on a scale that makes it difficult for them to accumulate any assets or real power. We have a group of intellectuals, women in public service, and others who own their businesses who manage to obtain a certain degree of economic autonomy. The last group, in particular, accumulates monetary wealth and women in it are able to help their partner in building the family assets in a more concrete way. Yet, women in all groups will lose their property and assets in case their spouse dies. When a sudden or unexpected death occurs, the family of the deceased spouse is accused of causing his death to take possession of the couple's wealth. That is because wealth accumulated by the couple will not stay with the female widow but will go to the deceased's siblings, nephews, and nieces.

In the political sphere, women cannot speak in public at meetings between the two families. Their power is not visible because they are not the ones who publicly declare the decisions taken by the families. But that does not mean that women lack real power in family relations. It means, rather, that this power must be exercised through discreet means. Behind the scenes, women are the ones who work to change their spouse's mind or the minds of other men with authority in the family system.

Socially, women's power is largely concentrated in motherhood. And not just the fact of being a mother, but the fact of mothering male children. For it is the boys who inherit things and manage the political and economic affairs of the family. In any case, there is still another detail worth noting. The male heirs, primarily the firstborn, are not heirs to their own parent's property, but to their maternal uncle's property. Therefore, your parents' older siblings are also called mama and papa and children are expected to obey and respect them as such.

One factor that seems worthy of emphasis is the way in which patriarchy, even in the face of the matrilineal tradition in Angola, contributes to rivalry between women. By that I mean that the power a woman has in the family is most often in tension with another woman. For example: a woman can disqualify and humiliate her sister-in-law, her brother's wife, if she is unable to have children. She also has the power to order her male children to take hold of her brother's property in the event of his death, leaving the widow—the sister-in-law—alone and empty-handed.

Bruno Madureira Sucumula explains the fact that the Angolan family system is matrilineal does not mean that women are empowered. While the system does not necessarily empower the husband as the head of the family, it still grants authority to the wife's older brother. The high role ascribed to the uncle creates many layers of tensions, especially in the relationship between women.[6] Thus, the political and economic rights and duties of a family are managed by the men on the mother's side. In concrete terms, I would say that my children play a role in my older brother's family life insofar as he is responsible and has authority over them. Moreover, my children are entitled to my older brother's inheritance while my brother's children will exercise the same right in connection to the family on their mother's side.

As I mentioned above, in the case of the death of the father of the family, his nephews, his sister's children, will have the right to inherit his property. So do the brothers and sisters of the deceased. At the root of this cultural practice is the assumption that they will have the obligation to care for the widow until she remarries and also take care of the orphans until they reach adulthood. When this is not observed, a fact that is becoming more common nowadays, we observe the dire suffering of widows and orphans. This is an instance where the power of women is being used not to build solidarity and to care for and protect another woman. To the contrary, when this happens what we see is the demeaning of a woman by another woman.

The Angolan government passed laws that support the rights of widows and orphans, but the social force of the practices I described in here remains strong. Laws are not always enforced, either due to the inefficacy of the legal system or because of the ingrained nature of the cultural practices themselves. Despite the integration of Christianity in the country, churches too struggle to disseminate a culture of care and protection of widows and orphans. In my view, there is much work to be done by church leadership so that the most vulnerable in our society are honored and cared for.

---

6. Sucumula, "A Constituição da Família Angolana."

Marriage in Wesleyan Thought

Wesleyan theology has contributed considerably to changing mindsets about cultural and spiritual practices in Angola. For example, the majority of United Methodists in Angola—especially those born and raised in the tradition—tend to disbelieve in the power of an uncle to curse them and impact their lives negatively. It is possible to understand Methodism as empowering women insofar as its teachings interrupt the patriarchal power exercised by uncles and older brothers and ensuring that assets and social power remain with women, regardless of their marital status. Unfortunately, there are few churches that value this dimension of Methodism and it often seems that the institution keeps this powerful teaching to itself. In my view, a frank and open dialogue between the Methodist tradition and the traditional expressions of Bantu culture could maintain the relational principle and the collective decision-making process that sustain family systems in Angola while, at the same time, questioning the type of power that uncles exercise over women in their family.

In my descriptions of the family and community assumptions that involve a marital union in the Angolan context, I hope I have made it clear how very significant is the commitment that families have in marriage as a social institution. The Bantu view of marriage transcends the affective relationship of a couple and also the legal dimension of marriage. In my view, we could perceive three dimensions of marriage. First, that our existence as a person is activated when it is linked to another with whom one shares life. Second, that as one walks and lives with the other, one's humanity is affirmed. And, third, that socialization is what makes a person a human being. When we are with each other we can determine the difference between what is real and what is not real. Alone you are a "puppet" or a thing, as it is often said in Bantu traditions, because everything you do is just for you and you cannot differentiate between the I and the you, to use Martin Buber's terminology. This epistemology and cosmology do not think that the human person can live alone.

This implies that single people struggle to find their place in society and in the church. They are forced to marry. Their families make arrangements so that they can be married and when that does not happen there is great stress. Angolans are not given the right to choose to be alone for life. When the parents realize that the young man or woman has already reached adulthood, they look for a spouse. When a partner is not found, families might accept that a family member remains single, not by virtue of their choosing but due to the lack of choices. Still, relatives are not happy and will communicate that to the single person whenever they have the opportunity. They will do so vehemently. In general, Angolan society does not have a positive outlook at the unmarried person who has made the decision to remain single. This person will not be allowed to have an independent life. For example, even when professional life is stable, she or he will be expected to live with family members.

This cultural predisposition is exacerbated in church environments, where the social pressure to marry takes on a spiritual dimension. For Methodist communities, the curious thing about this situation is that the Wesleyan tradition brought by the missionaries has in its founder, John Wesley, someone who embraced nearly monastic ideals. Marriage, of course, was not a requirement for itinerant preachers in the Methodist movement in England. However, upon entering Angolan lands, the Puritan vestiges present in Methodism, especially with regard to the ideal of the family and domestic life, became radicalized when they met with local traditions. Today, it is common sense among United Methodists that marriage is a mandatory tradition, particularly for pastors. While Methodist doctrines were very well assimilated in Angola, it is rather difficult to demystify the absolute importance of marriage. It was not even possible to cultivate a neutral and respectful posture toward the person who wants to dedicate their life exclusively to ministry.

As I said earlier, taking Wesley as a model for the "Methodist view" of marriage is simply impossible. What is found in his writings and in what other authors wrote about him allows us to perceive that his focus was to announce the gospel, neglecting responsibilities that could change the course of his missionary goals. Wesley is notorious for his apparent disregard for his romantic relationships and for his frustrations during his marriage to Mary Vazeille. It is worth noting that my intention here is not to make moralistic analyses of Wesley's marital life. On the contrary, I would like to start from the affective tensions in the *personal* life of the founder of Methodism to discuss the *cultural* tensions that emerge from the encounter of the Methodist tradition with the Bantu tradition in the Angolan context.

Writing in the early twentieth century, the Reverend W. H. Fitchett tells us that "all Wesley's love affairs were disasters, but his marriage was a tragedy."[7] This statement is no doubt strong but nevertheless accurate. In

---

7. Fitchett, *Wesley and His Century*, 456. For a psychological account of family dynamics and how it may have impacted John Wesley's marriage, see Headley, *Family Crucible*.

his journal, we find Wesley's reports that attest to his apathy and resentment toward his wife and he ranked the celibate life as a higher state than marriage. It certainly appears that, for him, marriage would be more the fulfillment of a social obligation than a necessity. In this sense, we could say that, for the founder of Methodism, when it comes to the holy life, celibate life was the rule and married life the exception.

Fitchett describes Wesley's position as "semi-monastic."[8] He references his treatise, *Thoughts on Marriage and a Single Life*, compiled by Wesley in 1743.[9] In this text, Wesley does not treat celibacy as an "imperative and universal obligation," but lets it transpire that he considers it a "loftier state," higher than marriage. Fitchett concludes by saying that, for Wesley, marriage constituted a "concession to human weakness, and ought to be postponed as long as possible in all cases, and foregone absolutely where there was sufficient grace to enable this to be done."[10] Wesley even stated that marriage could damage the soul, consequently causing the person to lose the kingdom. This position generated controversy at the Conference in London in June 1748, and it was then that Wesley changed his view. He writes: "Several brethren then objected to the 'Thoughts on Marriage,' and in full and friendly debate, convinced me that a believer could marry without suffering damage to his soul."[11]

Regardless of the amicable resolution and Wesley's apparent change of heart, this account astounds an Angolan Methodist. That is, to think that the revered founder of Methodism once thought that marriage could "damage one's soul" is a foreign idea. Indeed, any remnants of this form of monastic pietism never influenced the Methodist movement in Angola. In any case, I have been hinting at the fact that I believe that Wesley's example and proclivities for the monastic ideal could benefit us in the Angolan context. To be clear, I do not mean that I endorse Wesley's reference to how a marriage could harm a person's soul, but rather his respect and consideration of the possibility of a pious and unmarried life as a way to accept the call to serve God's kingdom. That is because, for me, the overvaluation of marriage and procreation in Angolan cultures impacts Methodist communities and harms the individuality of those who do not want to marry. What I propose

---

8. Fitchett, *Wesley and His Century*, 456. For a similar discussion, see Heitzenrater, *Elusive Mr. Wesley*, 141–46.
9. Wesley, *Thoughts on Marriage*.
10. Fitchett, *Wesley and His Century*, 456.
11. Fitchett, *Wesley and His Century*, 457.

here is that we seek a middle ground that allows for a joyous and prosperous life for both married and unmarried people.

The social pressure that possibly influenced Wesley to eventually get married puts him in a similar position as many Angolan pastors today. This is because Angolan society wants to make its young people marry at all costs, neglecting the harm inflicted on those who have no existential reason to seek a spouse or who lack the means to do so. In United Methodist environments, we see young pastors who decide to remain single to better give themselves to the gospel being pushed into marriage. This degree of social pressure is cruel and can cause a person to be emotionally and spiritually unstable. The church, as an institution, does not take a firm stand. It ordains single pastors but does not support them as single ministers. Church communities often assume that single pastors are not responsible enough, that they will get romantically involved with the youth or with married people in the congregation, that they will destabilize families in the community, and that they lack legitimacy as care-providers for couples and families. People ask: what pastoral authority will they have for children and parents if they themselves have no experience as parents or spouses?

Soon enough, questions like these become rumors, and rumors become reasons to distrust a pastor. The single pastor is therefore faded to a ministry that lacks harmony and peace. The United Methodist Church in Angola does not have any policy or effort to educate its members about a necessary change of attitude. As it currently stands, single United Methodist ministers find no dignity, acceptance, and support from their denomination.

Thoughts upon Cultural Encounters with Difference

As I have been suggesting, marriage was not part of the categories considered noble or of vital importance for Wesley. It is true to say that this aspect of the Methodist tradition, at least as conceived by its founder, did not impact the cultural roots of the Angolan people. Our analysis leads us to realize that Angolan Methodists continue to be loyal to cultural practices that tend to treat marital life as essential to the human person.

I believe that this situation needs to be understood in two angles. On the one hand, we need to emphasize the relational dimension of Bantu culture. For the Angolan, it is inconceivable that a person can live alone. The existence of a person is conditioned to another person. That is, the human being concretizes their existence in the relationship with other persons. This principle remains strong and intact regardless of the input of missionaries and other forms of Western influence. The arrival of Methodism and the contribution of Wesleyan thought did not take away the force of this conception. In my view, this ideal is laudable and needs to be constantly reaffirmed.

However, one must guard against reducing the relational principle to the context of matrimony. The human disposition toward the other person cannot be reduced to one's relationship with a spouse. This reduction poses considerable challenges for single people, especially in an ecclesiastical context where single pastors are treated as "incomplete" leaders. In Angola, this is a situation where the lack of intercultural dialogue between Methodist missionaries and local communities causes many tensions to this day.

Cultural dialogue is one of the highest phenomena for the development of the relational principle. But this importance only makes sense when it is not imposed. It only has relevance when the parties are equal, where the spirit of ethnic superiority is rejected. Methodist missionaries in Angola, in their way of transmitting the gospel message, tended to ignore the culture of the people. They brought their habits and customs and often represented them as part of the gospel message. The message brought by Methodists too often failed to acknowledge its Western cultural background. This can be found, for example, in prohibitions imposed to movement and dance during worship or drumming, both aspects that are ingrained with spiritual meaning in the Bantu worldview.[12]

Methodist missionaries in Angola, in their understanding of the importance of marriage, did not differ much from local customs. Apparently, upon entering the Angolan culture, they assumed that local communities shared a similar concern for marriage and the importance of having children. However, what is harder to realize is that, in the meeting between different cultures, the epistemological basis for the understanding of married life was not the same. The Bantu epistemology and cosmology that inform the Bantu understanding of marriage is unique. If marriage was affirmed in the reception of Methodism in Angola, the epistemological basis of the relational principle in the Bantu tradition was diminished. That meant that the social structures and the structures of authority present in the encounter between two families to arrange a marriage were fractured. With time, marriage was crystallized as a merely formal, bureaucratic, and

---

12. On this topic, see chapter by Elvira Moisés Cazombo in this volume.

highly hierarchical institution. This can be seen very clearly in the way in which the Methodist tradition and other traditional heirs to Western countries encouraged a split between the family ceremony and the religious ceremony. The mismatch between the family sphere and the ecclesiastical sphere was a new factor in the culture.

The elaboration of civil laws that forced the couple to have an official government license granted some degree of social power to married women over the goods acquired within the relationship, as well as their children. But the law assumes that marriage is an agreement only between two individuals, which conflicts with the Bantu understanding that marriage is a union between two families. Given the instability of this situation, the power of traditional culture imposes itself and reinscribes male dominance.

Meanwhile, Christianity, as a missionary religion, contributed to the questioning of the spiritual authority that uncles and aunts have over their nieces and nephews. The custom of perceiving them as people who could curse the youth has been largely challenged. I believe this has been an important contribution that tends to empower women in the community. Many Angolan Christians, especially young people, affirm that their faith in Jesus Christ means that no uncle or aunt can unilaterally determine their fate.

Conclusion

For Angolans, marriage remains a site where a person's existence is affirmed by means of this person's commitment to another person. As I indicated, this often means that single people are not well regarded in society. I have suggested that I dispute this disposition and that I want to affirm the value of single life, particularly as a form of honoring the vocation of pastors who want to devote fully to their congregations and their ministry work. I believe this vocation and commitment resonates with the Bantu relational principle insofar as it suggests that all people, married and single, must actively participate in the process of giving rise to life. From a Wesleyan perspective, this position is equally valuable insofar as the tradition affirms that some have a vocation to a life in celibacy for the sake of service to God and others.

The decolonial perspective is important due to its emphasis on epistemologies and the politics of knowledge production. I have described that the Bantu conception of marriage is based on a particular epistemology and cosmology, one that finds the meaning of life in social and family relations. The formation of a sense of kinship is paramount and that speaks to how Angolans seek so much in their relationship with their spouses. At the same time, a decolonial perspective does not romanticize a precolonial past nor seeks to presume that cultures are detached from the power of colonialism. Rather, this perspective thinks of culture always in tension with power relations. This is where the authority of male family members over women and the social pressure imposed on unmarried people requires a decolonial intervention. Living a full life does not require one to live a married life. Living a life of absolute devotion to God and others does not require one to be married. A church and a society that can embrace those principles will be on their way to a positive and decolonial future.

As I come to my conclusion, I stress that not all aspects of Methodist spirituality have been transmitted in the process of its integration with Angolan society and culture. I have also argued that the matrilineal dimension in the culture does not mean that women are empowered. It appears that this is merely symbolic. This is something that I will address more directly in future research. For now, I should like to close by saying that the decolonial perspective can be useful in addressing—and hopefully undermining—the power of a woman's elder brother, the maternal uncle that gains power in family systems in Angola. In future work, I will explore how the authority of these uncles has been perceived and ultimately exacerbated in the colonial context.

Bibliography

Diop, A. S. *Aperçu sur les Cultures Pré-historique en Afrique*. Paris: Presénce Africaine, 1974.
Fitchett, W. H. *Wesley and His Century: A Study in Spiritual Forces*. London: Smith, Elder, 1906.
Gatti, Ellen Morgan Waddill, and Attilio Gatti. *The New Africa*. New York: Scribner, 1960.
Headley, Anthony J. *Family Crucible: The Influence of Family Dynamics in the Life and Ministry of John Wesley*. Eugene, OR: Wipf & Stock, 2010.
Heitzenrater, Richard P. *The Elusive Mr. Wesley*. 2nd ed. Nashville: Abingdon, 2003.
MacGaffey, Wyatt. "Lineage Structure, Marriage and the Family amongst the Central Bantu." *Journal of African History* 24.2 (1983) 173–87.
Nsaovinga, Camilo Afonso Nanizau. "Os Bakongo em Angola: história e cultura." *Wizi-Kongo*, December 22, 2018. http://wizi-kongo.com/historia-do-reino-do-kongo/os-bakongo-em-angola-historia-e-cultura/.

Oyebade, Adebayo. *Culture and Customs of Angola*. Culture and Customs of Africa. Westport, CT: Greenwood, 2007.

Sucumula, Bruno. "A Constituição da Família Angolana: A Desnecessidade do Casamento Civil e Tradicional; A Situação do Convidado Familiar." *JuLaw*, January 16, 2020. https://julaw.ao/a-constituicao-da-familia-angolana-a-desnecessidade-do-casamento-civil-e-tradicional-a-situacao-do-convidado-familiar-por-bruno-sucumula/.

Wesley, John. *Thoughts on Marriage and a Single Life*. Bristol: Cengage Gale, 1743.

Chapter VI

TRAPPED BETWEEN THE PEW AND THE ALTAR

Wesleyan Traditions and Decoloniality;
An African Feminist Perspective

LILIAN CHEELO SIWILA

THE HISTORY OF WOMEN's presence and activities in the church in Africa can be described in two ways. First is the group of women who form their own fellowship groups called by different names in different congregations. In the Methodist Church of Southern Africa this group is known by names such as the Manyano or women's fellowship group. The Manyano are the earliest women's group formed around the late 1800s through the influence of female missionaries. The second group is the one of ordained women who serve in the church either as pastors or deaconesses. The number of women who do not belong to any of these two groups in the church in Africa is very minimal. African women theologians have argued that women are church in Africa.[1] They embrace and value the church that they serve so faithfully. Be it traditional mainline/mission churches or Pentecostal charismatic churches, it is very rare to find a church that has more men than women, in most cases the majority of members are women and children. This is despite

---

1. See Bum, "Women and the Church," 8–16; Oduyoye, *Introducing African Women's Theology*.

the fact that we still have churches that do not ordain women or give the ordained women freedom to fully participate in offering sacraments in the church. For example, there are churches that still hinder women to conduct funeral services if the deceased is male. There are also still churches that struggle to allow a single female minister to provide marital counselling to a married couple. As a result of all these hindrances, women who contribute to the statistical and spiritual growth of the church continue to remain invisible when it comes to issues of leadership and the offering of certain sacraments to the congregation. In the works of The Circle of African Women Theologians, Mercy Amba Oduyoye and Isabel Phiri are among African women scholars who have contributed significantly to the scholarship on women being church in Africa.[2] In their various publications, the authors demonstrate how women have found space to be "church within a church" despite the many historical and cultural teachings aimed at hindering and alienating them from the church.

The aim of this chapter is to explore ways in which this "church within a church" group has been both a liberative and oppressive space for women. As I embark on this study, I'm aware of the amount of research that has been conducted by various scholars on these women groups, especially the Methodist women Manyano, whose work has attracted a great deal of research. In this paper, I take a slightly different angle by looking at the ambivalence found in these women groups which makes them become both spaces of oppression and women's emancipation. The questions I seek to interrogate are how church traditions and liturgical practices imposed on these women fellowship groups contribute to the way in which these women understand themselves as being church. What are some of the oppressive teachings that these women groups have embraced in the name of church traditions? To what extent did missionaries contribute to some of the oppressive teachings that these women groups keep passing on from generation to generation without critical analysis? What kind of decolonization of these church traditions and liturgical practices is needed in order to create liberative spaces for women in the church?

---

2. Phiri, *Women, Presbyterianism and Patriarchy*; Oduyoye, *Daughters of Anowa*.

The Development of Women Fellowship Groups in African Wesleyan Traditions

At the time when there was no space in theological education and on the pulpit for women to exercise their ministry, especially in Africa, women decided to form their own spaces where they became active contributors to the growth of the church and for their own spiritual growth. Within the Methodist church tradition, women's groups are traced from as far back as the time of the missionaries. Deborah Gaitskell argues that the establishment of Women's Manyano in Southern Africa was the effort of the wives of missionaries who contributed to the development of this organization by evangelizing African women through trainings such as sewing and instructing them on the roles of motherhood, wifehood, and worker.[3] This is confirmed by Beverley Haddad who argues that African women's expression of Christianity is intertwined with the process of colonization and missionary enterprise that took place in the late-nineteenth century.[4] Scholars such as Jacklyn Cock and Cherryl Walker see the emergence of these women groups associated with the work of female missionaries' desire to introduce a Victorian model of housewifery by placing emphasis on domestication of women in the spheres of the home.[5] As these groups grew they became circles of identity where women shared their stories of faith through Bible studies, singing, preaching, providing spiritual and moral support to one another, and learning other craft and hygiene skills taught by missionaries' wives. Marja Hinfelaar adds that in "southern Africa, women found other ways of being involved with the Christian missions through attending these prayer groups.... The groups also offered support for women with problems in their marriages, in raising their children as Christians, and with other common issues; for these reasons they were sometimes considered mothers' groups."[6]

Most of the women who joined these groups adopted new ways of life by abandoning anything that was said to be "unchristian" by the missionaries. Although these groups held a kind of Western spirituality and tradition in their organization, they are also a space where women share their indigenous expressions of African spirituality. According to Isabel Apawo Phiri,

---

3. Gaitskell, "Housewives, Maids, or Mothers," 241–45.
4. Haddad, "Manyano Movement in South Africa," 4–13.
5. Walker, "Gender and the Development"; Cock, *Maids & Madams*.
6. Hinfelaar, *Respectable and Responsible Women*, 44.

this combination of African culture and western Christian traditions is what mainly informs how these women do church in these circles.[7]

As evidenced above, the influence of these female missionaries to the African women and girls created a great impact in the work of these groups. In some countries, missionaries had an upper hand in the drafting of the constitutions so as to suit their preference of how an African Christian woman should behave and present themselves as Christians. As time went on some groups managed to revise some of the rules in order to suit their own cultural context. Despite these changes, most of the groups still hold on to teachings inherited from the missionaries, most of which create tension and divisions among the women. Mercy Amba Oduyoye, a Methodist woman theologian, contends that African Christian women have formed groups and founded religious organizations despite the cultural, religious, and social constraints. She further warns against patriarchal tendencies imposed on these groups in the name of church traditions that later divide the women.[8]

In terms of mission and vision these women's church groups carry the church on their shoulders. Their mission is visible in all the countries where they are established. Holding the Methodist tradition and teachings, their presence is mainly symbolized by their uniform and the days of their meetings, which are Tuesday, Thursday, and Saturday. The significance of these days will, however, not be discussed in this study but suffice to say that these women's ministry and outreach is embedded in the Wesleyan model of class society that was proposed by John Wesley himself.

Wesley, who started this evangelical work in 1738, recommended his followers form themselves into a sort of little society to meet once or twice a week in order to reprove, instruct, and exhort each other. This little society was called a class and the practice was adopted wherever the Methodists established themselves. Hinfelaar confirms that the Manyano adopted this model with the emphasis on discipline, lay leadership, and the practice of various activities such as prayer, Bible studies, and conversion of other women.[9] The group has strict rules concerning moral behavior, which is drawn from a mixture of African and western culture and traditions. Among the public roles Wesley encouraged Methodist women to assume was the role of visitor. This tradition has continued to thrive among the people called

---

7. Phiri, *Women, Presbyterianism and Patriarchy*.
8. Oduyoye, "Ecclesiology," 149–53.
9. Hinfelaar, *Respectable and Responsible Women*, 44.

Methodists.[10] In the case of women's fellowship groups, visitation is one of the key roles of ministry. Women are taught to visit the sick in hospitals and hospices where they even offer not only spiritual service, but social service such as donating food and clothing. When discussing Wesley's approach to women, John English further argues that

> Wesley used the term "sister" again and again. He intended to emphasize the point that women as well as men are full members of the Christian church. Both men and women have free access to the means of grace and both can receive the gift of entire sanctification. Note, by way of contrast, the house churches described in the New Testament. These churches were composed of men and women; sometimes, indeed, women were chosen for positions of leadership in them. Nevertheless, the contributions which women made to the churches' life were barely recognized.[11]

Wesley's model of community fellowship included care of the widows, displaced children, and the poor. In a previous study, I argued that in most of the Methodist traditions in Africa these acts of mercy are mainly carried out by women, especially women's fellowship groups. Leaving these acts of mercy to women only simply shows how the church has forgotten the words of Wesley, the model of the Methodist church, who during the period of his ministry stated that: "For I myself as well as the other preachers who are in town, diet with the poor on the same food and at the same table. And we rejoice herein as a comfortable nest for our eating bread together in our Father's kingdom."[12] John Wesley's approach to evangelism and the preaching of the Gospel was centered on acts of mercy extended to all, especially the poor. This kind of approach needs to be encouraged as a model in our attempt to reconstruct these women's fellowship groups so that they are inclusive and embracing to all women in the church.

Reconstructionist Feminist Theology

In an attempt to discuss how women's fellowship groups within the Methodist tradition can be a space for the redemption of all women in the church, I use a reconstructionist feminist theology approach as the lens through which to critique ways in which mission-oriented teachings

10. English, "Dear Sister."
11. English, "Dear Sister," 28.
12. For more information, see Wesley, "Plain Account," 268.

have affected the operations of these groups. The theory will also discuss the ambiguities that developed in the way in which these women's fellowship groups operated in relation to their response to teachings from African cultures as well. According to Anne Clifford, one of the advocates for a reconstructionist feminist theology, the goal is to seek a liberating theological principal for women from church tradition while envisioning a transformation that is life-giving.[13] Some of the church traditions that are imposed on women in these fellowship groups do require a kind of rewriting our own theology as women. Wesleyan traditions that have been sacralized and treated as gatekeeping rules for women to attain full humanity in Christ need to be revisited and reconstructed to suit the current context. Therefore, as Clifford argues, feminist reconstructionist theology calls for more than just revising and adjusting church traditions but rather a radical renewed vision of what it means to be church for women. Especially those women who feel segregated by their fellow women due to their human conditions such as being single or divorced.[14]

Another point that I wish to emphasize when addressing feminist reconstructionist theory is the need to reconstruct from within. For a long time, feminist theologians have pointed to men as problems to women's struggles of being church with less reflection on some of the ways in which women themselves have perpetuated the oppression of other women. In her book *Daughters of Anowa*, Oduyoye calls for women to account for their own internal struggles among themselves. She warns of the danger of women's failures to support each other in the fight against patriarchal structures in the church and society arguing that in some cases women forget who their real enemy is and instead focus on internal fights among themselves.[15] She further urges that maybe as church women we should aim at transforming Mother's Union groups into women's groups to gain inclusivity, arguing that the ecclesiology that marginalizes women is built upon theories of exclusion.[16] Oduyoye's comment on the naming of these groups resonates well with the initial intension of the missionaries in the formation of these groups, which was to work with married women who are also mothers.

13. Clifford, *Introducing Feminist Theology*, 26.
14. Clifford, *Introducing Feminist Theology*, 26.
15. Oduyoye, *Daughters of Anowa*, 198–200.
16. Oduyoye, *Daughters of Anowa*, 198.

Another challenge that Oduyoye brings out is the need to create a sisterhood of concern and solidarity among women. Using biblical narratives, Oduyoye cites incidents in the Bible where women created a spirit of sisterhood and stood in solidarity for a common purpose. Among the stories, she cites the story of the salvation of baby Moses in Exodus chapter 2.[17] My summary of this story, which I think resonates with this study, is on the kind of women involved in the salvation of Moses from the wrath of Pharaoh. These women came from different backgrounds in terms of economic status/condition, class and race, and yet they put their differences aside and collaborated together in the spirit of sisterhood.

Reconstruction from within as proposed by this study then entails dealing with the struggles mentioned by Oduyoye in order to create equality among women.[18] Some of the restrictions placed on women in some circles of Methodist traditions, are those associated with bodily purity. For example, in some churches you find that women who are observing their menstrual cycle cannot serve or partake in Holy Communion even if they are members of these women's fellowship groups. Women who are suspended due to pregnancy outside of marriage or other sexual misconducts too are excluded from the Lord's table and are not allowed to wear the uniform, especially on occasions such as Holy Communion Sunday. What is very clear in this case is that these teachings on taboos and stigma associated with women's bodies can be traced from the teachings of the early fathers supported by African cultural practices that are also oppressive to women. These practices continue to haunt women and restrict them from full participation in worship and other forms of liturgy in the church. In an attempt to address these practices, both Musimbi Kanyoro and Oduyoye call for a feminist cultural hermeneutics that will put into scrutiny both the African culture and church traditions in the quest for women's liberation.[19] Therefore, feminist reconstructionist theology becomes relevant in reconstructing some of these teachings that have been upheld in the life of the church for a long time without much analysis of their essence in the present context.

---

17. Oduyoye, *Daughters of Anowa*, 201.

18. Oduyoye, *Daughters of Anowa*, 200.

19. Kanyoro, *Introducing Feminist Cultural Hermeneutics*; Oduyoye, *Introducing African Women's Theology*.

Decolonizing Wesleyan Traditions through a Feminist Lens

Decolonization has become one of the buzzwords in the work of many African scholars. For a long time now, theologians in the global South have lamented over the negative effects of colonization and mission influence in the church and society without providing much critical reflection on ways of addressing the damage it has caused. However, recent studies on colonization have seen a shift in academic discourses where many scholars are calling for the need to decolonize some of the negative effects of colonialism. In this chapter, I use the term decolonization consciously bearing in mind its broader usage and meaning. In an attempt to speak of decolonizing Wesleyan traditions, especially those that affected African women, I chose to focus my study on some of the traditional practices found in the African women's fellowship groups that are associated with Methodist traditions across Southern Africa.

Uniform as a Western Ideology

One of the common features that you see in most of the mission churches in Africa is the dress code. The church uniform as introduced by missionaries play an important role in the life of an African Christian. A visitor from other parts of the world visiting African churches will be fascinated to see the display of different designs of uniforms during Sunday service. In the Methodist tradition uniforms range from as young as the boys and girls brigade to the men and women's fellowship groups. There have been different opinions on the origin and colors of the uniform of women's fellowship groups. Scholars such as Hinfelaar argues that the uniform borrowed the colors from the Queen's battalion in South Africa, which at the time of the Boer War was stationed in Pietermaritzburg.[20] According to data I collected, the battalion wore white helmets, red coats, white polo-necked collars, and black trousers. The women from Transvaal also decided that they too, as soldiers of the cross, should wear a uniform similar to that worn by these soldiers.[21]

The uniform was then adopted across the continent as the prescribed dress code for women joining the women's fellowship groups. The uniform

20. Hinfelaar, *Respectable and Responsible Women*, 52.
21. Hinfelaar, *Respectable and Responsible Women*, 52.

is also seen as the traditional Christian way of dressing which, according to the missionaries, helped to give African women decency and identity, which is still being emphasized today. As Hinfelaar observes, Europeans were pleased with the uniforms for women because they made the Africans look "civilized" and "Christian" and gave them a sense of discipline. The uniform was also introduced in order to bring respect to these African women whose dress code was seen as a shame and disrespect to the Christian faith.[22] Hinfelaar shows that missionaries complained about women who came to meetings with torn and dirty clothes and others with only a small piece of cloth covering their bodies.[23] What is sad about this kind of expression is the fact that the very church whose leaders introduced the idea of wearing uniforms to African women for the purpose of being decent in the church did not encourage their women to do so. Instead, what we see in most cases is a situation where the very kind of dressing that was seen as improper to African women is what is prevailing in these churches. If they do, it's those who are ordained or are members of the choir. What we see as a bone of contention here is *the need to cover the African women's body for purity purposes.* These are the kinds of teachings drawn from the historical past that continue to be perpetuated, especially in colonized countries. While the protagonists of the tradition have moved on, the colonized remain bound in the tradition.

Another thing to consider are the restrictions imposed around the uniform, some of which include the wearing of accessories, which is forbidden. Things such as earrings and bracelets are not allowed when a woman is wearing her uniform. In as much as I do have great respect for one to appear decent before the house of the Lord, my concern is based on the extent to which some of the restrictions are purely based on missionaries and Victorian model housewives, which is out of context for Africans. When emphasis is placed on decency, where do we place Scriptures when it says, "But the Lord said to Samuel, 'Do not look on his appearance or on the height of his stature, because I have rejected him, for the Lord does not see as mortals see; they look on the outward appearance, but the Lord looks on the heart'" (1 Sam 16:7)? Hence the need to decolonize some of the rules that inform how this group should present themselves before the house of the Lord. There is need to allow the uniform to be a liberative tool that they embrace as part of what defines

22. Hinfelaar, *Respectable and Responsible Women*, 52–53.
23. Hinfelaar, *Respectable and Responsible Women*, 52–53.

their identity and unity in sisterhood. Haddad argues that the uniform is a symbol of power for Manyano women.[24] While I concur with Haddad, it is important to note the contestations the uniform brings to these women groups, especially when it comes to issues of disciplining members who are found to have created some sinful acts.

Membership

Another issue I wish to address is that of membership. When we talk about membership, we are talking about one's sense of belonging to a particular society or species. In every society membership plays a very important role to either build or destroying the members of that particular group. Membership can also build animosity on those who are outside that particular group by treating them as alien. In some cases, membership can also develop a closed society that is authoritarian in nature. In the case of the women's fellowship groups there are rules that are laid down for women to adhere to once they become members.

Historically, one of the rules that was discriminatory was on who qualifies to be a member of this group. Since the group was started as space for women to learn how to be good housewives, mothers, and mentors to young girls who wish to get married, until recently one of the criteria for someone to join women's fellowship group was marriage. To those who are married if they wanted to become members of the women's fellowship group, they had to obtain permission from their husbands. The husband had the right to tell the leaders when and if the wife is ready for the blousing occasion (a ceremony when women who have passed the test were ready to wear their uniforms and obtain full membership).

The missionary women's ideal of domesticity did not do African women any good. The idea of getting permission from the husband for one to belong to a women's group simply empowered men further to control women's lives and how they should live out their Christian lives. Although some churches within the Wesleyan tradition have challenged some of these rules, there are some churches that still encourage and perpetuate these rules as church teachings. Involving the husband in the decision on the wife's readiness to join a woman's group is sometimes tantamount to selling the woman's soul to the devil. This kind of approach gives men an upper hand to control their wives to the point of promoting gender-based

24. Haddad, "Manyano Movement," 4–13.

violence. To some women the freedom to serve God is curtailed by this decision as since the husband gains an upper hand in informing how the wife will participate in the women's fellowship group.

Marriage

The last issue I would like to highlight is the issue of marriage. Since female missionaries focused their attention on the value of marriage and family life among African women, the formation of these women groups could not operate without defining the type of marriage that would be acceptable by their masters as the correct model of Christian marriage. At the same time, the teachings of missionaries on marriage resonated with the African understanding on marriage, which saw marriage as the highest order of human existence. For missionaries, being a good household manager, a good mother, and a good wife were the attributes of a good native Christian woman.[25] Hence a woman's honor and spirituality were hidden in being a wife of someone. The combination of these cultures contributed to the way in which marriage was placed on the agenda of women's church. Later as time went on single women were also incorporated in these groups but with some degree of segregation, which meant that a group for unmarried women was called young *Manyano*. This is despite the age of the members in the group. As long as they were not married, they belonged to this group. This kind of elevation of marriage does not seem to leave room for women to choose how to live their lives. It also creates a notion that to be married is to be holy. One then is bound to ask where the social holiness that is promoted by Methodists is placed on this matter?

Other Teachings Requiring Decolonial Analysis

Besides the themes addressed above, women's fellowship groups also inherited some regulations that continue to be embraced and applied to members in some churches. For example, the notion regarding how a member appears in terms of hygiene, quarrelling, abstinence from alcohol, and alcohol avoidance also meant women were not longer allowed to brew alcohol. As Hinfelaar states, all these were part of a blueprint for

---

25. Sebastian, "Reading Archives," 13–25.

African women's mode of living as good Christians.[26] While I appreciate these rules as guiding principles for holy living, the main problem one observes are the dynamics in the way in which these rules are applied to Africans. For example, in most African contexts, the issue of beer drinking for believers became a contested matter with missionaries. This is because in some cases when missionaries spoke of prohibition of beer, they meant the African traditional beer that was made by Africans in their communities. Other intoxicating drinks such as wine were not prohibited by the church. In this case, one could find people who are comfortable drinking wine and condemn those drinking African traditional beer or women who brew African beer as part of their economic survival. It is these kinds of ambiguities that we seek to decolonize if the church has to be faithful to its call for holy living that is inclusive and without bias. Let alcohol be judged of its intoxication level and not by branding.

Have the Walls Collapsed?

As much as Christianity created a great impact in the continent of Africa, there are also aspects of this faith that need to be critiqued if Christianity is to be a truly liberating religion for all, especially women. For example, some of the rituals and traditions that inform our being church have also, to a certain extent, contributed to the subjugation that women face in the church. Scholars such as Haddad argue that women's fellowship groups such as Manyano are ambivalent in their operation in that they are both a space for women's liberation from patriarchy and a space of power and contestation among women themselves.[27] These power dynamics are mostly demonstrated through their adherence to the prescribed teachings such as membership and the rules around the uniform. One thing that needs to be taken into consideration in our quest to find redemptive ways of addressing these issues is the way in which our liturgies find themselves incorporated in these teachings. For example, the issue of who partakes in the holy communion is also associated with membership and uniform.

Therefore, we find many members trapped between the pew and the altar when it comes to the celebration of the Lord's table. A study of liturgy in the African context means a continuous process of border crossing—a process that is forcing liturgists in Africa to seriously rethink liturgical

---

26. Hinfelaar, *Respectable and Responsible Women*, 86.
27. Haddad, "Manyano Movement," 4–13.

studies in their own particular context. As an African church, we cannot afford to do business as usual when addressing issues that bring contestation when dealing with particular liturgical practices. We ought to be a church on the move. In a previous study alongside Roderick Hewitt, we have shown that throughout human history, liturgical practices have carried a gendered identity.[28] While liturgy bears the good mark of being a way of embodying one another in fellowship, it has also been used as a form of oppression and segregation between race, class, gender, and sexual orientation. Teresa Berger argues that as long as liturgical history continues to be written as a history of male rites and traditions, with males carrying leadership responsibilities, women will continue to be invisible in liturgical practice.[29] This is supported by Cláudio Carvalhaes, who states that liturgies are powerful weapons that can create and destroy identities of people, thus, liturgical spaces can also be contested.[30] Therefore, as I argued elsewhere, there is need to reinterpret liturgical traditions through gender lenses and other forms of marginalized discourses.[31]

Feminist Reconstruction of Ecclesiology: An African Perspective

In this chapter I have used feminist reconstructionist theology to demonstrate the need for a change in the way in which the church has dealt with issues of women especially those who belong to women's fellowship groups. The first point to consider in this call for the reconstruction of the church in Africa is to learn to live with ambivalence, as Natalie Watson argues, to make sense of oppression and empowerment, of liberation and suffering, of silence and speaking out.[32] The ambivalence that the church finds itself in goes beyond just the issues mentioned above to how the church responds to interpretation of the Scripture and church traditions. Rosemary Radford Ruether contends that when dealing with Christian traditions there is need to create a distinction between what is appropriate and what is credible. This is because for a long time in Christian history, issues that oppress women have been accepted as appropriate for Christian

28. Siwila and Hewitt, "Liturgy and Identity."
29. Berger, *Gender Differences*.
30. Carvalhaes, "Liturgy and Postcolonialism," 7.
31. Siwila, "Do This in Remembrance of Me."
32. Watson, *Introducing Feminist Ecclesiology*, 4.

living without weighing their credibility.[33] For example, most of the teachings handed down by female missionaries on African women's conduct as Christians were labeled as appropriate for Christian living. While I agree that the primary symbols of any tradition need to be returned and maintained, the content needs to be modified in order to suit the context. As people of Wesleyan tradition, we cannot just throw away our tradition but rather we want to come to these traditions in the twenty-first century with hermeneutical tools to reconstruct these traditions using particular lenses. The African cultural context needs to be seen as the fertile ground for decolonizing these traditions.

The second point I want to raise is the role that the Bible plays in the African church. One of the prominent statements that you hear so often when particular teachings are imposed in the church is "the Bible does not allow this . . ." During the mission/colonial era, the Bible was given a very prominent status. Both missionaries and colonizers used the Bible in ways that helped them to evangelize Africans. Using the literal reading approach, selected Scriptures were imposed on African Christians to help support the missionaries' teachings of the natives. As a result of that, the Bible gained so much popularity among Africans such that the bare fact of having the Bible in your home was seen as a ticket to heaven, even if it is not read. Oduyoye, speaking about the importance of the Bible in Africa, argues that for African people the Bible is the focal point of one's faith, it has been and continues to be absolutized as the most consulted oracle. It's found in homes, business places, schools, read or not read.[34] Musimbi Kanyoro points to the challenges of rural women in interpretation of the Bible. The author narrates her experience of how rural women used the Bible stories to justify certain African cultural practices such as child marriage.[35] She calls for a feminist cultural hermeneutics that considers the African culture and biblical culture, arguing that both cultures need to be taken into scrutiny if they are to be liberative to women. This is supported by Madipoane Masenya who argues that biblical interpretations that are not challenged have prevented women from exercising their God-given talents. It is through biblical interpretation that Africans began to hate their identity, their land was taken away, and their culture modified.[36]

33. Ruether, *Sexism and God-Talk*.
34. Oduyoye, *Daughters of Anowa*.
35. Kanyoro, *Introducing Feminist Cultural Hermeneutics*.
36. Masenya, "The Sword that Heals!"

The last point I wish to raise is the challenge of dealing with grassroots theology. Most of the women found in these women's groups have very little or no theological background. Therefore, their theologizing is based on the local knowledge shared among themselves and their faith experience. One of the dangers of grassroots theology is its lack of hermeneutical analysis, especially when dealing with the Bible. Therefore, in some cases when grassroots theology meets the colonial matrix, the result of that becomes oppressive to women.

Conclusion

Decolonizing Wesleyan tradition should not be seen as an idea that remains in the shelves of our libraries but rather an act that calls for transformation of the church's teachings for the liberation of all who belong to the body of Christ. As discussed in this chapter, the history and development of groups such as women's fellowship groups may be seen as less significant in the life and growth of the church and yet the groups themselves carry the church in Africa. Therefore, liberating these groups from the colonial matrix is like liberating the entire church.

In this chapter, I have also argued that at the core of every teaching or tradition is an emphasis on the foundation and constitutive nature of the particular teaching being pursued. Teachings applied in the church are meaningless without actual interpretation by the custodians of those particular teachings. Lastly, religious traditions fall under crisis when they become a source of abuse to exclude others from the sacraments in the name of received interpretations. This becomes more evident when the structures that transmit these traditions have become dissolute. Unless the church allows itself to take serious introspection on how and what needs to be decolonized within its Wesleyan traditions, the call for the salvation of all humanity remains questionable.

Bibliography

Berger, Teresa. *Gender Differences and the Making of Liturgical History: Lifting a Veil on Liturgy's Past.* Burlington, VT: Ashgate, 2011.
Bum, Brigalia. "Women and the Church in (South) Africa: Women are Church." In *On Being Church: African Women's Voices and Visions,* edited by Isabel Apawo Phiri and Sarojini Nadar, 8–16. Geneva: World Council Churches, 2005.

Carvalhaes, Cláudio. "Liturgy and Postcolonialism: An Introduction." In *Liturgy in Postcolonial Perspectives: Only One Is Holy*, edited by Cláudio Carvalhaes, 1–20. New York: Palgrave Macmillan, 2015.

Clifford, Anne M. *Introducing Feminist Theology*. Maryknoll, NY: Orbis, 2001.

Cock, Jacklyn. *Maids & Madams: A Study in the Politics of Exploitation*. Johannesburg: Ravan, 1980.

English, John C. "'Dear Sister': John Wesley and the Women of Early Methodism." *Methodist History* 33.1 (1994) 26–33.

Gaitskell, Deborah. "Housewives, Maids or Mothers: Some Contradictions of Domesticity for Christian Women in Johannesburg, 1903–39." *Journal of African History* 24.2 (1983) 241–56.

Haddad, Beverley. "The Manyano Movement in South Africa: Site of Struggle, Survival, and Resistance." *Agenda* (Durban) 18.61 (2004) 4–13.

Hinfelaar, Marja. *Respectable and Responsible Women: Methodist and Catholic Women's Organisations in Harare, Zimbabwe (1919–1985)*. Utrecht: Bookcentrum, 2003.

Kanyoro, Rachel Angogo. *Introducing Feminist Cultural Hermeneutics: An African Perspective*. London: Academic, 2002.

Masenya, Madipoane. "The Sword that Heals! The Bible and African Women in African-South African Pentecostal Churches." In *On Being Church: African Women's Voices and Visions*, edited by Isabel Apawo Phiri and Sarojini Nadar, 47–59. Geneva: World Council Churches, 2005.

Oduyoye Mercy Amba. *Daughters of Anowa: African Women and Patriarchy*. Maryknoll, NY: Orbis, 1995.

———. "Ecclesiology in African Women's Perspective." In *On Being Church: African Women's Voices and Visions*, edited by Isabel Apawo Phiri and Sarojini Nadar, 146–56. Geneva: World Council Churches, 2005.

———. *Introducing African Women's Theology*. Sheffield: Sheffield Academic, 2001.

Phiri, Isabel Apawo. *Women, Presbyterianism and Patriarchy: Religious Experience of Chewa Women in Central Malawi*. Zomba: Kachere, 1997.

Ruether, Rosemary Radford. *Sexism and God-Talk: Toward a Feminist Theology*. Boston: Beacon, 1983.

Sebastian, Mrinalini. "Reading Archives from a Postcolonial Feminist Perspective: 'Native' Bible Women and the Missionary Ideal." *Journal of Feminist Studies in Religion* 19.1 (2003) 5–25.

Siwila, Lilian Cheelo. "'Do This in Remembrance of Me': An African Feminist Contestation of the Embodied Sacred Liturgical Space in the Celebration of the Eucharist." In *Liturgy in Postcolonial Perspectives: Only One Is Holy*, edited by Cláudio Carvalhaes, 83–93. New York: Palgrave Macmillan, 2015.

Siwila, Lilian Cheelo, and Roderick Hewitt. "Liturgy and Identity: Exploring Possibilities for an Alternative Reading of Liturgy." Introduction to *Liturgy and Identity: African Religio-Cultural and Ecumenical Perspectives*, edited by Lilian Cheelo Siwila and Roderick Hewitt, xviii–xxviii. Pietermaritzburg: Cluster, 2019.

Walker, Cherryl. "Gender and the Development of the Migrant Labour System c. 1850–1930: An Overview." In *Women and Gender in Southern Africa to 1945*, by Cherryl Walker, 168–96. Cape Town: David Philip and James Currey, 1990.

Watson, Natalie K. *Introducing Feminist Ecclesiology*. Sheffield: Sheffield Academic, 2002.

Wesley, John. "Plain Account of the People Called the Methodist." In vol. 9 of *The Works of John Wesley*, edited by Rupert E. Davis, 253–80. Nashville: Abingdon, 1989.

Chapter VII

DECOLONIZING THE CHURCH OF EMPIRE

The Church on the Move for Justice, Peace, and Life

J. C. Park

> We are called to break down walls and seek justice with people who are dispossessed and displaced from their lands—including migrants, refugees, and asylum seekers—and to resist new frontiers and borders that separate and kill (Isaiah 58:6-8).
>
> —The Arusha Call to Discipleship

Introduction

IT HAS BEEN FOUR decades since I began my MDiv at the Candler School of Theology, Emory University, in the fall of 1979. For the last forty years the landscape of world Christianity has drastically changed. In this chapter I would like to reflect on the new realities of world Christianity from my personal and professional perspective, that is, from the perspective of Korean Methodist theologian who represents the World Methodist Council as its first Asian president. In this capacity, I have traveled the world and encountered Methodist communities dealing with the harsh realities of a walled world. This reality calls me to the work of peace and reconciliation and to a desire for what I will be calling a church on the move, a Spirit-filled movement of communities that cross unjust boundaries. This is a movement of people away from the centers of power and from the Christianity of empire.

During my study years at Candler my existential struggle in the depth of my soul was heavily concentrated on a theological reflection on the doctrine of reconciliation in the tragic reality of a divided Korea. In 1988, two years after I went back to Korea, the National Council of Churches in Korea announced its historic declaration on the "Peace and Reunification of the Korean Peninsula." Not too long after that, in 1989, the Berlin Wall went down. The Cold War seemed to melt down and a new springtime would bring about peace soon. In 1992, I participated for the first time in the Oxford Institute of Methodist Theological Studies where my former teacher, Prof. Theodore Runyon, had initiated what I consider a process of *decolonizing* the Wesleyan traditions by editing a volume on *Sanctification and Liberation*.[1] At that time, I was one of the progressive but naive Christians in Korea who expected with great enthusiasm to celebrate the fiftieth anniversary of national liberation from Japanese imperialism in the year of 1995. This would be the Jubilee Year to mark the overcoming of our national division.

Yet, the awaited *kairos* year was a farfetched dream. Instead of the sweet climax of peace, we witnessed the bitter anticlimax brought by the prospect of another war in Korea. The military tension between North Korea and the US increased in 1994 as North Korea rejected the International Atomic Energy Agency's inspection of nuclear sites in the country. The suspicious development of nuclear weapons provoked the US to go ahead with a preemptive attack on North Korea.[2] The Peninsula was again on the edge of war. Through this experience I realized the critical distance between my own perception and the reality of the ideological conflict and national division in Korea. In this context, I was also facing the fundamentalist theology and anti-communism rhetoric of Korean churches, particularly the Korean Methodist Church, which in the fatal year of 1992 excommunicated two progressive theologians, both of them colleagues of mine who advocated religious pluralism and who, according to the judgment of the church's court, embraced postmodernism.

---

1. Runyon, *Sanctification and Liberation*.

2. Rev. Dr. James T. Laney, appointed as ambassador of the United States to South Korea by President Bill Clinton, was instrumental in helping defuse the nuclear crisis with North Korea in 1994.

By a sequence of events that I consider to be part of divine dispensation, my vocation to develop a theology of reconciliation continued to be nurtured in me. In Korean, that represented a theology of *sangsaeng* (相生/living together). That moment of truth occurred when I gave my keynote address at the 19th World Methodist Conference held in Seoul in 2006. The theme of the conference was "God in Christ Reconciling" (2 Cor 5:19). It was in the same conference that the World Methodist Council and its member churches affirmed their fundamental doctrinal agreement with the teaching expressed in the landmark ecumenical document, "Joint Declaration on the Doctrine of Justification" (JDDJ) signed at Augsburg on October 31, 1999, on behalf of the Lutheran World Federation and the Roman Catholic Church. Articulating their common understanding of basic truths of the doctrine of justification by God's grace through faith in Christ, the JDDJ expresses a far-reaching consensus in regard to the theological controversy, which was a major cause of the division in Western churches in the sixteenth century.

In my own journey and in my own commitment to decolonizing the Christian faith, I find strong support in the spirit of the JDDJ. In this chapter, I would like to interpret the theological, ethical, and missiological meanings of the JDDJ in light of what I consider one of the most pressing issues of our time—migration. First, I situate the theme of justification in creative tension with this challenging situation and, secondly, elaborate my ecclesiological analysis through the concept of the "church on the move." I will propose a new perspective of church on the move for peacemaking evangelism as a guiding metaphor for world Christian citizenship for peace and *sangsaeng*. This latter piece supports my vision of a scriptural and Spirit-filled Christianity decolonizing the walled world of global apartheid.

From Conflict to Communion

The present Joint Declaration has this intention: namely, to show that on the basis of their dialogue the subscribing Lutheran churches and the Roman Catholic Church are now able to articulate a common understanding of our justification by God's grace through faith in Christ. It does not cover all that either church teaches about justification and shows that the remaining differences in its explications are no longer the occasion for doctrinal condemnations.
—The Joint Declaration on the Doctrine of Justification

The JDDJ-Lund event in Sweden on October 31, 2016, both commemorating the 500th year of the Protestant Reformation and celebrating the JDDJ, was an ecumenical milestone on the path from conflict to communion. The first imperative mentioned in the document, "From Conflict to Communion," is to begin our ecumenical dialogue "from the perspective of unity and not from the point of view of division."[3] The Joint Statement of the Lund event claimed: "Our common faith in Jesus Christ and our baptism demand of us a daily conversion that impede the ministry of reconciliation."[4] The statement looked beyond the JDDJ, it called for our commitment to the common witness to the gospel of Jesus Christ, which "summons us to be close to all those who yearn for dignity, justice, peace and reconciliation."[5] Besides the three open questions about the church, the eucharist, and ministry in the dialogue between Lutherans and Catholics, there was an urgent warning that ethical issues—especially about the beginning and end of life, and on family, marriage, and gender—were now divisive issues within and between churches.

It is appropriate to remind us of the concluding remark of *The Biblical Foundations of the Doctrine of Justification: An Ecumenical Follow-Up to the Joint Declaration on the Doctrine of Justification* (2011).[6] The exegetical insights of the document, especially in relation to the elaborate Pauline version of the theology of justification, refer to the following three points: first, the theology of justification is the basis for a universal theology of mission; second, the theology of justification is the basis of a theology of *koinonia*, which constitutes the church as a reconciled diversity of people of different ethnic, cultural, and religious backgrounds as well as different theological and spiritual insights; third, the theology of justification offers the deepest insights into the human condition before God.[7] Only in the light of God's all-encompassing and reconciling love in the death of his Son on the cross, only through the recognition that God has already done all that is necessary to reconcile us with him, not only the extreme distance and even enmity between human beings and God is visible, but also our incapacity as human beings to do anything to restore the broken

---

3. The Lutheran World Federation and The Pontifical Council of Promoting Christian Unity, *From Conflict to Communion*, 87 (para. 239).
4. Pope Francis and Younan, "Joint Statement," 1–2.
5. Pope Francis and Younan, "Joint Statement," 3.
6. The Lutheran World Federation et al., *Biblical Foundations*.
7. The Lutheran World Federation et al., *Biblical Foundations*, 128–29.

communion with God becomes apparent. It is significant to notice that the filial faithfulness of Jesus precedes our own faith and repentance. "But now, apart from the law, the righteousness of God has been disclosed, the righteousness of God 'through faith/faithfulness of Jesus Christ' (*dia pisteos jesu christi*) for all who believe" (Rom 3:21–22). In the spirit of Gal 3:17, we can say with McLeod Campbell that "the filial is prior to the judicial."[8]

Therefore, the historically critical recovery of the concrete, communal context of the Pauline dispute over justification is crucial for the full-blown realization of the principle of *sola gratia*. Paul saw Peter in Antioch who "did not walk straight to the truth of the gospel" (Gal 2:14a) because Peter, separating himself from Gentile Christians, denied the equality of the people of God of all who are justified by grace through faith. Justification is God's declaration that "in Christ Jesus you are all children of God through faith," as well as our assurance that we are children of God since "God has sent the spirit of his Son into our hearts, crying, '*Abba*! Father!'" (Gal 4:6b).

The assurance of our common filiation is what connects and reconciles us deeply with siblings in diverse faith traditions. *Biblical Foundations* states the following: "If God, the Father of our Lord Jesus Christ, is not only the God of the Jews, then he is also not only the God of Christians, but also the God of the Muslims, the Hindus, the Buddhists and even the atheists, nay, indeed, of the whole creation."[9] One of the most precious gifts that the Christian tradition has to offer to reconciliation among different faiths is the prayer Jesus taught, the "Lord's Prayer." We need to learn again how to pray to our Father in heaven. Our Father is the one God of Jews, Christians, Muslims, and the rest of humankind. The core and common confession of the Abrahamic religions is powerfully expressed in Jesus' own exhortation: "And call no one your father on earth, for you have one Father—the one in heaven" (Matt 23:9). We need to recognize that the principle of *sola gratia* is derived from and fundamentally undergirded by Jesus' own filial-faithful relation to his heavenly Father who is eternally faithful in God's covenant love.

Beyond sharing the common heritage of the Abrahamic religions, I would like to propose to reach out to the deepening of the humanistic understanding of faith in both the secularized West and the Confucian

---

8. For a review of Campbell's work, see Torrance, "Contribution of McLeod Campbell."

9. The Lutheran World Federation et al., *Biblical Foundations*, 131.

East. Creatively appropriating Jesus' parable of a merciful father who has two sons (Luke 15:11–32), the apparent believers in God ought to reflect self-critically on the sin of the unconscious, unnoticed obstruction of the mercy of the Father for the prodigal sons and daughters in our times. Similarly, Confucius calls the most fundamental ethos of human heartedness *xiao* (孝/filial faithfulness). *Xiao* is a universal anthropological need to believe in investing oneself in another human being who cares for the child, paying tribute to the primordial care of the mother for the child as well as for the primary identification to the father. The ontological ground of the *xiao* for the parents on earth is the *xiao* for the heavenly Father; and the epistemological ground of the *xiao* for the heavenly Father is the *xiao* for the parents on earth.

Jesus' prayer for the forgiveness of our neighbor's sins is grounded on the faith in the faithfulness of the merciful *Abba*/Father in heaven. We are all members of God's family. This liberating witness of the Holy Spirit needs to be recognized as a core message of our evangelical and ecumenical pilgrimage of justice, peace, and life.[10] The symbol of the bilingual expression of *Abba* Father is fundamentally undergirded by the semiotic irruption of the divine energy only through and in which any binary opposition of discrimination and oppression will finally collapse. John Wesley's exhortation is noteworthy on this matter: "I beseech you, brethren, by the mercies of God, that we be in no wise divided among ourselves. Is thy heart right, as my heart is with thine? I ask no farther question. If it be, give me thy hands. For opinions, or terms, let us not destroy the work of God. Dost thou love and serve God?"[11] Indeed, "There is no longer Jew or Greek, there is no longer slave or free, there is no longer male or female; for all of you are one in Christ Jesus" (Gal 3:28). Furthermore, there is no longer Easterner or Westerner, there is no longer conservative or progressive, there is no longer straight or gay; for all of us are one in Christ Jesus. The crucified and risen Christ embraces us in our singular identities while granting us a new

---

10. The World Council of Churches 2013 Busan assembly invited Christians and people of good will everywhere to join in a Pilgrimage of Justice and Peace. See "Invitation to the Pilgrimage of Justice and Peace." According to the document, "The word 'pilgrimage' was chosen to convey that this is a journey with deep spiritual meaning and with profound theological connotations and implications. . . . It is a transformative journey that God invites us to in anticipation of the final purpose for the world that the Triune God brings about. The movement of love, which is essential to the triune God, manifests itself in the promise of justice and peace. They are signs of God's reign to come which is already visible here and now wherever reconciliation and healing are seen" (384).

11. Wesley, "Character of a Methodist," para. 18.

identity and a new belonging that corresponds to his own risen life. We are all the members of God's family. This liberating witness of the Holy Spirit needs to be recognized as a core message of our evangelical and ecumenical pilgrimage of justice, peace, and life. We are the people of *Abba* Father who are on the pilgrimage of justice, peace, and life.

The Methodist contribution to the ecumenical dialogue around the doctrine of justification has been to emphasize the "deep connection between forgiveness of sins and making righteous, between justification and sanctification."[12] One of Wesley's latest sermons, "On the Wedding Garment" (1790), is his final theological testament for the people called Methodists to keep a healthy, critical, and dynamic tension between the imputation and the impartation of the righteousness of Christ. "By the former we become members of Christ, children of God, and heirs of the kingdom of heaven. By the latter we are 'made meet to be partakers of the inheritance of the saints in light' (Col 1:12)."[13] The former, which is necessary for our "entitlement to heaven," is based on the principle of *sola gratia*, that is, the filial (faithfulness) is prior to the judicial. The latter, which is necessary for our "qualification for heaven," is derived from the promise and gift of God of Israel: the covenantal (holiness) is the telos of the filial.[14] "(The God of love) saith: 'Choose holiness by my grace, which is the way, the only way, to everlasting life. He cries aloud, be holy, and be happy; happy in this world, and happy in the world to come.' 'Holiness becometh his house forever!' (Ps 93:5). This is the wedding garment of all that are called to 'the marriage of the Lamb' (Rev 19:7)."[15]

The call for repentance and reconciliation for the unity and sanctity of being the church demands costly, transforming discipleship: "and if children, then heirs, heirs of God and joint heirs with Christ—if, in fact, we suffer with him so that we may also be glorified with him" (Rom 8:17). The motif of suffering is crucial for our contemporary call for both

---

12. World Methodist Council, "World Methodist Council."

13. Wesley, "On the Wedding Garment."

14. The covenantal holiness is derived from the Torah of Israel and from the *logion* of Jesus: "I am the Lord your God; consecrate yourselves and be holy, because I am holy" (Lev 11:44); "Be perfect, therefore, as your heavenly Father is perfect" (Matt 5:48). Wesley calls the Methodist doctrine of Christian perfection "the doctrine of Jesus Christ." Wesley loved to point out that a perfect Christian is the one who "has the mind that was in Christ and who walks as Christ walked." For Wesley, Jesus Christ is the perfect embodiment of the covenantal holiness of Israel. See Wesley, *Plain Account*, para. 27.

15. Wesley, "On the Wedding Garment."

transformative spirituality and transforming discipleship. The suffering of disciples has nothing to do with heroism because it begins with acknowledging and participating in the very vulnerability of the marginalized: "We know that the whole creation has been groaning in labor pains until now; and not only the creation, but we ourselves, who have the first fruits of the Spirit, groan inwardly while we wait for adoption, the redemption of our bodies" (Rom 8:22–23).

The transformative spirituality for the transforming discipleship requires us to learn the Lord's Prayer in the power of the Holy Spirit who "helps us in our weakness; for we do not know how to pray as we ought, but that very Spirit intercedes with sighs too deep for words" (Rom 8:26). Saint Augustine says, "The words that our Lord Jesus Christ has taught us in his prayer are the rule and standard of our desires. You may not ask for anything but what is written there."[16] Praying constantly our Lord's Prayer, we shall complete our pilgrim journey together toward life. As the Apostle Paul writes, "consider that the sufferings of this present time are not worth comparing with the glory about to be revealed to us" (Rom 8:18).

Christ calls us to the obedience of faith. The crown of the transforming discipleship is taking up our cross to follow Jesus. As the faithful community of Christ, we have to encounter the suffering of being exposed to ridicule and persecution grown out of the fallen state of rebellion and sin in our contemporary age. This may lead us to the martyr's path, which is indeed a reality for many brothers and sisters in Christ today. We can say together to the fellow pilgrims gone before us on the martyr's path: I was not there, but we were there. Just remember that we are the people on the move living in the eschatological interval between Christ's Resurrection and the ultimate redemption of the world. At the peak of Romans 8, Paul quotes Ps 44:22: "For your sake we are being killed all the day long; we are regarded as sheep to be slaughtered." The faithful people of the transforming discipleship are suffering with Christ (Rom 8:17: *sympaschomen*) and thus their suffering has the quality of vicarious suffering.[17]

In the last thematic plenary of the 2018 Conference on World Mission and Evangelism, entitled "Embracing the Cross," Rev. Kathryn Mary Lohre, Lutheran theologian from the United States, stated on our faithful response when our neighbors of another religion become targets of hatred and violence:

16. Harper, *Pocket Guide to Prayer*, 103.
17. Hays, *Echoes of Scripture*, 62–63.

> There is a unique role . . . for the churches to play. We are just beginning to understand that equipping disciples for mission and evangelism today must include not only religious literacy and interreligious competences but also the courage and humility to embrace the cross for the sake of our neighbors of other religions and worldviews, and to defend them against discrimination, bigotry, racism, and violence, regardless of its source.[18]

Therefore, we must always be mindful of the margins of our world from which *missio dei* starts. God's mission from the margins is a pilgrimage moving in the Spirit together toward life. In other words, mission from the margins implies affirming the agency of those marginalized, overcoming the marginalizing tendencies, and resisting and confronting the forces of marginalization in our contexts of the world.

Church on the Move in the Walled World of Apartheid

> As we, participants in the Roundtable, work toward peace and reunification on the Korean Peninsula, we pray for God-given visions and dreams! By the grace of the living God, we are witnessing a miraculous event unfolding, raising hopes that the people of God will return from their Babylonian captivity to Jerusalem on the Korean Peninsula. . . . When the old era of *"sang-geuk"* (inter-killing) is over and the new era of *"sang-saeng"* (inter-living) begins on the Korean Peninsula, we will see the body joined as God has envisioned. . . .
> —The Atlanta Statement of the Third Roundtable for Peace on the Korean Peninsula

We are living in times when our shared life is threatened, uncertain, fragile, and fragmented. In the midst of unprecedented geopolitical shifts, widespread violence and war in and among nations and peoples disrupt the livelihoods of families in the Middle East, especially in Syria and Iraq, Africa and Asia and Central America, setting millions of people fleeing for refuge or migrating to more promising locales. Forced migration leaves the vulnerable subject to trafficking. Indeed, violence and mistreatment seem inordinately to affect women and girls, whose gifts are undervalued, whose bodies are often violated, and whose very education is often opposed. In this

---

18. Lohre, "Moving in the Spirit."

section, I would like to propose a metaphor for peacebuilding evangelism of scriptural and Spirit-filled Christianity today: *church on the move* in the walled world of apartheid. This same image is reflected on the theme of the 2024 World Methodist Conference, which is titled "On the Move" and has three sub-themes: migration, pilgrimage, and illumination.

In his message to participants of the 33rd Prayer for Peace Meeting, "Peace with no Borders," convened in Madrid on September 15–17, 2019, Pope Francis said: "This year its itineracy reaches Madrid, to reflect on the theme 'Peace without Border.' The mind flies to the past, when, thirty years ago, the Berlin Wall fell in the heart of Europe and the division of the continent, which caused so much suffering, was put to an end. From Berlin to the whole Eastern Europe, new hopes for peace were lit up that day, then spreading all over the world. It was, indeed, the prayer for peace of many sons and daughters of God that had contributed to accelerate the fall of the wall."[19]

Unfortunately, after the fall of the Berlin Wall it took the European Union only six years to create with the Schengen Agreement in 1995 a new division only 80 kilometer offset to the east of Berlin. Over the first two decades of the twenty-first century, we have witnessed that "peace on earth" (*pax civitas terrena*) has been dissipated by new wars and by new walls and barriers being raised. We are living in the "Walled World"[20] in which 73 percent of the world's income is held by the 14 percent of the world's population in the global North, while 27 percent of the world's income is held by the 86 percent of the world's population in the global South. The six prominent walls are DMZ–Korea, Australian Northern Approach, the United States–Mexico Wall, the Melilla Border Fence/the Ceuta Border Fence in Northern Africa, Schengen Border in Europe, and the Palestine Wall. These walls represent a worldwide system that contains an exclusive society. The rise of a system of militarized global apartheid has created a racialized world order to securitize the global North and foster violence in the global South and to gate the global North while imprisoning the global South.

On July 31, 2019, a forty-two-year-old mother, Ms. Han, and her six-year-old son were found dead at her apartment in a rundown part of Seoul. The police announced that they were found about two months later and that they starved to death. Ms. Han was a North Korean refugee who escaped her

---

19. Francis, "We Must Come All Together."
20. "Walled World—Project."

country in 2009 by way of China and Thailand. It reminds me of another tragedy in June 2019 in the Rio Grande, Mexico. The bodies of Oscar Alberto Martinez and his twenty-three-month-old daughter, Angie Valeria, lay face down in murky waters. They made the dangerous journey from El Salvador and drowned as they were crossing the river.

These are the cases of social exclusion and economic inequality. And we are facing "a globalization of indifference" because we are "incapable of feeling compassion at the outcry of the poor, weeping for other people's pain."[21] Brazilian theologian Jung Mo Sung, Korean by birth, likens the international capitalist system to altars. While ancient idolatry had visible altars, the postmodern altar of the global market gods is invisible, but still demands human sacrifices. The most dangerous idols sacrifice millions of people upon the altar of wealth. The idol worshippers in our consumerist society take the sacrifice for granted in the name of an inevitable social cost for the economy of prosperity, which is wrongly sanctioned by a theology of the prosperity gospel. Referring to Jesus' word that God desires mercy, not sacrifice, Sung claims: "Idol demands the sacrifice of human life. It neither forgives the poor nor pays attention to their cry. But God listens to the cry and provides His mercy as gift. He never demands sacrifice."[22]

The official visit of the World Methodist Council (WMC), the General Board of Global Missions of the United Methodist Church (GBGM) and the Methodist Church in Great Britain to Palestine in July 2019 marked the seventh anniversary of the Methodist Liaison Office (MLO) in Jerusalem. The annexation wall in the West Bank as well as the blockade of the Gaza Strip clearly demonstrates "the bitter fruits of military occupation that have fallen disproportionately upon the Palestinian people."[23] I also saw the radical vulnerability of the native Christian minority despite the increasing number of Christian pilgrims from all over the world. We have to share the suffering of our Palestinian Christian sisters and brothers in our pilgrimage of justice, peace, and life. A mere listening to a native Palestinian Christian, in my case, Ms. Samar Hashweh, who works for the MLO, challenges you to go through the circumcision of the heart. Too many times we have been brainwashed by the inhumane ideology of Christian Zionism. This is the *kairos* time to be converted to the warm-heartedness of Jesus Christ who

---

21. Francis, *Evangelii Gaudium*, para. 54.
22. Sung, "Liberation Theology."
23. The World Methodist Council et al., "Statement on Occupation."

invites us to follow him in his footsteps through *via dolorosa*, which ends at the Holy Sepulcher, the empty tomb of hope against hope.

Looking through the window of the bus, I felt the dark color of the sea on the beach of Da Nang muddy and threatening. My first short visit to Vietnam from November 4–7, 2019, was made possible as I joined my wife in her district's annual meeting for the next year's ministry. In the morning devotion, a Korean Methodist pastor preached on the miraculous healing of Naaman. Suddenly, I overheard in my mind the paraphrased words of Aloisius Pieris: "Can you be immersed by the murky water of Da Nang Beach?" Of course, I can gladly jump into the emerald sea at Cancun Beach anytime, as I did in September 2019 after the Executive Meeting of World Methodist Council in Mexico City. But I told myself: "Oh, gracious Lord, please forbid me from doing it here!" In many ways my trip to Vietnam was guilt-laden. I still clearly recall a Vietnamese student who refused to shake hands with me at my first international students' party at Emory University in the fall of 1979. I was upset at that time, but now I am rather grateful for his indignation against South Korean soldiers who massacred the innocent Vietnamese people during the Vietnam War. Korean soldiers, who went through the hellfire of the Korean War, became the mercenaries of the US to create another hell in Vietnam. They are also suspected to take part in the massacring of their own people during the Kwangju Uprising in 1980.

The *New York Times* reported in 1999: "For almost 50 years, South Korean villagers have insisted that early in the Korean War, American soldiers machine-gunned hundreds of helpless civilians under a railroad bridge near a hamlet some 100 miles southeast of Seoul."[24] For half a century, survivors and victims' relatives have tirelessly told their story though they met only rejection and denial from the US as well as their own government. According to the three Associated Press reporters who won the Pulitzer Prize in 1999, about 400 civilians, who were largely elderly people, children, infants, and women, were killed by the US army at Nogunri on July 28, 1950. They found 120 names of victims. Among the 120, seventy were women and most of the men were over fifty. There were also twenty-five children and infants under five.

"Massacre in Korea" is an expressionistic painting completed on January 18, 1951, by Pablo Picasso. It depicts civilians being killed by anti-communist forces. It is inspired by reports of American atrocities in Korea. Picasso's painting is marked by a bifurcated composition, divided

---

24. Associated Press, "G.I.'s Tell of a U.S. Massacre."

into two distinct parts. To the left, a group of naked women and children are seen situated at the foot of a mass grave. A number of heavily armed knights stand to the right, also naked, but equipped with gigantic limbs and hard muscles similar to those of prehistoric giants. What is more, none of the soldiers have penises. This representational feature is highlighted by the pregnant state of the women on the left side of the panel. Soldiers, in their capacity as destroyers of life, have substituted guns for their penises, thereby castrating themselves and depriving the world of the next generation of human life.

Theological work requires the priestly inscription of the traumatic memories of the victims of atrocities in history. Postcolonial critic Homi Bhabha writes that "[remembering] is never a quiet act of introspection or retrospection. It is a painful re-membering, a putting together of the dismembered past to make sense of the trauma of the present."[25] Proper theological work in such inscription should discern a critical difference between the totalizing and universalizing history of God of the center and the singularity of the individual sufferers of the margin whose images of God and of their own history resist colonial representations of their unique past. Only through discerning such difference can one be open to the ruptures of history and the traumatic experiences of those uprooted from history.

Difference, *differend* in French, an essential concept of Jean-Francois Lyotard's thought, "is the unstable state and instant of language wherein something which must be able to put into phrases cannot yet to be."[26] To deconstruct a sham theology of false reconciliation, which is co-opted by the imperialistic ideology of the center, we have to make sure that to theologize is not to reconcile quickly, but to inscribe patiently that which refuses to be reconciled. A lullaby from the Binh Hoa village in Vietnam gives testimony to this. This is the site where the Blue Dragon Division of South Korean Marines massacred 430 civilians in December, 1966. The lullaby goes like this:

> Baby, remember this.
>
> Korean soldiers threw us into a pit of bombs, and shot us all to death.
>
> Shot us all to death.
>
> Baby, surely remember this when you grow up.

---

25. Bhabha, *Location of Culture*, 90.
26. Lyotard, *Differend*, 13.

Next to the pit, a memorial to the Binh Hoa Massacre was set up. Indignation is engraved with the phrase: "The sin of reaching up to heaven, I will remember ten thousand generations."[27]

Death always brings a suspicion of murder.[28] And the death of the others is "neither magical nor beautiful," writes Jacques Derrida.[29] Far too long has the Christian theology of the center uncritically misrepresented the cross of Jesus Christ in terms of magical or beautiful death "for the sake of" or "in order that." Injustice and wrong, which is a matter of *han* (unjustifiable suffering) caused by the unredeemed anguish in the context of the *differend*, cannot and should not be swiftly resolved as if it were damages that can be paid back or compensated in the context of litigation. Therefore, the punitive rhetoric implied in the legal theory of atonement (Augustine and Anselm) according to the West ought to be deconstructed by a reconstructed discourse of atonement as "recapitulation" (Irenaeus) and "assumption" (Gregory Nazianzen), according to the Eastern Fathers. Jesus not only symbolically represents the true Israel obeying God to sacrifice himself for the sake of redeeming the rebellious and exiled people (N. T. Wright), but also recapitulates the semiotic irruption of the abject state among the suffering *ochlos* from the womb (*chora*) of God. Indeed, "What is not assumed cannot be saved/healed," as Gregory Nazianzen famously stated.[30] In other words, what is disconnected with "the M-other" (J. Kristeva) of God cannot be atoned. Irenaeus said, "In as much as blood cries out (*vocalis est*) from the beginning (of the world), God said to Cain, when he had slain his brother, 'The voice of thy brother's blood crieth to Me.'"[31] Irenaeus' fatal omission of the last part of Gen 4:10 is "from the ground," that is, the M-other from which the *ochlos* cry out to God.[32]

---

27. "Lullaby of Binh Hoa."

28. Critiquing German existentialist Heidegger's ontological notion of death as nothingness, Levinas raises an ethical suspicion of murder in every death, "In the being for death of fear I am not faced with nothingness, but faced with what is against me, as though murder, rather than being one of the occasions of dying, were inseparable from the essence of death, as though the approach of death remained one of modalities of the relation with the Other" (Levinas, *Totality and Infinity*, 234).

29. Author's notes from Derrida's lecture at Emory University in memory of Lyotard in the fall of 1999. For Lyotard's own remark on "Auschwitz" as the forbiddance of the beautiful death, see Lyotard, *Differend*, 100.

30. Nazianzen, "St Gregory's Letter to Cledonius."

31. Irenaeus, *Against Heresies*, ch. 14.1.

32. Park, "New Reading."

As a theologian working for decolonizing the Constantinian Christianity co-opted by the empire, I will never be exempted from the guilt as well as the shame of a survivor in the history of violence. Not even the best representation of the unrepresentable suffering of the others, the subaltern, the *minjung* in history, can make a good theology. A self-critical, contemplative language of silence, dwelling in the presence of the Spirit (Rom 8:26) and listening to the cry of the ruptured spirits (Rom 8:22), might create a space for doing theology responsible to the death of the others that are neither magical nor beautiful.[33]

It was not so much an accident as a providence of God that I encountered Ocean Vuong, a young Vietnamese American poet and novelist, when I watched CNN just a few days before my departure for Da Nang. Vuong's debut collection, *Night Sky with Exit Wounds*, was published in 2016, and made him just the second poet to win the T. S. Eliot Prize for a first book. In one poem, he writes, "An American soldier fucked a Vietnamese farmgirl. Thus my mother exists. / Thus I exist. Thus no bombs = no family = no me."[34] As a two-year-old, he had been brought to the US from Vietnam as a refugee and settled with his family in the working-class town of Hartford, Connecticut. No one in his family spoke English. Vuong couldn't speak English when he started school in Hartford, and couldn't read at grade level until age eleven. When his father left, his mother got work in a nail salon.

If *Night Sky* tackled the absent father as myth, then his debut novel, *On Earth We're Briefly Gorgeous*, reckons with the mother and grandmother who raised him.[35] It is the influence of these women—courageous, difficult, devastated by the ripple effect of the Vietnam War—that forms the spine of the novel. In it, Vuong asks the central question: how does one love after trauma? His was a violent household. Both his grandmother, who saw her village in Vietnam razed by US soldiers, and his mother, ripped from everything familiar for a new life in the US, where her husband beat her before leaving, were suffering from post-traumatic stress disorder. Violence was the ugly expression of this trauma, but with distance, Vuong could see a positive release of that energy—chiefly in the way that his mother

---

33. In the same vein, Joerg Rieger criticizes the universalist pretension of liberal contextual theology and demands attending to "what hurts" and what "lies below the surface." He adds, "One of the great advantages of the various liberation theologies over contextual theology is that they are trying to deal with context as *that which hurts*" (Rieger, *Christ and Empire*, 7).

34. Brockes, "Ocean Vuong."

35. Vuong, *On Earth We're Briefly Gorgeous*.

and grandmother told stories. In the stories these women, who counted for nothing outside, "turned themselves into myths and it had a rhetorical power. They turned themselves into the Odyssey."[36]

Vuong's parents, following a rural Vietnamese tradition of naming a child for something so worthless that the evil spirits might pass over the house and spare him, called him "Little Dog." Little Dog once accompanied his mother and grandmother to the grocery store, and his mom Rose had mistaken mayonnaise for butter. He wrote, "That night I promised myself I'd never be wordless when you needed me to speak for you."[37] In the family mythology, Vuong was the single last hope of these indestructible women and when, in the mid-2000s, Hartford was hit by the opioid epidemic, it's the thing that stopped him from leaning toward drugs. Vuong says,

> The great male writers of the European tradition, be it Proust, Tolstoy, Turgenev, deemed that those most inspiring to them existed in a white aristocracy. . . . You read those books and you wouldn't even know that people of color existed in Europe. To each his own, and that was their choice. But I wanted to say: these lives, of women, and even of poor white people—these lives are worthy of literature. As Turgenev looked at the crumbling Russian empire, I look at these folks in a different crumbling empire and deemed that these are inspiring lives to an artist.[38]

Ocean Vuong, the Little Dog, not only tells a story of surviving the violence of empire but also demonstrates the subversive power of being a small, queer, person of color.

Despite my shame and guilt for the last forty years, once again, I am eager to try shaking hands with another Vietnamese, Ocean Vuong. It is not merely my personal feeling but an imaginative and even inspiring perception that Vuong, the Little Dog, was a Little Christ to his mother and grandmother as well as to me and to many other marginalized people. Jesus' parable of The Sheep and the Goats says: "The King will answer (the righteous): 'Truly I tell you, just as you did it to one of the least of these who are members of my family, you did it to me'" (Matt 25:40). The text is Jesus' eschatological prophecy just before he went down the Mount of Olives to take up the cross. "The King," whom Jesus mentions in the parable, will paradoxically refer to Jesus himself as he will be crucified, raised,

---

36. Brockes, "Ocean Vuong."
37. Brockes, "Ocean Vuong."
38. Brockes, "Ocean Vuong."

and lifted up to the throne of the Lamb of God. The King/the Lamb is the future mode of Christ. But for the time being, before the Messiah comes again, what is the present mode that Christ will assume as a prefiguration of the Lamb of God? It is for me in the mode of the Little Dog, surely many other little dogs in many other instances all over the world. Discerning and encountering the hidden and anonymous Little Christs will increase the joy of peacebuilding evangelism as we will celebrate the polyphony of poems and stories powerfully demonstrated by a Little Dog's phrase, "On Earth We're Briefly Gorgeous."[39]

The *Shaliach* Principle, or the Law of Agency, suggests that "a person's agent is regarded as the person himself/herself."[40] Appropriating this principle, we can claim that Little Dog is not an abject patient of the crumbling empire but a subversive agent of Little Christ for the kingdom of God. Through his agency, Little Dog, as a mode of Little Christ, challenges and invites us to enlarge our christological vision even beyond the traditional dogma of *vere deus* and *vere homo* to incorporate the dimension of cosmic Christ, namely, *vere vita* (true life). Then, Jesus Christ is the Way/*Tao* of True Life (John 14:6) not only for humans but also for all living beings or all "sentient beings," in the Buddhist expression, or in the Confucian symbolism of "the ten thousand beings of heaven and earth" (*tiendiwanwu*). In the Christian tradition, one would say, the least of those who are members of the "*oikoumene*" (household) of God.

We are the people on the move, overspreading the earth where we're called to be briefly gorgeous to each other. We are on the move, we are pilgrims on the way of true life to reach the latter-day glory of the coming

---

39. Rieger's notion of a "Christological surplus" that cannot be assimilated by empire is relevant here: "The complex and transdisciplinary reality created by empire (a reality that cannot be limited to religion, politics, economics, and so forth) finds a stumbling block in the complex and transdisciplinary *real* of Christ (a real that cannot be limited to religion, politics, and economics either). The battle between *reality* (the commonly accepted vision of the way things are, upheld not by correspondence to a referent anchored in people's lives but by power) and the *real* (that which has been pushed below the surface and repressed in the formation of the dominant version of reality) is as uneven as any battle between dominant and repressed forces: reality seems to win every time. But where the dominant view of reality intersects with the repressed view of the real, things will never be quite the same. The real of Christ (repressed and pushed below the surface on the crosses of the empire, a form of repression that continues and is being repeated in many ways into the present) not only hold up a mirror to the reality of the status quo but also creates a Christological surplus that cannot be captured by this reality and thus points beyond it" (Rieger, *Christ and Empire*, 10).

40. Hare, *Matthew*, 396.

Messiah, the Lamb of God. Many thousand years ago the prophet Haggai delivered the divine message to his people on the move: "'Be strong, all you people of the land,' declares the Lord, 'and work. For I am with you,' declares the Lord Almighty" (Hag 2:4). God confirmed them through reminding them of the covenant as well as promising them of the spiritual presence: "This is what I covenanted with you when you came out of Egypt. And my Spirit remains among you. Do not fear" (Hag 2:5). This has been the common vision of Scriptural and Spirit-filled Christianity on the move, decolonizing the Complacent, Constantinian Christianity in the history of empire.

Conclusion

It is intriguing as well as encouraging to peacebuilding Christians to reinvent Haggai's prophesy of the latter-day glory of God: "The latter glory of this house shall be greater than the former, says Yahweh of hosts. In this place I will give peace, oracle of Yahweh" (Hag 2:9). Peacebuilding evangelism of Spirit-filled Christianity as church on the move is profoundly implied in John Wesley's vision in his sermon, "The General Spread of the Gospel" of "faith filled with the energy of love" (*pistis di'agapes energoumene*, Gal 5:6). Envisioning the dawn of the latter-day glory of God, the kingdom of God coming "not with splendor and pomp, or with any of those outward circumstances, which usually attend the kingdoms of this world," Wesley believes that the Kingdom of God "will silently increase wherever it is set up, and spread from heart to heart, from house to house, from town to town, from one kingdom to another."[41] Furthermore, the general spread of the Gospel of faith filled with the energy of love will be fulfilled "in the same order which God hath done from the beginning of Christianity." Wesley continues: "'They shall all know me,' saith the Lord, not from the greatest to the least (this is that wisdom of the world which is foolishness with God) but 'from the least to the greatest,' that the praise may not be of men, but of God."[42] Discerning the signs of our times, we should not miss God's glorious promises for making the least among the household of God "free agents: having an inward power of self-determination, which is essential to their nature." Indeed, "Least of all did God take away their liberty, their power of choosing good or evil; God did not force you; but being assisted by his grace you, like Mary, chose the better part. Just so has he assisted five

---

41. Wesley, "General Spread of the Gospel," para. 17.
42. Wesley, "General Spread of the Gospel," para. 19.

in one house to make that happy choice, fifty or five hundred in one city, and many thousands in a nation, without depriving any of them of that liberty which is essential to a moral agent."[43]

The prophetic call to be "on the move" represents the call of the Holy Spirit for the pilgrimage of justice, peace, and "life together" (*sangsaeng*). Life together is possible when there is peace between the forced migrants from the margins and the native citizens of empires at the center. Peace is possible when there is justice, not as justification of the perpetrators of violence but as vindication of the victims as equal moral and spiritual agents. Therefore, the integration policy of migration and border regimes in Europe and United States, and many other developed countries including South Korea, does not serve justice because it epistemologically and ontologically problematizes the existence of migrants, immigrants, and refugees. The quasi-proselytism of both post-Christian West and Communist China toward Muslim populations within their borders, if it ends up with a form of genocide, is not merely a crime against humanity but also an abomination of the glory of God who creates us in God's own image. For Christ's sake we need to stop it by collective metanoia in the spirit of Jesus Christ, who says, "First be reconciled to your brother or sister, and then come and offer your gift" (Matt 5:24).

During my pilgrimage to Palestine in July 2019 I saw an inspiring glimpse of Jesus' peacemaking politics of love among the Palestinian Christian and Muslim young people playing basketball at the court of a YMCA in the Gaza Strip. For me it was not a mere sports game. Rather, it was to practice a "liturgy before liturgy" to learn civility in exchange and courtesy in debate not only between fellow citizens but also between enemies. Bong Joon-ho, Korean director of the Oscar-awarded film *Parasite*, forthrightly puts "one's life, whether it sustains life together/*sangsaeng* without falling into a parasite living/*kisaeng*, depends on courtesy toward each other, in other words, respect for human dignity."[44] The urgent yet long-aborted metanoia of the ecclesial elites of the privileged churches in the global North has to begin with self-critical and self-withdrawing questioning of presumed moral and spiritual superiority in their condescending attitude toward the ignored multitude as if they needed to grow up.

Sympathizing with the prophet Isaiah's messianic vision, Wesley aspired to see the coming of the perpetual peace on earth (*pax civitas*

---

43. Wesley, "General Spread of the Gospel," para. 11.
44. Lee, "Bong Joon-ho."

terrena) as the opening of a new global Christian era: "At that time will be accomplished all those glorious promises made to the Christian churches, which will not then be confined to this or that nation, but will include all the inhabitants of the earth. 'They shall not hurt nor destroy in all my holy mountain.' 'Violence shall no more be heard in thy land, wasting nor destruction within thy borders; but thou shall call thy walls, Salvation, and thy gates, Praise' (Isa 60:18)."[45]

But alas! Look at our world today! Aren't the old walls still preserved and the new walls ready to be built that separate and divide heart from heart, house from house, town from town, nation from nation? Therefore, my fellow sisters and brothers in Christ the Way/*Tao* of True Life and the perfect embodiment of faith filled with the energy of love, my pilgrim companions on the move, do not stand at the crossroads between the church of the empire and the church on the move. We are the church in exile caught up between the vice of the empire and the virtue of the kingdom of God. We are summoned by our Lord Jesus Christ to move forward along the road and no longer stand endlessly at the crossroads. Let us continue our journey of peacebuilding evangelism, yearning for the decolonizing transformation of the dividing wall into "the Wall of Salvation," and for the decolonizing change of the cursed checkpoint to the "Gate of Praise"!

Bibliography

Associated Press, "G.I.'s Tell of a U.S. Massacre in Korean War." *New York Times*, September 30, 1999. https://www.nytimes.com/1999/09/30/world/gi-s-tell-of-a-us-massacre-in-korean-war.html.

Bhabha, Homi K. *The Location of Culture*. London: Routledge, 2004.

Brockes, Emma. "Ocean Vuong: 'As a Child I Would Ask: What's Napalm?'" *The Guardian*, June 9, 2019. https://www.theguardian.com/books/2019/jun/09/ocean-vuong-on-earth-we-are-briefly-gorgeous-interview.

Francis, Pope. *Evangelii Gaudium: Apostolic Exhortation on the Proclamation of the Gospel in Today's World*. The Holy See. https://www.vatican.va/content/francesco/en/apost_exhortations/documents/papa-francesco_esortazione-ap_20131124_evangelii-gaudium.html.

———. "'We Must Come All Together to Shout that Peace Has No Borders': The Message of Pope Francis to 'Peace With No Borders.'" Incontri internazionali preghiera per la pace, Madrid, September 15, 2019. https://preghieraperlapace.santegidio.org/pageID/3/langID/en/itemID/4304/We-must-come-all-together-to-shout-that-Peace-has-no-borders—the-message-of-Pope-Francis-to-Peace-with-No-Borders.html.

---

45. Wesley, "General Spread of the Gospel," para. 26.

Francis, Pope, and Munib Younan. "Joint Statement on the Occasion of the Joint Catholic-Lutheran Commemoration of the Reformation." Lund, October 31, 2016. https://www.lutheranworld.org/sites/default/files/joint_commemoration_joint_statement_final_en_0.pdf.

Hare, Douglas R. A. *Matthew, Interpretation: A Bible Commentary for Teaching and Preaching.* Korean Translation. Louisville, KY: Korea Presbyterian Publishing, 2001.

Harper, Steve. *A Pocket Guide to Prayer.* Nashville: Upper Room, 2010.

Hays, Richard B. *Echoes of Scripture in the Letters of Paul.* New Haven: Yale University Press, 1989.

"An Invitation to the Pilgrimage of Justice and Peace." *The Ecumenical Review* 66.3 (2014) 383–90.

Irenaeus. *Against Heresies.* In vol. 1 of *The Ante-Nicene Fathers*, edited by Alexander Roberts and James Donaldson. Grand Rapids: Eerdmans, 1977.

Lee, Ho-nam, "Bong Joon-ho: Courtesy Towards Humans Separates Parasitism and Symbiosis." *Joongang Daily* (Korea), May 29, 2019. http://www.joongang.co.kr/article/23482372#home.

Levinas, Emmanuel. *Totality and Infinity.* Pittsburgh: Duquesne University Press, 1969.

Lohre, Kathryn Mary. "Moving in the Spirit: Called to Transforming Discipleship." Unpublished paper from Conference on World Mission and Evangelism, March 8–13, 2018, Arusha, Tanzania.

"The Lullaby of Binh Hoa." *Hankookilbo News Paper*, September 30, 2014. https://hankookilbo.com.

The Lutheran World Federation and The Pontifical Council of Promoting Christian Unity. *From Conflict to Communion: Lutheran-Catholic Common Commemoration of the Reformation in 2017.* Leipzig: Evangelische-Verlagsanstalt, 2013.

The Lutheran World Federation, et al. *The Biblical Foundations of the Doctrine of Justification: An Ecumenical Follow-up to the Joint Declaration on the Doctrine of Justification.* New York: Paulist, 2012.

Lyotard, Jean-François. *The Differend: Phrases in Dispute.* Theory and History of Literature 46. Minneapolis: University of Minnesota Press, 1999.

Nazianzen, Gregory. "St Gregory's Letter to Cledonius." In vol. 7 of *Nicene and Post-Nicene Fathers*, edited by Philip Schaff and Henry Wace. Buffalo, NY: Christian Literature, 1894. https://www.newadvent.org/fathers/3103a.htm.

Park, J. C. "A New Reading of the Story of Atonement in Dialogue with Julia Kristeva's Maternal Semiology of the Abject/the M-other." Paper presented at the 13th Oxford Institute of Methodist Theological Studies. Institute Archives, 13th Institute (2013). https://oimts.files.wordpress.com/2013/09/2013-3-park-jc.pdf.

Rieger, Joerg. *Christ and Empire: From Paul to Postcolonial Times.* Minneapolis: Fortress, 2007.

Runyon, Theodore, ed. *Sanctification and Liberation: Liberation Theologies in the Light of the Wesleyan Tradition.* Nashville: Abingdon, 1981.

Sung, Jung Mo. "Liberation Theology and the Idolatry of Money." Speech at the Methodist Theological University, Seoul, Korea, October 21, 2014.

Torrance, James B. "The Contribution of McLeod Campbell to Scottish Theology." *Scottish Journal of Theology* 26.3 (1973) 295–311.

Vuong, Ocean. *On Earth We're Briefly Gorgeous: A Novel.* New York: Penguin, 2019.

"Walled World—Project." *TD Vrij Nederland*, 2006. https://the-department.eu/projects/show/walled-world/.

Wesley, John. "The Character of a Methodist." *Evans Early American Imprint Collection*, n.d. https://quod.lib.umich.edu/e/evans/N20188.0001.001/1:3?rgn=div1;view=fulltext.

———. "The General Spread of the Gospel" (sermon 63). In *Wesley Center Online*, n.d. http://wesley.nnu.edu/john-wesley/the-sermons-of-john-wesley-1872-edition/sermon-63-the-general-spread-of-the-gospel/.

———. "On the Wedding Garment" (Sermon 120). *Wesley Center Online*, n.d. http://wesley.nnu.edu/john-wesley/the-sermons-of-john-wesley-1872-edition/sermon-120-on-the-wedding-garment/.

———. *A Plain Account of Christian Perfection*. Edited by Randy L. Maddox and Paul W. Chilcote. Kansas City: Beacon Hill, 2015.

The World Methodist Council. "The World Methodist Council and the Joint Declaration on the Doctrine of Justification: Methodist Statement." Seoul, 23 July 2006. https://worldmethodistcouncil.org/wmcs-statement-of-assocation-with-the-joint-declaration-of-the-doctrine-of-justification/.

The World Methodist Council, et al. "Statement on Occupation of Palestine." July 17, 2019. https://worldmethodistcouncil.org/2019/07/17/methodist-delegation-sees-bitter-fruits-of-palestinian-occupation/.

Chapter VIII

WATER AND SAND

Illuminating Native Theologies with a Wesleyan Lens of Spiritual Experience

AMELIA KOH-BUTLER

Grounding: Acknowledgement of Country

Warami Ngallowah Mittigar [Darug, translates into English as "Hello, Come sit down, Friend"][1]

I write from the Barramattagul Country of the Darug-speaking peoples. Barramattagul is the place where the eels lie to spawn. It is a place of creativity. It is also a bustling cosmopolitan commercial population centre, now known as "Parramatta," the heart of Western Sydney, on the Pacific coast of Australia. Indigenous peoples invite us to consider our interactions, not just with other people, but also with and within "country." *Where* our spirits are embodied impacts our worldviews and attitudes to theology. In this place, people from Oceania/Pasifika and Australasia/*Down Under* interact with waters under Southern skies. I pay my respects to the First Peoples and those who have kept and will keep law (lore) and custom on this Land.[2]

---

1. A welcome song, sung in some of our Western Sydney elementary schools, introduces the language of greeting, Icry2u, "Warami Ngallowah Mittigar."

2. Aboriginal Christian leader Brooke Prentis says, "An Acknowledgement of Country is more than just words, it's about heart and mind coming together through a genuine want and act of building relationship with Aboriginal peoples." See "Acknowledgement

Glistenings of light on water: Oceania—the wettest continent

While other continents are defined by their land masses, Oceania is the wet continent. It is characterized by the vast ocean. The wilderness is experienced on and in waters where no land can be seen, where the seascape is excited by waves and whales. God is experienced in the grandeur of the leviathan and its smallness within the waters. The sound of the conch shell calls from beyond the horizon.

Wisdom from above and below: Ancient dreaming from the driest land, known as Australia

While other cultures are defined by property and boundaries, the Southern Land (Latin: *terra australis*) is the driest of the human-inhabited continents.[3] Bordered by coastlines, with rivers that flood, it is home to an array of Deserts. The ancient landscapes are joined by what is seen in the stars: the Seven Sisters (Greek: *Pleiedes*). Wisdom for humanity comes from above and below. When night turns to day, we know the stars are still there, but the memory fades until we turn off the lights and look into the dark. Each star is worthy of wonder, even when it is but a speck in a vast sky with depths beyond imagining.

Introduction

WHAT FOLLOWS IS A celebration of the influences of country and water, of wisdom from ancients, interacting with postcolonial faith. Historically, across the Pacific and in Australia, faith-talk has been shaped by the language of Wesleyan theology. Yet, this language has been associated with oppression, disruption, and struggle. Searching for holiness, people of faith are recognizing the limitations of human greed and privilege. In these lands and oceans, colonization has danced with increasing anthropocentrism, in places where

---

of Country." Offering Acknowledgement has become for us a way of identifying our relationship with the Land and her peoples. For Methodists in Australia, this is connected to relationships. The National Superintendent of the Wesleyan Methodist Church is Indigenous Elder, Rev. Dr. Rex Rigby, and the Uniting Church in Australia, partly founded out of Methodism, has a Covenant with Uniting and Aboriginal and Islander Christian Congress. Both denominations are committed to the work of reconciliation between First and Second Peoples.

3. The Antarctic is drier, but has temporary human "guests," rather than any indigenous or permanent population.

creation and created order previously had a privileged position. The loss of harmony with creation challenges hermeneutics. How can we talk about a God of creation, when the works of the Creator's hand are in need of salvation? Perhaps a sign of sanctification is when souls gather, outside buildings, to celebrate the wonder of God's cathedral?

In this chapter, I intentionally resist bringing a linear (Western-style) approach. Instead, I seek to push the hermeneutical spiral into experiences of *talanoa* circles, *corroborees*, and *campfire* conversations among the family of faith. Each of these practices contribute to our discussion, as they have provided the opportunity to unearth sacred stories. The stories allow us to see links to eucharistic rite, with shared testimony, thanksgiving, wondering, sharing, and blessing, effectively sending the community beyond the gathering into a transformed way of being.

In the Pacific, we often talk about talanoa, meeting and talking around the grass mat or *tapa* cloth (Tongan), or *masi* cloth (Fijian). Whether it is the woven mat, made from people weaving the grass together and incorporating their conversations and patterns, or whether it is the papery cloth made from pounded mulberry back and decorated with symmetric symbols, the gathering incorporates past relationships and conversations physically. Talanoa is a traditional word used in Fiji and across the Pacific to reflect a process of inclusive, participatory, and transparent dialogue. The purpose of talanoa is to share stories, build empathy and to make wise decisions for the collective good. People gather and talk, sharing Kava (a muddy drink made from powdered root). Talanoa is not free from problems. Some conversations are helpful and some are less so. There need to be courtesies for us to truly listen and hear one another. Learning the courtesies takes time.

The indigenous (Aboriginal) peoples in Australia often consider linear thinking to be naïve and superficial.[4] Deep wisdom conversations are often more circular. In these ancient cultures, time is allowed to narrate experience and integrate bodily developed learnings. In Corroboree, reflection and contemplation are enhanced by dancing, singing, and feasting. Formal

---

4. In Australia, the term *indigenous* refers to *Aboriginal* Australians and to *Torres Strait Islanders*. This usage is sometimes extended to other islanders, although most Micronesian, Melanesian, and Polynesian Islanders will come under the collective *Pacific Islanders*, or, colloquially, *PIs*. Australian Aboriginal Peoples (from over 300 people groups) are also known as *First Peoples*, recognizing they were first on this land, but also the oldest continuing culture groups in the world, with heritage dating back more than 60,000 years.

and informal explorations are given complementary spaces in developing ideas. Such circles do not always come to conclusions or fixed positions, but offer ways to live with questions and negotiate next steps. Like talanoa, learning how to be in such an environment takes mentoring, patience, and generosity of companion-elders along the way.

For people beyond the Pacific, perhaps the easiest way to enter this process is to remember the experience of a campfire. As we sit in a circle, the illumination from the campfire highlights the faces around us. The light is not conducive to reading books or papers, which could only be seen in shadow. We remain aware of the influence of the past, but our focus is in this moment of presence around the dancing flames and glowing coals. Our attention is drawn to each narrative and we expect the storyteller to draw us into participation in their story. We are not asked to listen objectively, but to become involved as active listeners.

Soong-Chan Rah explains the required attitude: "Cultural intelligence requires knowledge about our own cultural framework and the immediacy of our cultural environment. But it also requires a willingness to go to another place and to reflect on your own culture and see the cultures of others from a new angle."[5] Because the native theologies of Pasifika-Oceania develop in interactive communities, this chapter will feature several prominent voices from this region. Therefore, I start with a series of stories and invite you to hold particular questions in mind while we share a range of responses to the stories.

A Story of Pasifika-Oceania: Earthquakes and Tsunamis, Cyclones (Tropical Storms)

In early 2022, the Pacific Island nation of Tonga faced an underwater earthquake and resulting tsunami. Nearly two decades earlier, the tsunami of 2004 claimed the lives of more than 230,000 people. Whether due to tsunami or cyclone, a tropical paradise can quickly turn into the waters of the underworld. The increasing frequency of storm events counters opportunities for recovery. Tropical dwellers are used to cyclone seasons, but not to the relentless persistent catastrophic events happening *at the same time* as rising sea levels.

Our images of tsunamis often present as the tall waves towering over people and boats, usually when they have suddenly ascended over

5. Rah, *Many Colors*, 84.

a coastal shelf or rocky outcrop. The first indicator of a tsunami is often the recession of water. The water goes out, sucking into the ocean as if collecting in a black hole, disappearing from its normal places. Then the water comes in and comes in and keeps coming in. The problem passes when the water comes in, but continues as the water recedes again, when it drags everything back into the deep.

I penned this "Tsunami Confession of Hope" in 2017:

Creeping up on us,
slowly, insidiously,
the waters rise.
Forces beyond us
drag us
into the unknown.
The oceans teeming with life
also salt the earth with death.
The beaches and reefs of paradise-welcome
become a graveyard
where salty tears mingle with the receding tide.
A sense of inevitability drives away hope.
Resignation to depression takes hold.
What is this state of sin?
Hopelessness?
The loss of belief in possibility
becomes its own obstacle to experiencing life.
Yet, walking on water
and commanding the waves
invites us to believe
in miracles.[6]

Those of us who live around the Pacific learn to read the ocean. Waves are a good sign of the health of currents and tides. Where there is dark and calm water, there is more likely to be a "rip"—the kind of flow that drags you out to sea—the kind you cannot swim against. Tourists come to our beaches and get caught in rips. We have life savers to fish them out. Beware the dark and calm waters.

---

6. Koh-Butler and Floyd, "Growing Up," 17.

People who swim under water become aware of refractions of light. Underwater light bends and plays. It shifts and reflects. When we are surrounded by water-light, we see differently. Our imaginations respond differently. Some things are magnified, some things draw our attention. Things we previously thought of as important seem to fade into insignificance. Aids to seeing underwater, such as goggles, change our perceptions yet again.

The Pacific is vast. It is a wet wilderness, sometimes described as "Paradise." The ocean, as country, forces us to read the stories of Scripture differently. In the first breath of creation, God forms heaven and earth (Gen 1:1–2, 6–8). Before the dry lands are created (Gen 1:9–10), the earth is the water. It is a good place for the beginning. Consider, then, how tsunamis and cyclones challenge how we might read stories of wilderness and water. These are sometimes stories of paradise disrupted and in torment.

A Story of Rising Waves

Forty days of wilderness is relevant on an outrigger canoe on the oceans between visible land points. Currents flow to a different time. When explorers and missionaries came to the Pacific, they encountered the "doldrums," where the lack of wind made sailing tall ships impossible. Pacific sailors, with their outrigger and paddle canoes, knew when to rely on currents and paddles, rather than relying on "wind in sail." The first recognition in listening to Pasifika voices is to recognize the relationship with country and ocean prompts different questions. In the same way, scholars from Oceania ask: How shall we read Scriptures written by people who could not swim and only bothered fishing on lakes? People like Peter seemed to panic at a few waves![7]

At a conference around 2005, a graduate student posed the question: "How do I go home and tell people to stop teaching that God will never let another flood destroy humanity? The flood is already destroying us." I cannot reference which student it was, for too many of my friends from

---

7. The story of Peter's relationship with water often amuses ocean-living fishing communities. Reading Matt 14:22–33, Mark 6:45–52, and John 6:16–21 with Pasifika Bible study groups can lead to much laughter, as people discuss walking on water and how to catch fish. In a study group with Australian-Fijian young people, I heard of their wondering about Jesus paddle-boarding (on boards you stand on and paddle from and which make it look like you are walking on water). They were sure he would enjoy the ocean with them.

too many island nations have had to say the same thing over the years. Nations are literally drowning. Our consciousness of water, as source of life and harbinger of death, is entwined.

Reading through Eurocentric and North American missionary lenses, there can be a tendency to revert to historical interpretations that make limited sense in this climate. I use the term climate in the full geographic sense. The islands of Tuvalu and Kiribati (Kiribas) are archipelagos—stretches of coral islands of low altitude. Some of the islands are only two meters above sea level. As we think about climate change and rising sea levels, a one- centimeter rise or a two- or a five-centimeter rise translates into scarcity, starvation, or annihilation. Biblical scholars from these islands have for a couple of decades come to Australia and New Zealand to be able to try to remove themselves from the immediate *emic* (insider) perspective, in order to stand back and experience *etic* (outsider) observations, rearticulating their thinking so that they might advocate between communities.

People, whether from the North or the South, the East or the West, bring their own worldviews, shaped by experiences. Their understanding of truth, their questions, their experiences provide the benchmarks by which they measure the understandings of others. However, our worldviews, formed in a particular culture in a particular place, may be challenged as we are exposed to other cultures and other places. The experience of those who have been colonized involves receiving and conforming to conflicting narratives, shaped by worldviews from other places. The new story takes over, dominating previous stories. Sometimes, the old stories can only be remembered or retold when the dominating colonizing presence is not focused on the act of colonizing. It is ironic that many Pacific scholars come to Aotearoa (New Zealand) or Australia to participate in the colonizers' education system in order to be able to articulate postcolonial hope.

Even toward the end of the twentieth century, indigenous spiritualities were termed "folk religions." Writing about theological assumptions regarding personal salvation in relation to evangelism and discipleship in missions, Hiebert, Shaw, and Tienou contrast corporate faith with that which is understood and acted on apart from the community. As anthropologists, conscious that conversion is more than either-or, they highlight problems of syncretism resulting from uncritical acceptance or denial of old beliefs and practices.[8] Perhaps the task of the Pasifika-Oceania faithful, who have been previously colonized, is to be sent with missionary zeal

---

8. Hiebert et al., *Understanding Folk Religion*.

to those places who previously sent missionaries, in order to assist with reflexive critiquing of the colonizer-cultures. To be more explicit, Western thinkers may not fully grasp the vast depths of what Oceania offers until Western culture and theology are critiqued through Talanoa lenses. Could we consider the possibility that Talanoa might expose Western theological methods, based on linear thought processes, as syncretistically linked to Greek philosophy and enlightenment individualism?

Living with Our Stories

Decolonization must recognize the depth of colonialism and how it has impacted us on multiple levels, regardless if our ancestors were among colonizer or colonized. Decolonization must seek differently structured relationships, liberated from previous power abuses and imbalances. Liberation becomes possible with justice, restoration, and mutuality in relationships. Overcoming colonial privilege and subjugation requires commitment to learning the perspective of the "other," or, as we say in Australia, "truth-telling."[9] Both colonizer and colonized may attribute motivations to one another or make assumptions about benefits or hardships. Moves toward reconciliation can be strengthened by developing narratives that can be told as truth by both parties to be reconciled. Just as it is inappropriate to justify the pain of colonial experience by editing the stories of pain, it is inadequate to cast out any appreciation of anything that was gained in the interactions.[10] Justice and reconciliation in this case is not mere "retrieval" of these stories. It entails acknowledgment of the colonial forces that led to the loss of life, land, and wisdom. It demands accountability from people and institutions that benefited from colonialism. And it means giving primacy to the voices of formerly colonized peoples as agents of their own history, empowered to lead others into peace with justice and reconciliation.

At the 2022 Assembly of the World Council of Churches in Karlsruhe, Fijian leader James Bhagwan, General Secretary of the Pacific Conference of Churches, offered perspectives on human security and climate change.

9. "Voice, treaty and truth" was the major theme of the 2021 NAIDOC Day in Australia (National Aboriginal and Islanders Day Observance Committee).

10. This argument is supported by the work of Tracy Spencer, whose research into the lives of missionaries Jim Page and Rebecca Forbes among the Adnyamathanha people tells stories of encounter and enculturation that provide an alternative to colonizer and colonized. She refers to the work of Adnyamathanha-missionary "life-writing" as a task of story-hybridity. Spencer, "White Lives," 5.

He assisted a group of young indigenous islanders to present in song and dance their readings of faith from the oceans.[11] Their contributions were dramatic and profound, seeming to wake delegates from their wordsmithing into deeply considering the urgency of climate crisis.

In the Pacific, decolonizing Wesleyan theology requires:

1. making fresh translations of Scripture that do not simply translate English words and concepts into islander languages, recognizing that some Islander concepts may shed light on new readings of Hebrew and Greek stories;
2. redefining tradition to include the wisdoms revealed in the oceanic islander cultures;
3. reasoning by talking around the mat, in interactive conversations of many voices, *prioritizing understanding others, rather than being understood*;[12]
4. experiencing the spirituality of the blue planet, remembering that the dominion of God we experience on this earth is covered by 71 percent water.

Combining *emic* (insider) and *etic* (outsider) approaches allows for walking in the shoes of the other, while conscious of one's own feet. An islander translation of the concept might be to walk in the footprints of the other, learning from the country beneath by treading the trodden path. Developing *emic-etic* awareness invites movement toward a "both-and" approach, rather than the dualistic choice of "either-or." Decolonizing Wesleyan theology may require us to dance, with feet intentionally encountering ground, as both "insiders" and "outsiders," translating how lived experience transforms the spirit.

Tongan scholar Jione Havea points toward reading native theologies.[13] How does a starting point of oceanic spiritual reflection change the lens or

---

11. I attended the WCC Conference in Karlsruhe, Germany, in September 2022. A group of young people from across a number of different island-nations led reflections at a number of sessions, focused on worship of Creator and confession of humanity's failure to care for creation.

12. Rah, *Many Colors*, 85.

13. Jione Havea uses clusters of *Roots* (an indigenous reading of tradition), *Reads* (theologies informed and inspired by written and oral texts and missionary contact), and *Routes* (an attempt to cast off into the ocean of ongoing theological navigation and voyaging). Havea, *Theologies from the Pacific*.

lenses through which we read "Christian" Scriptures? What is particular to Talanoa is the expectation of participants to evolve through conversation with each other. We enter into authoring as part of a community, so I forewarn the other authors in this collection that I hope to meet and converse with you. This commitment becomes an act of faith in a God who we believe to be loving and engaged enough to have been revealing Godself throughout history and story, generation upon generation, language upon language, place upon place, and culture upon culture.

Reframing how we talk about the sacred stories and interpretations of Scripture is not a discarding of faith in Jesus Christ, but an invitation to regard the Gospel as engaging with existential exploration by humans. Instead of overlaying colonizing languages and concepts, it is a commitment to be attentive to the Spirit of God at work in God's creation and among those who carry God's image. Attention to native theologies allows spiritually faithful people to speak into a Christocentric church of the learnings of Creator-and-Creation.

A Story of Transition: The Path from Ocean to Desert

If you go from one island to another, you are said to have wet feet. It is only when you have been in a place long enough for your feet to be dry that you are ready for listening and conversation. We hear echoes of Gen 1:9–10, as our feet dry and we see the waters divided. Too often people never take the time to situate themselves and let their feet dry. Australia, although it is an island continent surrounded by Pacific (to the east), Indian (west), and Southern Oceans, and the Arafura Sea to the north, has vast tropical areas and ten deserts.[14] Geologists talk of the inland deserts

---

14. Australia's ten deserts are: the Great Victoria Desert (348,750 square kilometers), the Great Sandy Desert (267,250 square kilometers), the Tanami Desert (184,500 square kilometers), the Simpson Desert (176,500 square kilometers), the Gibson Desert (156,000 square kilometers), the Little Sandy Desert (111,500 square kilometers), the Strzelecki Desert (80,250 square kilometers), the Sturt Stony Desert (29,750 square kilometers), the Tirari Desert (15,250 square kilometers), and the Pedirka Desert (1,250 square kilometers). To get a sense of scale, this compares with the United Kingdom (243,610 square kilometers) or Texas (695,662 square kilometers). These deserts are dry, but not all are sandy dunes. Some are scrubby, teeming with life, adapted to the conditions over millennia. In some places, there may be no rain for eight years, but when it does rain, fish appear!

as having once been an inland sea. Where there was once water is characterized by red (iron-laden) dust.

"Dusty feet" is a term used by Australian Aborigines. The Dusty Feet Mob are a group of Aboriginal Christians, living in Port Augusta, South Australia, who perform rite, dance, and story. Port Augusta is a crossroads town, where desert meets sea and different people groups would interact. The First Peoples in Australia include more than 250 distinct languages with more than 800 dialects. Although I was born in Australia, of Chinese-Scottish ethnic descent, I have been adopted into the Adnyamathanha peoples of the Ikara-Flinders Ranges. My late-husband's ashes were received back onto country near Ikara Wilpena Pound, on sacred site—where we tell stories of how God's Spirit, in the form of giant serpents, formed the land.

When Adnyamathanha people read Genesis 2, the instruction to the serpent to slither on the earth is welcomed as God's first act of redemption. The serpent becomes involved in God's work of creation, bringing into being the earth's form, where humanity will live and the revelation of God's purposes will come into being. The serpent's punishment is also an activity of restoration and sanctification. The serpent is sent to contribute to God's mission of creation.

In the Genesis stories of migration, we hear of Abram and Sarai being renamed Abraham and Sarah, reflecting the change of place and culture. Eventually, they are buried under the Oaks of Mamre, far away from where they were born. In their new places of rest, we sense God is there—on country. Yet, we also hear that God was on their journey, being worshipped on the way at Peniel and Bethel. Indeed, God was to be found in the wilderness and in the places of rest. God is to be found among people and in the places where no people dwell.

The explorers and colonizers of Wesley's era made the mistake of describing Australia as *terra nullius* (unclaimed land or land of no-one). In so doing, they categorized Australian Aborigines as fauna—not human. Decolonizing Wesleyan theology invites us to ask, what must we do to confront Wesleyan concepts of what it means to be human and what it means to be created in the *imago dei*?[15]

---

15. Colonizers did not always see the subjects of colonization as "being made in the image of God." Oppression and discarding of language and culture became an act of dehumanizing, enshrined in the "White Australia Policy," which saw Aboriginal people only being counted in the census from 1967. Prior to that, Aboriginal relations were often managed in different states and territories by Departments of Fisheries and Wildlife. Aboriginals sometimes received official government correspondences referring to the

A Story of Stars and Deserts: The Seven Sisters

We hear of God's promise to Abraham and Sarah (Gen 15:5 and 26:4) that there will be prolific descendants, as many as the stars in the sky. Traveling into the desert, away from the light pollution of the coastal cities in Australia, the night is dominated by a sky vibrant and alive with light. It is the same sky that is reflected in the oceans, but in the desert, the light shines upon scurrying and hunting. Dusk sees the movement of kangaroos and wallabies. As the stars appear, the nocturnal animals of the desert come out and the scorching dead heat of day turns into the night of feasting, journeying, and campfire gathering. It is easy to imagine Abraham in the desert, trying to count the uncountable lights of promise.

So many cultures have looked to the skies, seeking spiritual revelation, seeking signs, seeking beyond ourselves and our own self-referencing. Among the most ancient of stories known and shared in humankind is the story of the Seven Sisters. These are the seven stars, also known as the Matariki (Maori), Pleiades (Greece), 昴 mǎo (China), Subaru (Japan), and by many other names. They appear in Job 9:9, Job 38:31, and Amos 5:8.

My husband and I attended the *Songlines* exhibition at the National Museum of Australia in 2019. The story of the Seven Sisters was curated in a series of weaving, stories, music, and paintings. The offerings came from many different indigenous communities from the northwest to the center. Story after story followed, episodes in a grand narrative, tracking the development of characters in their journeys across the country. As we moved from chapter to chapter, we could sense the characters evolving as they encountered different landscapes. As we journeyed though the galleries, we felt the desert and sky speaking ancient lessons. Abruptly, the stories stopped with the last of the paintings, from Pitjantjatjara land. We could feel people leaving the last work, satisfied that they had encountered wisdom. We felt stunned, incomplete, and bereft. We knew the next chapter, the untold Adnyamathanha story that continued the epic drama. We were filled with wonder at the significance of knowing, but it also came home to us how few people hold sacred stories, how precious they

---

(nonexistent) "Flora and Fauna Act." Such social dehumanizing was reinforced by missionaries and churches when any attempts to image Christ as Aboriginal or Islander were labeled syncretistic, and when so many book illustrations and stained-glass windows depict Christ as white European.

are, and how we were being immediately challenged to learn how best to keep the story alive.¹⁶

As a direct result of colonization, past Adnyamathanha elders oversaw the burying of the law (lore) into the earth. They could not trust the colonial social systems and relationships and decided it was safest to preserve knowledge without the corruption of continued colonial contact. They hoped that one day it would become safe enough to unearth what is buried and that other, stronger indigenous communities would be in a position to help them reclaim their culture and heritage. Decolonizing Wesleyan theology in such a situation means finding good news that does more than make a fresh start, as if there was no humanity before the arrival of Wesleyan missionaries. The idea of "fresh start" is offensive when it means ignoring the brokenness and pain in front of us. God was already in this place, before the arrival of colonizers and missionaries. God was being revealed in land and spirit, in sacred stories, and in rite and law (lore). Jesus Christ came, not to abolish the law (lore), but to fulfill it (Matt 5:17). How often has law (lore) been abolished in the name of Christ?

A Story of Dreaming

Waka Waka woman Brooke Prentis places herself within the law (lore) that is known as Dreaming,

> I, Brooke, belong to peoples who have a Dreaming—a Dreaming that for over 60,000 years taught us and continues to teach us of the Creator, how to care for creation, and how to live in right relationship with one another. I belong to people who, for over 2,000 generations, have left footprints on these lands now called Australia. I belong to peoples who are the world's oldest living culture. I also belong to peoples, however, who understand what it is to live the politics of the postponement of justice in Australia, a people who have been crying out for justice for nearly 250 years in this land we are told is "young and free," this land of the "fair go" in this so-called "lucky country."¹⁷

I was born in this "lucky country," where we were taught at school to treat historical interpretations of history as truth, while relegating

---

16. To get a sense of the people groups across the country today, it is helpful to look at a contemporary map, see "Map of Indigenous Australia."
17. Broughton and Prentis, "Recognition without Dignity," 1.

Dreaming stories as fictional mythologies, as if they were tarnished by sunburn. I was blessed to be brought up by a couple of atheist grandparents who cared for country and dispossessed indigenous returned soldiers who lived in the bush close to their home. I learned, as a child, about stories being told for different reasons and with different claims being made about the stories. Sometimes we tell our stories for discovering truth or wisdom or identity. Some stories are disparaged and discarded and sometimes storytellers are intentionally and brutally silenced. Stories change over time, revealing different perspectives on what is true.

Dreams of biblical characters are treated as sacred. We continue to interpret them, Sunday by Sunday, in the light of Scripture, reason, tradition and experience. Could the Dreaming stories of indigenous peoples be one of the ways the Spirit of God prompts us to work toward wisdom? Methodist missionaries have often documented indigenous stories and wondered at links to the stories in Scripture. Some Dreamings function as parables, while others show models of behavior, for example, the journeying of Magi holds similarities to following the Songlines of the Seven Sisters.

Sending Storytellers and Reclaiming Stories

In recent years, I learned stories connecting the Wesleyan missionary heritage of the early colonies in Australia with the Pacific Islands. I served at Parramatta Mission from 2017 to 2020 and was a member of its Leigh Fijian Congregation, named after Samuel Leigh. It is both the place of the first Methodist missionaries to Pasifika-Oceania, and the place where some wonderful Fijian theologians do some of their current postcolonial thinking.

The first British colony in Australia was established in 1788 and the first Wesleyan missionary to arrive was Staffordshire-born Samuel Leigh in 1815. Three years later, his colleague, Walter Lawry, would arrive. Both men embraced Arminianism, committing themselves to "word and deed" among all people. This led them to look beyond settlement and colony boundaries and travel to New Zealand and Tonga. While both were advocates for justice, preached compassion for the poor, and the abolition of slavery, they were also "of their age."[18] Wittingly or unwittingly, missionaries were often pressured to reinforce a social system that saw Aboriginal people as targets

---

18. De Reland, *All Love's Excelling*, 13–17.

of salvation, rather than sources of wisdom, and their lands as inhospitable places of danger, rather than revealing of God's grace.[19]

One of the themes that came through the *Songlines* exhibition is the importance of "what is told to whom."[20] Through the period of colonization, Aboriginal people in Australia learned that there was a time to speak and a time to be silent. Speaking language could result in punishment in a society where speaking English was a requirement for access to identity, resources, and privilege. The "White Australia Policy," primarily focused on limited non-white immigration, came into being in December 1901 and its deconstruction did not start until 1966. At the time of Federation in 1901, Aboriginals were described as being part of a dying race. They were not recognized as citizens until 1967.

Fifty years later, Brooke Prentis would write,

> I am a volunteer community Aboriginal pastor as there is little to no funding from Australian church denominations for Aboriginal ministry, to see me employed by the church, any church. This vocation has enabled me to follow Jesus into the realities of Australia in 2017 where I see, hear and feel the impacts of racism, the impacts of poverty in the apparently "Lucky Country," and the impacts of colonialism still present in Australia—and ultimately the impacts of the lack of Reconciliation.[21]

Today, the task of decolonizing Wesleyan theology is overdue and urgent. Gabi Gabi man, Rex Rigby, is the National Superintendent of the Wesleyan Methodist Church and the only indigenous head of denomination in Australia. He writes social cohesion theory and practice. By looking at migration through indigenous lenses, systemic problems of colonial racism and dispossession are understood to limit our capacity to converse respectfully and learn from one another. He challenges us to reject the notion that a dominant narrative is required for social cohesion. As he tells his own family's story of the breaking of kinship relationships through "stolen generations"[22] and his work to reconcile people and groups, we hear that

---

19. There were exceptions, with some missionaries embedding themselves in country. However, they were often disparaged for "going native." An example of such behavior involved missionaries Jim Page and Rebecca Forbes. See Spencer, "White Lives."

20. Young, "On Revealing and Concealing."

21. Broughton and Prentis, "Recognition without Dignity," 116.

22. *Stolen Generations* refers to the practice of removing Aboriginal and "half-caste" children from their families through the twentieth century in Australia. The extent of the genocidal experience was documented in a Royal Commission, led by former Uniting

reconciliation is not the majority adopting a particular version of a story, but being able to sit in company of difference, bound by a value of grace.[23] Rigby writes, "A problem can occur with the notion of building shared values if it implies the imposition of one's values onto others (which is a commonly held view for some regarding immigration). This leads to the problematic idea of assimilation."[24]

In an ironic twist, in Australia, the argument for *assimilation* comes from those colonizers who could not possibly have considered assimilating into Aboriginal communities. The terms assimilation, colonization, and domination carry connotations of abusive and coercive power.

Wrogemann makes a helpful contribution to the discussion about cultural terminology as we consider what is next for decolonizing. It is as if *multiculturalism* and *interculturality* have been strategies where it has been assumed that cultures can be shaped into systems for the purposes of social cohesion. The analogy of *melting pot* proposed that subgroups would assimilate and conform into a dominant culture. The analogy of *salad* allowed for different ingredients coming together to form a whole. Yet, *culture*[25] and *civilization* (preferred in some parts of Europe until the 1940s) are terms that separate behaviors from place. The more recently used terms of *hybridity*, *mélange*, and *creolization* expected an amalgamation of cultures.[26] Yet, I believe it is worth taking a "both-and" approach rather than an "either-or" attitude.

Bringing different cultures together can be experienced as both *amalgamation* and *takeover*. It becomes difficult to tell the story of lived experience without making judgments about the good and evil associated with what we perceive to be "just, right, and fair." Hybridity may be critiqued as tarnished due to arising from a context of power imbalance. The

---

Church President Sir Ronald Wilson. It is documented in Wilson, "Bringing Them Home."

23. Privileged to be his supervisor, I learned a great deal from Rex in our conversations and following his path of discovery. His attitude toward honoring a broad variety of migrant cultures and traditions, from the position of the most marginalized indigenous peoples in our society, has encouraged me to "push back" when faced with the dominance of Western theological method.

24. Rigby, "Social Cohesion," 19.

25. While culture contains the stem from Latin "cultus," referring to land and cultivation, the German "kultur" expanded the concept, by taking on connotations of social behavioral characteristics, including art and creativity.

26. Wrogemann, *Intercultural Hermeneutics*, 350–58.

claim can be that the "purity" assumed by colonizer is challenged by the encounter.[27] Nevertheless, we cannot hope that decolonization will return us to precolonial naivety. Hybridity (different contributors generating a new form of being) is an expression of generative energy, even when it has been painful and costly. Cultural shifts may be experienced as both mutuality and oppositionality, so decolonizing needs to account for both positive and negative narratives.

A Story of Space for Grace

Between 2009 and 2016, I worked with the National Multicultural Ministry Reference Committee of the Uniting Church in Australia, both as member and chairperson. The interactions of culturally diverse ministry leaders enabled higher-order theological listening and reflection. We called our way of working "space for grace," based on the work of Eric Law.[28] Voices from Pasifika-Oceania, Asia, Africa, South America, and the Middle East sang together, ate together, listened, and reflected on stories together. This was a gift of time.

> When the Multi/Cross-cultural Ministry Reference Committee faced important matters in the life of the Church we created what we described as a "Space for Grace" by carefully and respectfully using the gift of time to include the stories and experiences of the diverse people in our group as normative.... It highlights the critical place which the Grace of God plays in the whole of our lives, and our responsibility to expect and wait upon it.[29]

The Uniting Church in Australia's story is one of ecumenical experience and commitment, hence the terminology of Uniting, rather than United, which might only go to describing the foundational heritage of Methodist, Presbyterian, and Congregational. The Wesleyan Quadrilateral is commonly used to inform the church's methods used for the work of spiritual discernment: where tradition, reason, and experience are grounded by scriptural reflection. While experience is often criticized as opening the door to use any story to justify any position or opinion, the received tradition is being critiqued in our living postcolonial sharing:

---

27. For thinking about "Third Space," see Bhabha, *Location of Culture*, 37.
28. Law, *Inclusion*.
29. Koh-Butler and Floyd, "Growing Up."

> We struggled together and there were tears and laughter. We did not get to having end-solutions to complex questions and issues. But we found the Spirit spoke to us in ways we could not have foreseen, leading us into deeper awareness of and acceptance of our diversity, differences, and ability to live by grace with the tensions within which we are called to live faith and life cross-culturally.[30]

As our community peeled back layers of storying and shared from the pain of colonization, we gained a heightened awareness of Aboriginal pain. In this, Budden's work on doing theology on invaded space has helped us continue to question the fine balance between humility and dominance, oppression and liberation.[31] People who had migrated from places where they had been colonized learned that they had become invaders. Our greatest learning was to discover we were colonizers and colonized at the same time. The work of decolonizing is to confront the system that has captured our identity.

As new migrants in an ancient country, we started to appreciate Aboriginal Dreaming as comforting, rather than threatening. Dreaming practices do not need to stress uncertainty, rather they can nourish faith in the mystery of God, who is beyond our understanding and naming, yet who meets us in the circle of story and relationship. Although all the members of the committee were well-versed in Western linear academic method, we found energy and enthusiasm in what we variously called Talanoa, Corroboree, and Campfire.

With the majority of committee members being first generation migrants from countries where they had been indigenous, there was already a deep longing for a noncolonizing approach to method. To survive and be successful in ecclesial leadership, we gain credibility from mastering the methods approved by missionaries. Yet, there is always a sense of loss of identity, when the hearing and valuing of theological contribution requires us to reflect white Western thought processes and language. Decades of liberation and contextual theology have seen Latin Americans, African Americans, Africans, and Asians contribute to global thinking, and their writings are devoured with appreciation and wonder.

Many of the liberation writings have emerged from places of vast populations and numerous communities, recording their struggles and using reasoned words to narrate their stories and claim new ground. While there

---

30. Koh-Butler and Floyd, "Growing Up."
31. Budden, *Following Jesus*.

are certainly voices from the Pacific following their lead, I am prompted to return to Aboriginal friends dismissing of much Western thinking method as being too quick, too linear, and too naïve. A story might help.

A Story of Two Great White Gum Trees

Husband and wife stood tall, surrounded by offspring. They had grown and matured together in this place. It was their home. Birds would flit between their branches. Breeze would share their whispering conversation. Their shade took a daily dance around them.

The road came.

Children were cut down and taken away. The road moved between them, dividing them. Their branches were hacked, so they could no longer touch. When the kangaroos came to sit under their shade, they smeared the road red as roadkill.

The road went between the trees, but few saw the ancient couple and their dwelling-place.[32]

An Aboriginal Way of Gathering in Wisdom

Some Aboriginal communities will not tell particular stories except on country in the place of the story. Part of the story is to be there, to feel the dryness and breathe the red dust. To tell the story in another place may not carry the full sense of the story. The sun feels different in the northern hemisphere. The sounds and smells are different. How can we tell stories of foreign country? How can we sing our songs in a strange land? (Ps 137:4).

Anthropologists have recorded and republished many stories, but putting the stories onto pages can feel like containing and caging them. In writing the story of the Two Great White Gum Trees, I am tempted to move to conclusions and comments about significance. If I am on country, the story sits longer. We do other work before coming to conclusions. We take different time.

The diagram below was developed to help school and college teachers with Aboriginal children and families to understand respect when using stories. It may also become useful for us in decolonizing Wesleyan theology.

---

32. This is my version of a story learned, from an oral telling on country, with my sister Auntie Rev. Dr. Denise Champion.

The diagram serves as a map, helping us to negotiate the different elements of seeking wisdom. Our interactions may start anywhere, but once we enter the process, we are not free to simply jump steps. Rather, we may follow the pathways from one element to another.

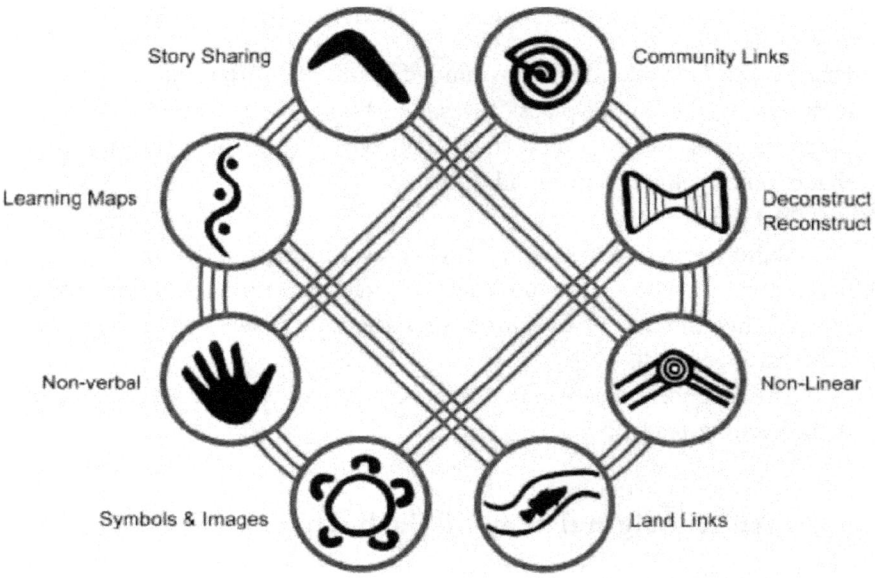

Aboriginal Eight Ways of Learning. Source: NSW Department of Education, Western NSW Regional Aboriginal Education Team (2019).

Sometimes, an element is not accessible. When I tell you the story of the Two Great White Gum Trees, you are not able to easily call up the senses of being on country or understand the *land links*, whatever words I may use. In writing, it is difficult for me to offer you *non-verbal* communications. I might start with *story sharing* and offer you some *non-linear* questions or prompts: How do you feel when you think of the trees? What was it like when the children were removed? Do you know trees like that? We could then move in two possible directions. The first option would be to name *land links* (other places with two trees and a road) and the second option would be to do some *deconstruction and reconstruction*. If we had chosen the latter, we could then choose between exploring *symbols and images* or discovering *community links*.

In following such a process, we might be taking the time to learn of the communities whose children were taken away down this road.

We might hear of the fear of leaving home. We might see the remains of dead branches as the symbols of those taken. We might hear the sounds of birds in the distance and realize they have been banished. The deep encounter with story may become a tsunami, receding and flooding us. Perhaps such a method may inform our encounter with sacred stories of other kinds, both the biblical texts and the sacred stories of our sisters and brothers around the world?

A Continuing Story

Talanoa, corroboree, and campfire do not reduce the cultures in the circle to a single culture, nor do they emphasize distinctive difference. In the Pacific, where talanoa has been possible with different language and culture nationalities from Polynesia, Melanesia, and Micronesia, thinking and behaviors can be quite different. My Pasifika experiences, pastoring highly community-oriented Samoan and Fijian congregations, were very different from my teacher Sherwood Lingenfelter's experiences, who served on the island of Yap with highly individualistic values.[33] Likewise, gathering indigenous Aboriginal Australians together involves sharing different stories about common ingredients, based on different landscapes. In *Songlines*, the story of the common stars was reflected by country in different ways. The stories were different, yet related. Learning the different chapters enabled different peoples to relate to one another in new linked ways. The absence of continued story highlighted the limitations of knowledge. How do we walk together if we have not sat and shared the stories that guide us?

Walking together requires multiple parties orienting themselves, choosing a direction and discarding competing views. Understanding how people view the world and set their course is helpful to find a shared alternative.

Inspired by the vision "in which there is neither Jew nor Gentile, slave or free" (Gal 3:28), the Wesleyan theological community has before it the invitation to affirm its own diversity. We might embrace the value of respecting difference and rejoicing in the unifying love of God. Our Methodist identity and methodology can be contextually and continually reframed by both people and places. Our varied worldviews could enhance our experience of sanctification, creating opportunities for intercultural conversations, shaping transcultural behaviors to serve God

33. Lingenfelter, *Leading Cross-Culturally*.

and God's purposes. We could experience different approaches to hospitality and faith, mission and worship. Decolonization might lead to an appreciation and affirmation of pluralistic and postmodern contextual community. We could move toward a new polydoxy, where the one God is understood and worshiped in many ways.[34]

Bibliography

"Acknowledgement of Country." *Common Grace*, n.d. https://www.commongrace.org.au/acknowledgement_of_country.

Bhabha, Homi K. *The Location of Culture*. London: Routledge, 2004.

Broughton, Geoff, and Brooke Prentis. "Recognition without Dignity." In *Enacting a Public Theology*, edited by Clive Pearson, 1–14. Stellenbosch: African Sun Media, 2019.

Budden, Chris. *Following Jesus in Invaded Space: Doing Theology on Aboriginal Land*. Eugene, OR: Pickwick, 2009.

De Reland, Elizabeth. *All Love's Excelling*. Parramatta: Parramatta Mission, 2021.

Grau, Marion. *Rethinking Mission in the Postcolony: Salvation, Society and Subversion*. New York: T. & T. Clark, 2011.

Havea, Jione, ed. *Theologies from the Pacific*. New York: Palgrave Macmillan, 2021.

Hiebert, Paul G., et al. *Understanding Folk Religion: A Christian Response to Popular Beliefs and Practices*. Grand Rapids: Baker, 1999.

Icry2u (username). "Warami Ngallowah Mittigar." Youtube video, 1:59. April 2, 2019. https://youtu.be/mevonIdrYn4.

Koh-Butler, Amelia. "Tsunami Confession of Hope." In *Wide and Deep*, by Amelia Koh-Butler, 23. Adelaide: Mediacom, 2017.

Koh-Butler, Amelia, and Anthony Floyd. "Growing Up and Redesigning Home: Space for Grace." *Growing Up Uniting: The Proceedings of the Third Uniting Church National History Conference 11–13 June 2021*, 135–52. Australia: Uniting Church National History Society, 2021.

Law, Eric H. F. *Inclusion: Making Room for Grace*. St. Louis: Chalice, 2000.

Lingenfelter, Sherwood G. *Leading Cross-Culturally: Covenant Relationships for Effective Christian Leadership*. Grand Rapids: Baker, 2008.

"Map of Indigenous Australia." AIATSIS, n.d. https://aiatsis.gov.au/explore/map-indigenous-australia.

NSW Department of Education, Western NSW Regional Aboriginal Education Team. *The Aboriginal 8 Ways of Learning Pedagogy*. 2019. https://www.virtuallibrary.info/the-aboriginal-8-ways-of-learning-pedagogy.html.

Rah, Soong-Chan. *Many Colors: Cultural Intelligence for a Changing Church*. Chicago: Moody, 2010.

Rigby, Rex E. "Social Cohesion Through the Eyes of an Indigenous Australian Elder and its Application in the Intercultural Church." PhD diss. Tabor College, 2022.

"Songlines: Tracking the Seven Sisters." National Museum of Australia, n.d. https://www.nma.gov.au/exhibitions/songlines.

---

34. Grau, *Rethinking Mission*.

Spencer, Tracy. "White Lives in a Black Community: The Lives of Jim Page and Rebecca Forbes in the Adnyamathanha Community." PhD diss., Flinders University, 2011.

Wilson, R. D. "Bringing Them Home: Report of the National Inquiry into the Separation of Aboriginal and Torres Strait Islander Children from Their Families." Human Rights and Equal Opportunity Commission, 1997. Canberra, Australia.

Wrogemann, Henning. *Intercultural Hermeneutics: Intercultural Theology*. Vol. 1. Downers Grove, IL: IVP Academic, 2016.

Young, Diana. "On Revealing and Concealing." In *Songlines Catalogue*, by Diana Young, 72–73. Canberra: NMA, 2019.

INDEX

Aboriginal Australians, 137–58
Abraham (Abram) [biblical], 147–48
Abraham, William, 6–7
Abrahamic religions, 119
Abya Yala, 27n4
Acts, Book of, 62
Adam [biblical], 36n34
Adnyamathanha people, 144n10, 147–49
Africa and Africans
    and Angolan liturgical practices, 66–71, 73–78, 80–82
    and Angolan perspective on Methodism and marriage, 85–86, 87n5
    and decolonizing the Church of Empire in Korean Methodism, 123–24
    feminist perspective of Wesleyan traditions in, 99–113
    and Wesleyan perspective of Native theologies, 153–54
alambamento [traditional marriage], 84, 87–88
Alves, Rubem, 26
Amos, Book of, 148
Anabaptism, 15n53
analogia fidei [analogy of faith], 21
Andean region, 11, 40
Andrews, Jonathan, 52
Anglican Communion, 3n8
Anglicanism, 2, 3n8, 14–15, 18–19
Angola and Angolans, 66–82, 84–97
Anselm of Canterbury, 128

Antarctic, 138n3
Antioch [historical], 119
Anzaldúa, Gloria, 11
Aotearoa, New Zealand, 143
Arafura Sea, 146
Argentina and Argentinians, 30, 32–33, 34n27, 49
Arias, Mortimer, 27n6, 29–30, 31n16
Armed Forces Museum, Luanda, 68
Arminianism, 150
Army, U.S., 126
Articles of Religion, 15
Arusha Call to Discipleship, 115
Asia and Asians, 115, 123, 153–54
Assembly of the World Council of Churches (Busan, 2013), 120n10
Assembly of the World Council of Churches (Karlsruhe, 2022), 144, 145n11
Assmann, Hugo, 33n25
Associated Press, 126
Atlanta Statement of the Third Roundtable for Peace on the Korean Peninsula, 123
Augsburg, Germany, 117
Augustine, Saint, 122, 128
Augustinians, 68
Auschwitz, 128n29
Australasia, 137
Australian Aboriginal Peoples (First Peoples), 137–58
Australian Northern Approach, 124

INDEX

Babylonians [historical], 123
Bachelard, Gaston, 51
Baia das Cabras, 68
BaKongo people, 86, 86–87n5
Bantu Ministry, 80
Bantu people, 85–86, 91–92, 94–97
Barcala, Martin, 1n1
Barramattagul people, 137
Bastian, Jean-Pierre, 29n11
Bauman, Zygmunt, 26
Benjamin, Walter, 14n47
Berger, Teresa, 111
Berlin, Germany, 76, 124
Berlin Wall, 116, 124
Bethel [historical], 147
Beyond the Spirit of Empire (Míguez et al.), 37
Bhabha, Homi, 8, 13n44, 127
Bhagwan, James, 144
The Biblical Foundations of the Doctrine of Justification: An Ecumenical Follow-Up to the Joint Declaration on the Doctrine of Justification (Lutheran World Federation et al.), 118–19
Binh Hoa Massacre, 128
Binh Hoa, Vietnam, 127
Blue Dragon Division, South Korean Marines, 127
Boer War, 106
Boff, Leonardo, 40n46
Bonino, José Míguez, 27n6, 29n11, 31–32, 34, 38–39
Book of Common Prayer, 15
Book of Discipline of the United Methodist Church (United Methodist Church), 3–4
Borck, Igor Sulaiman Said Felicio, 76
Boyle, Robert, 55
Brazil and Brazilians
  and Angolan liturgical practices, 69, 71, 78–79, 81
  and decolonizing the Church of Empire in Korean Methodism, 125
  and liberation and Wesleyan theology in Latin America, 32–33
  and the Wesleyan quadrilateral, 21, 22n66
British. *See* England and the British
British Empire, 15
British Isles, 15
Bruno, Daniel, 30–31, 32n22, 33
Buber, Martin, 91
Budden, Chris, 154
Buddhism, 119, 131
Buenos Aries, Argentina, 32–33
Busan, South Korea, 120n10

Cabral, Amílcar, 68
Cain [biblical], 128
Cambridge, England, 1n1
Campbell, McLeod, 119
Campbell, Ted, 2n4, 3n6, 15, 119n8
campfire culture, 139–40, 148, 154, 157
Cancun Beach, 126
Candler School of Theology, Emory University, 115–16
Canguilhem, Georges, 51–52, 54
Cardoza-Orlandi, Carlos, 35
Carey, William, 69
Caribbean Ocean, 8, 10, 27
Carvalhaes, Cláudio, 111
Carvalho, Emílio Júlio de, 81
Casas, Bartolomé de las, 28n8
Castro, Emilio, 27n6, 31
Catholicism, 30–31, 37, 76, 118
Cazombo, Elvira Moisés, 66–82
Central Africa, 87n5
Central America, 27n4, 123
Ceuta Border Fence (Melilla Border Fence), 124
Champion, Rev. Denise, 155n32
Chaterlain, Heli, 69
China and the Chinese, 124, 133, 147–48
Chiziane, Paulina, 81
Christian Student Movement, 31
Christianity
  and Angolan liturgical practices, 67–69, 75–78, 80–81
  and Angolan perspective on Methodism and marriage, 85, 88, 90, 96

INDEX

and decolonizing the Church of Empire in Korean Methodism, 115–17, 119, 120n10, 121n14, 122–23, 125, 128–29, 131–34
and feminist perspective of Wesleyan traditions in Africa, 101–3, 106–12
and liberation and Wesleyan theology in Latin America, 27–30, 33, 35, 37, 40, 42–43, 45
and Wesley on medical science, healing, and the ecology of knowledge in Methodism, 50
and Wesleyan perspective of Native theologies, 137n2, 146–47
and the Wesleyan quadrilateral, 4–8, 10, 12–17, 19–22
Christocentrism, 146
Christology, 37–42, 37n38, 38n40, 43, 131
Church and Society in Latin America (ISAL), 31
Church of England, 15
Circle of African Women Theologians, 100
Clifford, Anne, 104
Clinton, Bill, 116n2
Cobb, John, 5
Cock, Jacklyn, 101
Cold War, 116
Colón-Emeric, Edgardo, 38
Colossians, Book of, 121
"Come, O Thou Traveler Unknown" [hymn], 14n48
Communism, 133
Comte, Auguste, 52
Cone, James, 32, 81
Conference on World Mission and Evangelism (Arusha, 2018), 122
Confucianism, 119, 131
Confucius, 120
Congregationalism, 153
Connecticut, 129–30
Conservative Methodism, 6
Constantine era, 15, 129, 132
Corinthians, Book of, 117

corroboree [Australian Aboriginal ceremony], 139, 154, 157
Costa Rica, 32–33
COVID-19, 36, 44, 51
Craig, Eleanor, 9

Da Nang Beach, 126
Da Nang, Vietnam, 126, 129
Daremberg, 54
Darug people, 137
Daughters of Anowa (Oduyoye), 104
Democratic Republic of the Congo, 87n5
Departments of Fisheries and Wildlife, Australian, 147n15
Derrida, Jacques, 128
Dickson, K., 32
différend [difference], 127–28
DMZ–Korea, 124
"Doctrine of Death" (Abraham), 7
Dominicans, 68
Dondo, Angola, 69
Dreaming, Aboriginal, 149–50, 154
Duque, José, 27n6, 31
Dussel, Enrique, 17, 28n7
Dusty Feet Mob, 147

Eastern Europe, 124
Egypt, 132
El Salvador, 39, 125
emic [insider], 143, 145
Emory University, 115–16, 126, 128n29
England and the British, 32, 59–60, 66, 69, 85, 92–93, 150
English, John, 103
English Baptist Missionary Society, 69
Enlightenment, 18, 56
etic [outsider], 143, 145
Eurocentrism, 75, 143
Europe and Europeans
and Angolan liturgical practices, 69
and decolonizing the Church of Empire in Korean Methodism, 124, 130, 133
and feminist perspective of Wesleyan traditions in Africa, 107

INDEX

Europe and Europeans *(continued)*
    and liberation and Wesleyan theology in Latin America, 28nn7–8, 31
    and Wesley on medical science, healing, and the ecology of knowledge in Methodism, 51, 64
    and Wesleyan perspective of Native theologies, 148n15, 152
    and the Wesleyan quadrilateral, 9
European Union, 124
Evangelical United Brethren, 3
Evangelicalism, 37, 38n40
"Examination of Mr. Wesley's Primitive Physic" (Hawes), 57
Executive Meeting of World Methodist Council (Mexico City, 2019), 126
Exodus, Book of, 105

Faces of Latin American Protestantism (Bonino), 29n11
Faculty of Theology, Methodist University of Sao Paulo, 1n1
Fanon, Frantz, 8, 75
Federation of Australia, 151
Ferrer, Pablo Manuel, 49–64
Fiji and Fijians, 139, 142n7, 144, 150, 157
First Peoples (Australian Aboriginal Peoples), 137–58
Fitchett, Rev. W. H., 92–93
Flora and Fauna Act, 148n15
Forbes, Rebecca, 144n10, 151n19
Foucault, Michel, 52n8
"four-fold syndrome." *See* quadrilateral/quartet, Wesleyan
Francis, Pope, 124
Franciscans, 68
"From Conflict to Communion" (Lutheran World Federation and the Pontifical Council of Promoting Christian Unity), 118

Gabi Gabi people, 151
Gabon, Republic of, 87n5
Gaitskell, Deborah, 101
Galatians, Book of, 119–20, 132, 157
Galilee [historical], 45

Gaza Strip, 125, 133
General Board of Global Missions of the United Methodist Church (GBGM), 125
General Conference of the United Methodist Church (Baltimore, 1984), 3–4
"The General Spread of the Gospel" [sermon], 132
Genesis, Book of, 128, 142, 146–48
Germany and Germans, 76, 117, 124, 128n28, 144, 145n11
Gibson Desert, 146n14
Glissant, Eduard, 10
Global Methodist Church, 6
González, Justo, 39
Great Britain, 125
Great Sandy Desert, 146n14
Great Victoria Desert, 146n14
Greece and Greeks, 15, 51–52, 61, 62n33, 120, 144, 148
Gregory Nazianzen, Saint, 128

Haddad, Beverley, 101, 108, 110
Haggai, Book of, 132
Haggai [biblical], 132
han [unjustifiable suffering], 128
Hartford, Connecticut, 129–30
Hashweh, Samar, 125
Havea, Jione, 145
Hawes, William, 57
Heidegger, Martin, 128n28
Heitzenrater, Richard, 37
Hewitt, Roderick, 111
Hiebert, Paul G., 143
Hinduism, 119
Hinfelaar, Marja, 101–2, 106–7, 109
Holy Communion Sunday, 105
Holy Sepulcher, 125
Homilies, 15

Ikara Wilpena Pound, 147
Ikara-Flinders Ranges, 147
India, 13n44
Indian Ocean, 146
International Atomic Energy Agency, 116

INDEX

"An Invitation to the Pilgrimage of Justice and Peace," 120n10
Iraq, 123
Irenaeus, Saint, 128
Isaiah, Book of, 115, 134
Isaiah [biblical], 133
ISAL (Church and Society in Latin America), 31
Islam, 69, 119, 133
Israel [historical], 121, 128

Japan and the Japanese, 116, 148
JDDJ (Joint Declaration on the Doctrine of Justification), 117–18
Jennings, Willie, 16
Jerusalem [historical], 123, 125
Jesuits, 68
Jesus Christ [biblical]
    and Angolan liturgical practices, 79, 81
    and Angolan perspective on Methodism and marriage, 96
    and decolonizing the Church of Empire in Korean Methodism, 117–22, 125, 128, 130–31, 133–34
    and feminist perspective of Wesleyan traditions in Africa, 104, 113
    and liberation and Wesleyan theology in Latin America, 29, 36–45
    and Wesley on medical science, healing, and the ecology of knowledge in Methodism, 60, 62n34, 64
    and Wesleyan perspective of Native theologies, 142n7, 146, 148n15, 149, 151
"Jesús was born in Guatemala" (Colón-Emeric), 38
Jews. *See* Judaism
Job, Book of, 148
John, Book of, 40, 44, 81, 131, 142n7
John Wesley's Sermons: An Anthology (Wesley), 37
Joint Declaration on the Doctrine of Justification (JDDJ), 117–18
Joon-ho, Bong, 133
Josgrilberg, Rui de Souza, 21

Jubilee Year, 116
Judaism, 119–20, 157

Kant, Immanuel, 17
Kanyoro, Musimbi, 105, 112
Karlsruhe, Germany, 144, 145n11
Keating, AnaLouise, 11
Kingdom of Congo, 68
Kiribati (Kiribas) Island, 143
kisaeng [parasite living], 133
Koh-Butler, Amelia, 137–58
koinonia [church diversity], 34, 118
Kongo. *See* State of Kongo
Korea and Koreans, 115–34
Korean Methodist Church, 116
Korean Peninsula, 116, 123
Korean War, 126
Kristeva, J., 128
Kuango River, 66
Kuanza River, 66, 69
kubula kilundu [breaking of the spirit], 72
Kwangju Uprising, 126
Kwok Pui-lan, 7n24, 12, 13n46

LALT (Latin American Liberation Theology), 27n6, 40
Lamb of God, 121, 131–32
Lambeth Quadrilateral, 3n8
Laney, Rev. James T., 116n2
Latin America and Latin Americans/Latinx, 8, 26–46, 49, 51, 154
Latin American Liberation Theology (LALT), 27n6, 40
Latin American Union of Evangelical Youth, 31
Law, Eric, 153
Law of Agency (*Shaliach* Principle), 131
Lawry, Walter, 150
Leigh, Samuel, 150
Leigh Fijian Congregation, 150
Levinas, Emmanuel, 128n28
Lingenfelter, Sherwood, 157
Little Christ, 130–31
Little Sandy Desert, 146n14
Lohre, Rev. Kathryn Mary, 122
London, England, 93

INDEX

Lord's Prayer, 119, 122
Luanda Island, 68–69, 79
Luke, Book of, 40, 62, 120
Luke [biblical], 62
Lund, Sweden, 118
Lutheran World Federation, 117
Lutheranism, 117–18, 122
Lwey River, 66
Lyotard, Jean-Francois, 127, 128n29

Macedo, Bishop Edir, 78–79
MacIntyre, Alaisdair, 16
Madden, Debora, 55–56
Maddox, Randy, 2–3, 15n53, 19, 59
Madrid, Spain, 124
Magi [biblical], 150
Maia, Filipe, 1–22
makudionda [African worship], 73
Malanje, Angola, 70
Malanje Mission, 70
Maldonado-Torres, Nelson, 17
Mamani, Fernando Huanacumi, 11
Mammon [wealth as evil], 29, 45
Manyano, 99–102, 108–10
Maori people, 148
Mark, Book of, 49–50, 60–62, 142n7
Mark [biblical], 60–62
Martinez, Oscar Alberto, 124–25
Martins, Mariana, 81
Marxism, 31
Mary [biblical], 132
Masenya, Madipoane, 112
"Massacre in Korea" [painting], 126
Matariki (Seven Sisters), 148
Matthew, Book of, 45, 62, 119, 130, 133, 142n7, 149
Matthew [biblical], 62
Mbanza-Kongo (Sao Salvador do Congo), Angola, 69, 86–87n5
Mbembe, Achille, 76
Melanesia and Melanesians, 139n4, 157
Melilla Border Fence (Ceuta Border Fence), 124
Messiah and messianism, 42, 45, 131–33
Methodist Church of Southern Africa, 80, 99
Methodist Liaison Office (MLO), 125

Methodist Revolutions: Evangelical Engagements of Church and World (Rieger and Vaai, eds.), 45
Methodist University of Sao Paulo, 1n1
Mexico, 124, 126
Mexico City, Mexico, 126
Micronesia and Micronesians, 139n4, 157
Middle East, 123, 153
Mignolo, Walter, 8, 9n30, 10, 12, 28n7
Míguez, Nestor, 28n8, 37, 39–40, 42
missio dei [work of God], 35, 42, 44, 123
MLO (Methodist Liaison Office), 125
Moses [biblical], 105
Mother's Union, 104
Mount of Olives, 130
Mozambique, 81
Multi/Cross-cultural Ministry Reference Committee, Uniting Church, 153
Muslims. *See* Islam
Mveng, Father Engelbert, 81

Naaman [biblical], 126
National Aboriginal and Islanders Day Observance Committee (NAIDOC) Day, 144n9
National Council of Churches in Korea, 116
National Museum of Australia, 148
Native Methodism, 137–58
nepantla [zone of potential], 11
"The New Creation" [sermon], 36n34
New Testament, 63, 103
New York Times [newspaper], 126
New Zealand, 143, 150
Ngungu ia isungu [spirit rites], 71
Nhangui-a-Pepe, Angola, 69
Nicene era, 15
Night Sky with Exit Wounds (Vuong), 129
Nkama Longo [delivery of dowry], 87
Nogunri, South Korea, 126
North America and North Americans, 5–6, 27n4, 28n8, 30–33, 143
North Korea and North Koreans, 116, 124
Novais, Paulo Dias de, 68
Nzambi [God], 72

INDEX

Oaks of Mamre, 147
Oceania, 137–38, 142, 144. *see also* Pasifika-Oceania and Pasifika people (Pacific Islanders)
Oduyoye, Mercy Amba, 100, 102, 104–5, 112
On Earth We're Briefly Gorgeous (Vuong), 129, 131
"On the Wedding Garment" [sermon], 121
Oscar Awards, 133
Oscar Romero, Saint, 39
Outler, Albert C., 2–7, 18–21, 37
Oviedo, Pablo Guillermo, 26–46
Oxford Institute, 32
Oxford Institute of Methodist Theological Studies, 116
Oxford University, 18

Pacari, Nina, 11
Pachamama [Mother Earth], 39
Pacific Conference of Churches, 144
Pacific Islands and Pacific Islanders (PIs). See Pasifika-Oceania and Pasifika people (Pacific Islanders)
Pacific Ocean, 137–43, 145–46, 155, 157
Paco, Félix Patzi, 11
Page, Jim, 144n10, 151n19
Palestine [historical], 61, 125, 133
Palestine Wall, 124
Parasite [movie], 133
Park, J. C., 115–34
Parramatta, Australia, 137
Parramatta Mission, 150
Pasifika Bible, 142n7
Pasifika-Oceania and Pasifika people (Pacific Islanders), 137, 139n4, 140, 142–43, 148n15, 150, 153, 157. *see also* Oceania
Paul [biblical], 37n38, 119, 122
Pauline Christianity, 118–19
Peace and Reunification of the Korean Peninsula, 116
Pedirka Desert, 146n14
Pembenji, Angola, 75
Peniel [historical], 147
Pentecostalism, 67, 78–82, 99

Perkins School of Theology, Southern Methodist University, 2n3
Peter [biblical], 119, 142
Pharaoh [biblical], 105
Phiri, Isabel Apawo, 100–101
Picasso, Pablo, 126
Pieris, Aloisius, 126
Pietermaritzburg, South Africa, 106
Pieterse, Hendrik, 1n1
Pietism, 2, 19, 30–31, 85, 93
Pilgrimage of Justice and Peace, 120n10
Piracicaba, Brazil, 32–33
PIs (Pacific Islands and Pacific Islanders). See Pasifika-Oceania and Pasifika people (Pacific Islanders)
Pitjantjatjara people, 148
Pleiades (Seven Sisters), 148
Polynesia and Polynesians, 139n4, 157
Port Augusta, Australia, 147
Portugal and the Portuguese, 68, 78, 87n5
Prayer for Peace Meeting, 124
Prentis, Brooke, 137n2, 149, 151
Presbyterianism, 153
Primitive Physic (Wesley), 49–51, 54–59, 61, 63
Proença, Paulo Sergio de, 81
Protestantism
    and Angolan liturgical practices, 69, 74–77
    and decolonizing the Church of Empire in Korean Methodism, 118
    and liberation and Wesleyan theology in Latin America, 28n8, 29n11, 30–32, 35n33, 37, 38n40
    and the Wesleyan quadrilateral, 4, 12, 14, 19
Proust, Marcel, 130
Psalms, Book of, 121–22, 155
Pulitzer Prize, 126
Pungo-a-Ndongo, Angola, 70
Puritanism, 15n53, 92

quadrilateral/quartet, Wesleyan, 1–22, 153
Quessua River, 70
Quijano, Aníbal, 9–10

INDEX

Quingua, 75

Rah, Soong-Chan, 140
Reformation, Protestant, 19, 118
Republic of Angola. *See* Angola and Angolans
Republic of the Congo, 87n5
Resurrection of Christ, 122
Revelations, Book of, 121
Ribas, Óscar, 72
Rieger, Joerg, 28n8, 36–37, 43, 129n33, 131n39
Rigby, Rev. Rex, 138n2, 151–52
Rio Grande, Mexico, 124
River Plate Basin, 30
Roman Catholicism, 14, 30, 33n25, 76, 117
Roman Empire, 15
Romans, Book of, 119, 121–22, 129
Rome and Romans [historical], 62n33
Rosenlee, Li-Hsiang Lisa, 51
Roundtable for Peace on the Korean Peninsula, 123
Royal College, 59
Royal Commission, 151n22
Ruether, Rosemary Radford, 111
Runyon, Theodore, 36n34, 116
Russian Empire, 130

Saharan Africa and Saharans, 85
Said, Edward, 8
Samoa and Samoans, 157
Samuel, Book of, 107
Samuel [biblical], 107
San José, Costa Rica, 32
Sanctification and Liberation (Runyon, ed.), 116
sang-geuk [inter-killing], 123
sangsaeng [living together], 117, 123, 133
Santa Ana, Julio de, 27n6, 31
Santos, Boaventura de Sousa, 8, 10–11, 18, 50, 58–59
Santos, Virgínia Inácio dos, 84–97
São Paulo, Brazil, 32–33
São Salvador do Congo (Mbanza-Kongo), Angola, 69, 86–87n5

Sarah (Sarai) [biblical], 147–48
Schengen Agreement, 124
Schengen Border, 124
Scotland and the Scottish, 147
Second Peoples, 138n2
Seoul, South Korea, 117, 124, 126
Seven Sisters, 138, 148, 150
Shaliach Principle (Law of Agency), 131
Shalom [peace], 40
Shaw, R. Daniel, 143
The Sheep and the Goats [parable], 130
Simpson Desert, 146n14
Siwila, Lilian Cheelo, 99–113
Society of Jesus, 68
sola gratia [by grace alone], 119, 121
sola scriptura [Bible as sole authority], 12–14
Songlines [exhibition], 148, 150–51, 157
Soranus of Ephesus, 62n33
South Africa, 99–113
South America and South Americans, 27n4, 28, 63, 153
South Korea and South Koreans, 116n2, 117, 120n10, 124, 126, 133
South Korean Marines, 127
Southern Ocean, 146
Souza, José Carlos de, 1n1, 21
Spain and the Spanish, 28n8, 124
Spencer, Tracy, 144n10
Spivak, Gayatri C., 8
Staffordshire, England, 150
State of Kongo, 86n5
Stobart, Andrew, 1n1
Strzelecki Desert, 146n14
Sturt Stony Desert, 146n14
Subaru (Seven Sisters), 148
Sucumula, Bruno Madureira, 90
Sudan and the Sudanese, 85
suma qamaña [good life], 40
sumak kausai [good life], 39
Summers, William, 69
Sung, Jung Mo, 37, 125
Sweden, 118
Sydenham, Thomas, 54–55
Sydney, Australia, 137
Syria, 123

INDEX

T. S. Eliot Prize, 129
Talanoa [sharing of ideas], 139–40, 144, 146, 154, 157
Tamez, Elsa, 19, 27n6, 31
Tanami Desert, 146n14
Taylor, Bishop William, 69–70, 78
Thailand, 124
Theological Study Commission of The United Methodist Church, 3
Theological Study Commission on Doctrine and Doctrinal Standards, 3n8
Thoughts on Marriage and a Single Life (Wesley), 93
Tienou, Tite, 143
Tirari Desert, 146n14
Tolstoy, Leo, 130
Tonga and Tongans, 139–40, 145, 150
Torah, 121n14
Torres Strait Islanders, 139n4
Transvaal, South Africa, 106
Trinitarians, 38
"Tsunami Confession of Hope" (Koh-Butler), 141
Turgenev, Ivan, 130
Tuvalu Island, 143

UMC (United Methodist Church). *See* United Methodism
United Kingdom, 1n1
United Methodism, 2–4, 6, 84, 91–92, 94
United States–Mexico Wall, 124
Uniting Aboriginal and Islander Christian Congress, 138n2
Uniting Church, 138n2, 151–52n22, 153
Universal Church of the Kingdom of God, 78–79

Valeria, Angie, 125
Vazeille, Mary, 92
Victorian era, 101, 107
Vietnam and the Vietnamese, 126–27, 129–30
Vietnam War, 126, 129
vincularidad [relationality], 11
Vizcaíno, Rafael, 17

Vuong, Ocean "Little Dog," 129–31
Vuong, Rose, 130

Waka Waka people, 149
Walker, Cherryl, 101
Walled World, 124
Walsh, Catherine, 10
WASPs, 4
Watson, Natalie, 111
Way/*Tao* of True Life, 131, 134
WCC (World Council of Churches), 42, 120n10, 144, 145n11
Webba, Nzengele Joao, 76
Wesley, Charles, 14n48
Wesley, John
 and Angolan perspective on Methodism and marriage, 85, 92–94
 and decolonizing the Church of Empire in Korean Methodism, 120–21, 132–33
 and feminist perspective of Wesleyan traditions in Africa, 102–3
 and liberation and Wesleyan theology in Latin America, 28–29, 32, 34, 36–38, 44–45
 on medical science, healing, and the ecology of knowledge in Methodism, 49–51, 54–64
 and Wesleyan perspective of Native theologies, 147
 and the Wesleyan quadrilateral, 2–3, 5, 13, 15–16, 18–19, 21
Wesley House, 1n1
Wesleyan Methodist Church, 138n2, 151
Wesleyan Week, 1n1
West Bank, 125
Westhelle, Vitor, 28n8
White Australia Policy, 147n15, 151
WHO (World Health Organization), 53
Williams, Colin W., 3n6
Wilson, Sir Ronald, 152n22
WMC (World Methodist Council), 115, 117, 125
Women's Manyano, 101
Wood, Charles, 2n3

World Council of Churches (WCC), 42, 120n10, 144, 145n11
World Health Organization (WHO), 53
World Methodist Conference (Gothenburg, 2024), 124
World Methodist Conference (Seoul, 2006), 117
World Methodist Council (WMC), 115, 117, 125
World Parish Webinar, 1n1
Wright, N. T., 128
Wrogemann, Henning, 152

xiao [filial faithfulness], 120
xinguilamento [Angolan worship ritual], 67, 71–73, 76, 79–80

Yap Island, 157
YMCA, 133
Yountae, An, 9, 17

Zaire, Angola, 86n5
Zaire River, 66
Zambezi River, 66
Zionism, 125

www.ingramcontent.com/pod-product-compliance
Lightning Source LLC
Chambersburg PA
CBHW020851160426
43192CB00007B/870